1989

Teaching Thinking in
K-12 Classrooms:
Ideas, Activities, and Resources

Teaching Thinking in K–12 Classrooms:

Ideas, Activities, and Resources

Iris McClellan Tiedt   Bert D. Howard

Jo Ellen Carlson   Kathleen S. Oda Watanabe

Allyn and Bacon

Boston   London   Sydney   Toronto

Library of Congress Cataloging-in-Publication Data

Teaching thinking in K–12 classrooms.

   Includes bibliographies and index.
   1. Thought and thinking—Study and teaching.   2. Cognition in children—United States.   I. Tiedt, Iris M.
LB1590.3.T44   1988   370.15′7   88–28500
ISBN 0–205–11729–5

Printed in the United States of America
10 9 8 7 6 5 4 3 2 1 92 91 90 89 88

Contents

11 Reflection: Infusing Thinking into All Instruction 301

Preface

Thinking is synonymous with *learning* in the classroom. Yet, we know little about the teaching of thinking and how thinking is infused throughout all instruction.

As teachers, working with a Writing Project, our first concern was emphasizing thinking skills as part of the teaching of writing. As we developed strategies for engaging students in writing activities, we gradually realized that what students are writing is "thinking." Quickly, we leaped to the further conclusion that what they read is also "thinking." Our purpose became therefore to teach students to write "thinking" as they communicated their ideas to others and to read the "thinking" of their peers as well as that of published authors.

Like you, we searched to clarify our own knowledge about thinking. What does research have to tell us? Just how do we define thinking? What kinds of objectives will lead to a student's learning to think? Which strategies will best support teaching for thinking in our classrooms?

As we read and encountered ideas, we found that many scholars are talking about thinking, but they have different perspectives. New research about the human brain, for example, has brought about interest in how the two hemispheres of the brain function and comparisons between linear thinking and the more creative leaps involved in synthesis. Many studies have sought to identify complexity levels of thinking skills and to develop new strategies for engaging students in problem solving. We rediscovered the scientific method with its stress on logic, discovery, questioning, both inductive and deductive methods. We recognized, too, the impact of earlier studies on creativity and the influence of work with self-esteem, attitudes, and values on thinking instruction. Planning for the development of thinking skills in the classroom is far from simple.

We found also that, in general, thinking and language are acquired in tandem, each supporting the other from the time a child is born. Thus, listening, speaking, reading, and writing language provide opportunities for students to engage in thinking. As they use language and thinking skills, students can learn the content of any field, but language and thinking remain foundational to learning in every classroom. Therefore, language arts strategies, using either oral or written language, provide methods of instruction for any classroom, no matter what the level or the subject of study.

Our intent in writing this book has been to identify and to share with you ideas for teaching that encourage thinking to happen in any classroom. We have designed sample lessons that demonstrate how you can provide scaffolding for thinking as students collect data and utilize it in meaningful ways. Using these ideas will add excitement to your classroom as you share learning with your students. Talking about the process with your students will guide them to understand what is happening as they brainstorm, question, discover, and create. You can lead students to respect the powerful tool each one possesses and to enjoy using their brains with greater effect.

Cheers!
The Authors
1988

Teaching Thinking in
K-12 Classrooms:
Ideas, Activities, and Resources

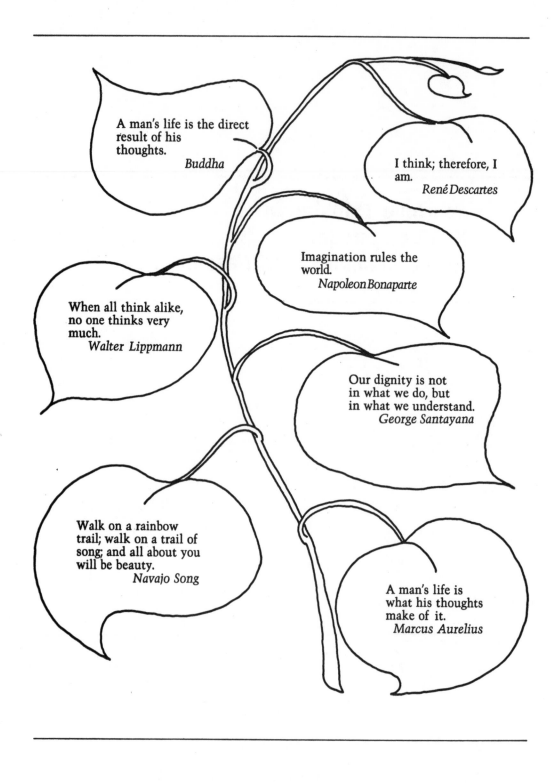

CHAPTER 1

Thinking About Thinking

Objectives

After reading this chapter, you will be able to

- *Define "thinking" operationally.*
- *Discuss various theoretical positions presented in the literature on thinking.*
- *Write objectives for stimulating student-thinking skills in all subject areas.*
- *Design a lesson plan that engages students in active learning that emphasizes independent thinking.*

When teachers talk about teaching thinking today, many refer to critical thinking. Some have become intrigued by studies of right-brain/left-brain thinking. For others, thinking is synonymous with creativity. Thinking, however, is all of these and much more.

As we review what has been written about teaching thinking in K–12 classrooms, we discover the following important categories of information:

> Human values and making choices
> Levels or frameworks for thinking
> Scientific or inquiry methods
> Whole-brain thinking
> Creativity and imagination
> Comprehension as thinking
> Composing as thinking
> Thinking with the computer
> Integrating thinking across the curriculum

These topics, logically, are subjects of chapters for this book: *Teaching Thinking in K–12 Classrooms: Ideas, Activities, and Resources.* In each chapter, we first present a summary of the theory and research associated with each topic. Perhaps more important, we apply these ideas in lessons that demonstrate just how you might stimulate student thinking in your own classroom. In this first chapter, we provide an introduction to the study of thinking and what is happening in education as teachers discover the importance of teaching thinking.

Defining Thinking

What is thinking? We use this term freely as we admonish children to "*Think* about what you're saying," "Now, *think* hard and you'll get the answer," and "What do you *think* happened next?" Clearly, the word *thinking* has many variations of meaning and connotations.

The kind of thinking that we do during any one day, furthermore, varies widely. Consider the difference in the way we think as we

- *play a favorite Chopin étude on the piano.*
- *ponder over the meaning of a poem by T. S. Eliot.*
- *ski down the slopes on Mt. Baldy.*
- *use the word processor to write a letter.*
- *compare the prices of cat food in the grocery store.*
- *experience a wild colorful journey in a dream.*
- *remember the pleasure of last summer's family reunion.*
- *call a friend on the telephone to offer condolences.*
- *visualize a new arrangement of furniture in the living room.*
- *plan a finesse in bridge.*
- *drive a car down a crowded freeway.*
- *choose a new television set for the family.*
- *hug someone we love.*
- *argue about the national space program.*

In all of these acts, the brain is functioning; *thinking* is going on. The kind of thinking varies tremendously, however, as varied kinds of intellect are employed. Howard Gardner argues in *Frames of Mind* that we have many kinds of intelligence—linguistic, musical, logical, spatial, kinesthetic, and personal.[1] Obviously, the study of thinking is complex.

What do you mean when you use the word *thinking?* Take a minute or two to jot down a few synonyms for *think* that come to your mind. *The Random House Dictionary of the English Language* includes such definitions as these:

- *To have a conscious mind capable of reasoning*
- *To employ one's mind rationally in evaluating*
- *To focus on a certain topic (think about)*
- *To call something to mind (think of)*

- *To consider a possible choice*
- *To invent something (think of)*
- *To have regard for someone*
- *To hold an opinion*
- *To consider or evaluate (think over)*
- *To analyze (think out)*
- *To devise (think up)*
- *To plan or intend*

Synonyms for *think* cover a wide range of skills, varying from simpler, information gathering to more complex activities involving analyzing and synthesizing. You might have students generate a web of verbs that mean a kind of thinking.

A Web of Thinking

Discussing the kinds of activities listed helps make students aware of the many kinds of thinking they themselves engage in every day, activities they may not have identified as *thinking*. Obviously, pondering and analyzing are different kinds of behavior. The web of ideas will vary, of course, according to the maturity of the students. You may help them extend their ideas by asking pertinent questions. For example, we might ask older students: Which word best describes the behavior of Rodin's *The Thinker?* Younger students might consider: What kind of thinking do you do as you begin drawing a picture? What do you think about as you begin to write a story?

You might discuss the following information with students, translating it to fit their varied ages. Thinking refers to *what happens between the moment we perceive or experience something and our response.* As a mediating process, it cannot be observed directly but is inferred from the relationship of stimulus, problem, question, and the response or effect. Although thinking or thought usually occurs very quickly, complex processes draw forth information stored in the brain, organize the data, and respond based on some conclusion. Multiples of these thinking acts take place as we engage in reading or writing. We codeswitch from one kind of thinking to another and back again rapidly, without being aware of the miraculous feats we are performing, as we carry on an ordinary conversation with a friend.

Thinking behavior is influenced by the individual characteristics of each human being—for example, intelligence, memory, personality, and experience. Thinking is also influenced by environmental conditions, physical as well as psychological. It is exciting to consider how we can stimulate these thinking processes as we work with learners of all ages.

Thinking, A Languaging Process

The aspect of thinking, which sets humans apart from other animals, is the use of language, verbalization, communication with other people. Although we know that thinking can occur without language, in this book we are going to focus chiefly on thinking that involves language.

Developing with language abilities from birth, thinking provides the foundation for all language learning. Yet, thinking is seldom listed when we refer to the language skills: listening, speaking, reading, and writing. The time has come to "think about thinking" and to recognize its presence as we use oral and written language in the classroom.

As Britton, Squires, and others point out, for most children language is the vehicle through which thinking occurs. Thinking abilities develop together with language abilities.[2] Studies of how children acquire language, therefore, should also demonstrate how thinking abilities are acquired.

Children begin learning to speak from the moment of birth. Indeed, Noam Chomsky argues that human babies are born with a special innate ability to learn language.[3] At birth, a child can potentially learn any language—Swahili, Tagalog, Russian, English, Chinese. Children learn whatever language surrounds them, and they readily become bilingual or trilingual. Their ability to learn language at this formative stage is astounding!

Children learn language through listening, but they do not learn to speak by parroting what they hear. Instead, through exercising highly skilled thinking processes, they abstract the rudiments of a complex grammar system. They create, first, a simplified grammar, a child grammar that has distinctive structure, carries meaning, and allows the child to communicate with the world. We all know what two-year-old Sarah means when she says "Water" or "Airplane." Her meaning becomes even clearer in two-unit sentences—for example: "Sarah go" or "All gone truck." Children are highly motivated to speak.

Children learn to use language and thus to think during the first several years of their lives. Before entering school, they have mastered a complex grammar system and have been using varied thinking skills in all kinds of situations. They have also acquired a large speaking and listening vocabulary that enables them to communicate their thoughts. Furthermore, this learning occurs naturally, without the assistance (or hindrance) of formal instruction. We can learn much about effective instruction by observing the child's acquisition of oral language abilities.

By simply observing the lives of children from birth to kindergarten, we see how naturally learning takes place:

1. Children are eager to learn. What children want to learn, they do learn.
2. Children exert much effort to learn when they are self-motivated. They practice speaking constantly.
3. Children learn from each other. They do not require adult instruction.
4. Children apply discovery methods, make hypotheses, and test them as they learn language.
5. Children play with language; they are creative and humorous.

First graders fracture proverbs[4]
Don't put all your eggs—in the microwave.
People who live in glass houses—better not take off their clothes.
All's fair—in hockey.
He who laughs last—didn't understand the joke.

The children we observe, the children who enter our schools, are eager, hardworking learners. Yet, teachers from elementary grades through high school decry the apathy of their students. What has turned these eager learners into nonresponsive students? This is a problem we need to solve.

One solution is to replicate the natural language-learning environment, including the positive learning experiences, described above, in the classroom. Teachers are discovering stimulating methods, such as the following, that do engage students in languaging and thinking:

1. Prewriting activities that emphasize oral language, thinking, and talking before beginning to write.
2. Student-generated topics of study that interest the learner more than those imposed by the writers of a textbook.
3. Integrating learning around a theme of universal concern that allows for individual choices.
4. Positive evaluation strategies and realistic expectations for individual learners that create a more comfortable classroom climate.

These are the kinds of ideas we will explore in this book.

Stimulating Thinking in the Classroom

The purpose of this book is to help you apply what theory and research about thinking tell us. We need to correlate this information with what we know about good teaching practices and learning theory. We also need to select or devise instructional strategies that will promote thinking, while questioning and discarding practices that stifle thinking. Planning thinking instruction is enjoyable and should lead to more effective teaching.

WHAT WE HAVE LEARNED ABOUT TEACHING THINKING

Through our work in classrooms at the elementary, junior high, high school, and college levels, we have learned much about good teaching. We have tried to integrate these generalizations about good teaching with studies of the thinking processes that we want to promote in the classroom. It is important to state these assumptions here because they form the foundation on which this book is based, the ideas that we are trying to help you carry out in your own classrooms. You may have questions about some of these ideas or wish to state them in different ways.

All Persons Think

At birth, thinking (cognition) begins as the brain functions. One of our major tasks is to help students become aware that they are thinking

An Example of a Junior High School Student's Creative Thinking[5]

(metacognition). We can help them become aware of what they are thinking and different kinds of thinking, and we can give them opportunities to apply more sophisticated ways of thinking. We can guide them to recognize the thinking processes they are using. We can also build their self-esteem as we help them recognize that what they think has value. See the cover of a student publication, *The Panther Prowl* (above), which gives students an opportunity to share their creative thinking.

Thinking Is Not Taught in Isolation

We usually think about something. These ideas may be already in the brain, based on prior experience, or the ideas may be new to the thinker, taken in through observation, experience, perhaps through listening or reading. In the classroom, we can scarcely teach thinking skills without involving language; student language abilities are directly correlated with their ability to think. Their vocabulary, for example, limits or enhances the range of possible thoughts, the concepts that can be considered. Ability to read enables the student to take in information at increasingly advanced levels. Thinking skills may be taught in a separate class that focuses on activities that engage students in higher-order thinking skills, but thinking must also be seen as the foundation for learning in all subjects and all classrooms.

Students Learn to Think by Thinking

Time on task studies in education affirm what common sense tells us: You learn to *do* what you *do*. If we want students to think, we must do more than talk about thinking; we must provide opportunities for students to engage in thinking. Time-on-task studies also emphasize the influence of the *quality* of the activities that learners engage in. Effective learning activities that stimulate thinking therefore will be active, not passive; student-generated, rather than teacher-mandated; interactive as well as individual; interesting; purposeful; and satisfying.

Students Learn to Think by Experiencing, Listening, and Speaking

Oral-aural language skills provide the foundation for successful work with written language. These primary language skills, and the varied experiences that individual children have, form the prior knowledge that any student brings to a learning task. We need to provide additional experience and the chance to develop oral-aural language abilities for students who have any disadvantage, including those who are learning English as a second language. Oral language activities, planned as part of prewriting and prereading experiences, engage students in thinking and prepare them to write and read successfully.

Students Learn to Think by Writing and by Reading

Writing is thinking expressed through the written language rather than speech. Effective student writing grows out of thinking and talking about ideas, using organizational strategies, and testing the shaping of their ideas for a given audience. Students discover what they want to say and learn how to express it in writing more effectively through these processes. Students also learn to think as they read for meaning, comprehension. Not only do they receive the input of knowledge about a subject, but they also experience vicariously the events and emotions depicted; they identify with the characters. They learn to observe the writing of a skillful author; they learn to perceive reading as "writing." And, they begin to identify the thinking and the assumptions of this writer with whom they may agree or disagree.

We Can Teach Students to Improve Their Thinking Abilities

We begin with the level of self-awareness, students' knowledge that they are thinking beings and that what they think is worth sharing with the world. We can show students techniques that will facilitate their probing into the rich storehouse of ideas in their brains. We can introduce or make students aware of varied ways of thinking and offer opportunities for them to engage in interactive learning experiences that involve independent thinking. We can plan experiences that show students how to deal with the thinking expressed by others orally or in writing. Teaching thinking skills should be explicitly stated in the objectives for every program.

As part of our plans for teaching thinking to children and young adults, we might well begin with discussing some of these understandings. Even young children could discuss, for example, the fact that all human beings think. Ask such questions as

- *How do you know you think?*
- *Are there different kinds of thinking?*
- *Can you describe a time when you knew you were thinking?*
- *What do you think about?*

At another time, introduce a different idea. These discussions will help students become aware of thinking as something we all do, the first step toward stimulating student thinking. Once these ideas have been introduced, you can reinforce them as they are demonstrated in classroom activities.

Writing Objectives for Teaching Thinking

What do we want students to know about thinking? What do we want them to be able to do? The following model for organizing thinking instruction depicts three stages in thinking development: data collecting, data processing, and data publishing.

TIEDT DEVELOPMENTAL MODEL FOR THINKING INSTRUCTION

Stage 1 is foundational for all learning activities, a time for collecting information through observation, experimentation, and reading. Stage 2 engages learners in processing the data collected as they compare, question, and analyze. During Stage 3 we encourage students to communicate their thinking through some kind of performance, usually speaking or writing. All these stages are recursive and are most effectively implemented in a spiral curriculum that engages students in varied sequences of collecting data, processing it, collecting more data, sharing their findings, rewriting the report, collecting more data, processing it differently, and eventually publishing their thinking in a class book (as depicted in the diagram, "The Spiral Thinking Process").

THE SPIRAL THINKING PROCESS

This developmental approach to thinking is open and flexible, the kind of learning that is not predictable and therefore not readily evaluated by objective tests ranked according to established norms. Such instruction encourages independent thinking and individual growth that can be evaluated only through such practices as self-evaluation and individual conferences, which do not lend themselves to traditional grading practices. Because of the nature of the learning in which students are engaged, how-

---

TIEDT DEVELOPMENTAL MODEL FOR THINKING INSTRUCTION

Stage 1: Data collecting

Learner Behaviors

Experience	Record
Experiment	Transcribe
Explore	Note
Observe (hear, see, smell, feel, taste)	Listen
Recall	Read
Brainstorm (cluster, map, web)	View
Copy	Interview

Stage 2: Data processing

Learner Behaviors

Sort	Compose	Diagram
Classify	Question	Transform
Categorize	Discuss	Verbalize
Organize	Analyze	Visualize
Compare	Integrate	Generate
Connect	Synthesize	Create
Define	Structure	
Conceptualize	Form	

Stage 3: Data publishing

Learner Behaviors

Communicate	Evaluate
Perform	Revise
Present	Rewrite
Review	Polish

---

ever, they are developing self-esteem, general savoir faire about working with other people, and positive approaches to problem solving and self-directed learning.

Objectives that we write for thinking appropriately focus on a "thinking" skill that can be developed within any subject area. They are achieved through student performance in such learning activities as those listed here.

The Spiral Thinking Process

Level A: Basic Thinking Activities

At this level, students will be able to

1. describe (an object or event).
2. state (the characteristics of an animal or person).
3. retell (the events in a story).
4. list (what a good writer does).
5. draw (a picture of a character described in story).
6. transcribe (the dialogue in a television show).
7. record (the progress of an experiment).
8. recall (the causes of the Revolutionary War).
9. give (directions for locating the school).
10. recite (a humorous limerick).

Level B: More Advanced Thinking Activities

At this level, students will be able to

1. discuss (reasons for selecting a poem to read).
2. compare (their lives with that of a character).
3. analyze (peer writing for a specific feature).
4. visualize (the effect of an event in history).
5. use (a Venn diagram to show how two books are alike and different).

6. keep (a Learning Log noting ideas and questions).
7. question (the assumptions in a history textbook).
8. create (a new recipe in home economics).
9. show (character traits through behavior in writing).
10. infer (character traits from behavior in literature).

Level C: Integrative Thinking Activities
At this level, students will be able to

1. write (an I-Search Paper).
2. create (an imaginary country in detail).
3. act out (an event in history).
4. rewrite (a story from a different point of view).
5. make (a film).
6. compose (a song).
7. change (the classroom into an Indian village).
8. interpret (a poem).
9. publish (an original children's book).
10. participate (in a town meeting).

The basic skills enumerated in Stage 1 of the Tiedt Developmental Model for Thinking Instruction are those used in Level A activities. They require observation and the gathering of data. The emphasis is on facts, close reading to determine exactly what the author said. Accuracy and care are necessary to record, list, or retell. These basic skills are important because they are used frequently to perform needed functions—the minutes for a meeting, directions for assembling an airplane, a list of words for different colors. These skills provide basic information for almost all of the more advanced thinking activities.

The more advanced skills listed in Level B activities require the student to process given information. We move beyond the collection of facts to interpretation, imagination, and organization. The student will evaluate, analyze, and apply data, drawing conclusions and making inferences. The more advanced skills are more difficult to teach. We need to model, to demonstrate, and to engage students in purposeful activities that require going beyond the facts.

Ideally, we frequently will plan such learning activities as those listed under Level C. These integrative learning experiences involve students in collecting data, processing it in many different ways, and producing a publication or a performance. Any of the thinking processes may be used and repeated, recursively, as presented in the diagram, "The Spiral Thinking Process." Students are involved thus in active, purposeful learning that permits them to make choices. Interaction with their peers and the satisfaction of the finished product make such self-motivated learning a joy.

Planning an Effective Thinking Lesson

The best lesson plan begins with our objectives. Before we can plan a lesson, we need to clarify for ourselves what we are trying to teach. Then, we can select appropriate teaching strategies.

In the preceding section, we discussed possible objectives for teaching thinking at different levels of difficulty and specificity. Each lesson you plan will be aimed at teaching at least one specific thinking skill. You will probably also plan the lesson to teach several skills specific to developing language skills or the content of a subject course such as American History. A sample set of objectives for one lesson (with specific applications suggested in parentheses) might include the following: Students will

1. brainstorm a list of words and phrases (related to life along the Mississippi in the 1850s)
2. write a story (set in a specific place at that time)
3. evaluate stories (on the basis of accuracy of the setting in time and place)

After selecting the objectives we want to achieve, we will plan a lesson designed to meet these objectives using such activities as those suggested. We will also draw on the understandings we have about effective teaching and how we can best help students learn. We will plan a lesson that includes four parts:

1. Stimulus
2. Activity
3. Follow-up
4. Evaluation

The beginning letters of these four parts spell out the acronym SAFE. We will follow the SAFE Demonstration Lesson Plan throughout this book because it ensures that each lesson includes the important warm-up period that promotes thinking and the follow-up that assists students in summarizing what they have learned. The plan, illustrated on the next page, also builds in student and teacher evaluation of the lesson presented. Each part of the lesson is described in more detail below, and sample lessons are presented to show you exactly how the model works.

SAFE Demonstration Lesson Plan
Title of Lesson _____
Grade Level:

OBJECTIVES

        Students will

        1. _____

        2. _____

        3. _____

BRIEF DESCRIPTION

PROCEDURES

Stimulus

Activity

Follow-Up

Evaluation

NOTES

SAFE DEMONSTRATION LESSON PLAN: PRESENTATION

Stimulus

        The stimulus for the activity in the lesson actually includes anything that happens before the students perform (act, speak, or write). This could include all prior knowledge and experience. In writing the lesson plan, however, we limit the stimulus to the talking and planning that immediately precede performing the learning activity. The stimulus could be viewing a film, listening to the teacher reading a newspaper article, or brainstorming words associated with a topic to be studied. The stimulus always includes talking and thinking that contribute directly to the learning task to be performed.

Activity

The activity is the specific task to be performed by students, the task that will be evaluated. It may be done individually or in peer groups. The work may be a form of writing, an art activity, or a spoken performance.

Follow-Up

The follow-up is whatever happens with what the students produce. It may be sharing with the whole class, comparing work in small groups, or publishing writing in a class book. Because these follow-up activities are highly motivating and lead to enthusiasm for continued work on a study, they should not be omitted. Students learn to work independently, to write for audiences other than teachers, and to evaluate (a thinking skill) the work of their peers. These activities can also remove the paper-load from a busy teacher's shoulders.

Evaluation

Teacher evaluation is based on the specified objectives. How well did this lesson achieve the objectives? Frequently, evaluation can be done through observation of student participation while students work independently. Work may be collected for checking in even though no grades are assigned. Sometimes, evaluation may take place on the following day as you see how well the students can apply what they have learned in the preceding lesson.

Involve students in evaluation also. Often, the student-evaluation activity will be part of the follow-up as students share what they have produced. Students can work with you in establishing criteria for grading as part of the activity; they can set up a point system, a credit/no credit arrangement, or specified quality indicators for each grade. Be aware that these evaluation activities engage students in important thinking processes.

SAFE Demonstration Lesson Plans 1.1 and 1.2 illustrate how this plan works. The first lesson is designed for a forty-five- to fifty-minute period. Each of the three main parts of the lesson requires about fifteen minutes each. The entire lesson is completed in school.

SAFE Demonstration Lesson Plan 1.1: Metaphors, a Way of Life
Grade Levels: 3-12

OBJECTIVES

Students will

1. compare two unlike concepts.
2. generalize a definition.
3. compose an extended metaphor.

BRIEF DESCRIPTION

Students compare themselves to animals metaphorically, explaining the reasons for their choice. They then compose extended metaphors in written form. They examine metaphors from literature to observe how metaphor enlivens writing.

PROCEDURES

Stimulus

Begin a dialogue with students; thus,

TEACHER: What color are you?
STUDENT: I'm green.
TEACHER: Why are you green, Steve?
STUDENT: I'm green because I like to start things, to get things going, to be on the cutting edge.

Continue with other students to present several examples. Then, ask everyone to answer these questions on paper. Encourage students to think of several ideas to explain their choices. Share some of the writing orally.

Activity

Tell students that they are now going to choose the animal with which they identify. Ask: "What animal are you?" Have students place the name of the animal they choose in the center of a sheet of paper. Then, direct students to jot down ideas suggesting how they are like that animal. Their ideas will develop a web like this:

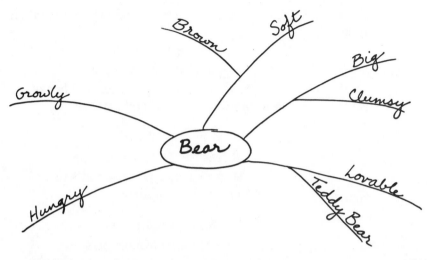

Have students write a paragraph beginning: I am a _____. They should include ideas noted on the web. Other ideas may occur as they write.

Follow-Up

Have students read their paragraphs in groups of four. Each group should choose one of the paragraphs to share with the whole class. After students share the best paragraphs, discuss what made the paragraphs interesting to read. List these features (quality indicators) of good writing.

Tell students that this kind of comparison of two unlike things is called a metaphor. (Note that a simile compares, using the words *as* or *like*, whereas the metaphor does not use these explicit words.)

Evaluation

As homework, direct students to create another web. This time they are to choose some other object to put in the center of the web: a rock, lemon, house, car, freeway, pen. Then, they are to choose a character from a book they are reading, for example, Anne Frank or Huck Finn. They are to compare this character with an object, writing a paragraph or poem about the comparison.

Have students evaluate the writing done for homework based on the list of quality indicators about writing done in class on the previous day.

NOTES

Sources of additional ideas for developing work with metaphors include *Activities to Promote Critical Thinking*, edited by Jeff Golub and others, National Council of Teachers of English, 1986; *Metaphors We Live By*, by George Lakoff and Mark Johnson, University of Chicago Press, 1980.

The following are examples of similes and metaphors taken from literature:

Smells (Junior)
CHRISTOPHER MORLEY

My Daddy smells like tobacco and books,
Mother, like lavender and listerine . . .

The Skunk
ROBERT P. TRISTRAM COFFIN

. . . He is a conscious black and white
Little symphony of night.

The Woodpecker
ELIZABETH M. ROBERTS

. . . the big, big wheels of thunder roll . . .

A Modern Dragon
ROWENA BENNETT

A train is a dragon
That roars through the night.

I Like to See It Lap the Miles
EMILY DICKINSON

I like to see it lap the miles,
And lick the valleys up,
And stop to feed itself at tanks;
And then, prodigious, step

Around a pile of mountains,
And, supercilious, peer
In shanties by the sides of roads;
And then a quarry pare

To fit its sides, and crawl between,
Complaining all the while
In horrid, hooting stanza;
Then, chase itself down hill

And neigh like Boanerges;
Then, punctual as a star,
Stop—docile and omnipotent—
At its own stable door.

Lesson Plan 1.2 is part of a unit of study on naming. At the end of this introductory lesson, we have included a list of other lessons that can be developed more fully for this fascinating venture into the folklore of names and naming practices. A stimulating topic that leads to multicultural understandings and develops self-esteem, this integrative study would fit well in either the social studies or the language arts class.

SAFE Demonstration Lesson Plan 1.2: How I Was Named
Grade Levels: 6–12

OBJECTIVES

Students will

1. analyze a short literature selection.
2. compose a personal narrative.
3. share their writing with peers and family.

BRIEF DESCRIPTION

Students listen to the first chapter of *Roots* by Alex Haley, which describes the naming of Kunta Kinte. They discuss the naming practices described and then find out how names are chosen in their families. Students write a paragraph about their names—what each name means, how they got the name, and how they feel about it (adapted from a National Writing Project workshop).

PROCEDURES

Obtain a copy of *Roots* by Alex Haley. You may wish to duplicate copies of the first short chapter for each student. This lesson requires two forty-five- to fifty-minute periods.

Stimulus

Write your own full name on the board. Tell students about each of your names. Include anecdotal information about how you got the names and how you feel about each name.

Ask students to fold a sheet of notebook paper in fourths. In each section of the paper, they will write one of their names. Discuss the fact that many people have three names, but some have only two, and some may have more than three. (If anyone has more than four, the extra names can be written on the back of the page.) Tell students to think about their names and to jot down words and phrases that they associate with the name in each square.

Activity

Direct students to write a paragraph about their name. They may tell why they especially like (or dislike) different parts of their names.

Follow-Up

Have students share their paragraphs in groups. Each group will choose one of the paragraphs (with the permission of the author) to share with the class. After students have shared, read the short first chapter from *Roots* to illustrate one very beautiful naming practice.

For homework, direct students to read the paragraphs they have written about their names to someone in their families. Then, they are to interview that person about how they were named and how children are named traditionally in their culture.

Evaluation

Observe student participation at each stage of the lesson by circulating around the room. At the end of the period, ask students to write a paragraph summarizing what they learned through this activity. They can share these paragraphs in small groups.

NOTES: DEVELOPING THIS FOLKLORE UNIT

This fascinating study can be titled *Names in America*.

1. Focus on personal names in class, beginning as described. Continue with lessons that engage students in searching and sharing:
   a. Naming practices; for example, Jewish
   b. Why so many children receive the same name
   c. The importance of names; why we have several names
   d. Characteristics of names in the classroom; for example, short Chinese names
   e. What your name tells about you
   f. Making a family tree
2. Move to more general information about names
   a. Origins of surnames
   b. Name societies; for example, Scottish clans
   c. Changing names legally
   d. Special naming problems of women—Ms., married names
   e. Geographic names; names in our community
   f. Genealogy

This integrative study, lasting over a period of a month or more as students engage in various aspects of the study, involves students in all stages of thinking: data collecting, data processing, and data publishing. Students can create a personal book, *Names in Our Family*, and a class book, *Naming-Practices in America*. Illustrations, photographs, maps, and other illustrative material will enhance these bound collections. Families can receive the personal books as gifts. Other classes in the school and the Parent Teacher Association can share the class book.

Teaching Strategies That Stimulate Thinking

As we consider what we know about teaching thinking and what we know about effective teaching, we can identify certain strategies that stimulate thinking. Described here are a few key strategies that will be incorporated in lessons that follow.

CLUSTERING

Gabrielle Rico, a professor at San Jose State University, California, describes clustering in her book *Writing the Natural Way*.[6] Both teacher and student can use this useful technique for any topic as a way of delving into the resources of the brain.

To introduce clustering to students, select a topic to which all can respond—for example, school, summer, or happiness (see the figure, "Clustering"). Write the topic in the center of the board and ask students to give you free associations with the word. Notice that related words are

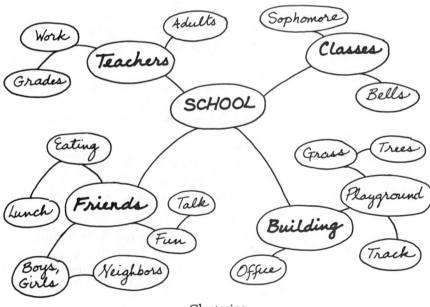

Clustering

hooked together. As more and more words are joined around one aspect of the topic, a cluster of ideas is formed. Clustering provides an informal, nonthreatening kind of outlining as ideas are categorized in groups.

For a second, independent clustering experience, ask students to cluster around a word that has little apparent meaning—for example, *up*, *over*, or *to*. Students will be surprised to find that these little words trigger ideas, and everyone's ideas are different. This experiment offers you the opportunity to discuss the source of these ideas (each individual student's brain) and to make clear that everyone has a brain full of interesting ideas to draw forth for thinking and writing about.

MAPPING

Constructing a map of a story, an event, or a concept is another way of organizing information as it is collected. In addition to the student's brain, the source of ideas may be reference books, interviews, or letters. Here is a map of an Observation Walk students took on a pleasant fall day around the school grounds (see the figure, "Mapping"). Following this Observation Walk, students readily composed poems using the structure of the map.

Observations

JANE MILLAND

I saw
    birds flying high over head,
    trees beginning to turn yellow,
    a colony of ants busy storing food.

I heard
    children playing four-square,
    two dogs barking furiously,
    an airplane heading across country.

I smelled
    freshly cut grass in the schoolyard,
    the bark of crushed cedar branches,
    the perfume of a warm, sunny day.

I touched
    the warm hood of a red Thunderbird,
    the crumbly earth beneath the cedars,
    the hand of a friend who smiled.

I tasted autumn in the air.

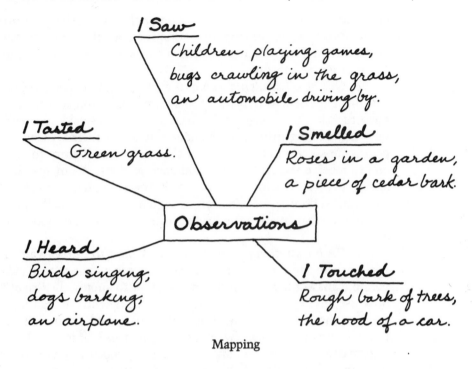

I Saw
Children playing games,
bugs crawling in the grass,
an automobile driving by.

I Tasted
Green grass.

I Smelled
Roses in a garden,
a piece of cedar bark.

Observations

I Heard
Birds singing,
dogs barking,
an airplane.

I Touched
Rough bark of trees,
the hood of a car.

Mapping

Teaching Behaviors That Stimulate Thinking (or Avoid Stifling It)

As teachers, we have almost complete control over how students engage in learning. If we want students to think, we must plan activities that engage them in thinking. Consider how these teaching strategies affect student response and involvement.

1. *Guiding students to generate criteria for editing papers.* Even young writers can generate a list of what good writers do. This list is highly individualized, beginning with what the class knows at the beginning of the year and developing as the students learn more about writing.

A Good Writer

uses sentence markers (periods, question marks, capital letters)
writes sentences of different lengths
uses colorful, interesting words to describe

Displayed on the wall, the list is changed as students themselves make suggestions or question a statement that appears on the chart. Students can discuss how this list varies when applied to narrative writing compared to expository writing. Preparing the checklist gives students ownership in the list, which all of them can apply to their writing as they begin to revise their work.

2. *Giving all students a chance for active participation.* Cooperative learning experiences that put students in small groups give each student opportunities to engage in healthy interaction—asking questions, explaining, getting immediate feedback. Reading their writing in pairs or peer groups gives every student a chance to read a story to an audience and to receive the stimulus of audience response. Compare the percentage of involvement for each student in these small-group activities with the teacher-dominated classroom, which relies on "call-and-response" techniques that involve the teacher interacting with only one student at a time.

3. *Giving students "time to think."* Count to thirty (wait time) after posing an interesting question. Give students a chance to ponder over a possible answer before calling on a student to supply the "right" answer or worse, giving the answer yourself. Students who are reading also need time to check the context of an unfamiliar word or to read the rest of that and maybe the next two or three sentences before they have enough information to make an educated guess. We need to give students time to learn, refraining from showing off our adult expertise.

4. *Planning broad studies in which students can become involved.* Units of study based on topics that interest students, studies that have purpose and relate to their lives, permit students to work at individual levels of ability. These broad topics—color, naming, communication, love, conflict—begin with personal involvement and move outward to the broader community and then to the world, our global village.

Organization of This Book

We believe that thinking instruction rightfully belongs in every classroom. We recognize, however, that teachers are busy and may not have time to attend workshops on right-brain/left-brain thinking, creative writing, values clarification, synectics, and all the other special concerns related to teaching thinking. We have tried therefore to analyze the different ideas about thinking and to consolidate them into an integrated approach that we hope you will find helpful.

For purposes of discussion, we have categorized ideas in separate chapters. We hope, however, to show you how these ideas go together and to point out how they are more alike than different, each with its place in an integrated curriculum. The following is a brief synopsis of the content of each of the following chapters.

VALUING AND DECIDING

Values and attitudes are essential aspects of thinking. They are hidden in everything we say, our opinions, and our behaviors. Although we do not presume to teach specific values or attitudes, we do want students to recognize the alternatives that are available. We also want to help them avoid the two-valued orientation to evaluation and decision making. Many of these understandings are best presented through examples in literature. In *The Red Badge of Courage*, for example, Stephen Crane provides insight into the reality of war and the courage of men who face death as they fight for their country.

MODELS OF THINKING

As discussed in Chapter 1, some thinking can be identified as basic, common to more advanced operations in thinking. One familiar hierarchy of "levels of thinking," developed by Benjamin Bloom, is presented with suggestions for implementing it in lesson form. We also discuss other theories related to the thinking processes.

DISCOVERY METHODS

The discovery or inquiry method of thinking has been closely associated with the scientific method. We discuss the scientific method and the logic that is subsumed within it as we suggest ways of engaging students in conducting, for example, research studies.

WHOLE-BRAIN THINKING

While the studies of right-brain/left-brain thinking have provided interesting insights based on research, we prefer to apply "whole-brain thinking" theories in the classroom. We try to make teachers aware of the difference between linear thinking and more creative thinking, but we want them to recognize the interdependence of these aspects of thinking.

CREATIVITY IN THE ROUND

We want to develop the creative skills of each student as they take risks, generating original ideas and ways of doing things. At the same time, we realize that creativity is not some weird, unusual way of thinking but is a fresh perception that is usually based on a knowledge base. Therefore, we do not segregate "creative" writing from "functional" writing but recognize all writing as creative to some degree. We encourage students to risk making creative leaps by providing opportunities for them to note relationships and to experiment with varied media.

EXTENDING COMPREHENSION SKILLS

Although we talk about *comprehension,* we do not always seem to understand that comprehension is thinking. In this chapter, therefore, we examine the term *to comprehend* in order to discuss the various aspects of comprehension. We look at specific thinking skills that add to understanding, gaining meaning in transaction with the author.

COMPOSING THINKING

We see writing as the expression of thinking. We examine the processes that make up the act of composing in order to identify specific skills that can be taught. We examine the contributions specifically of James Moffett and his modes of discourse. We also recognize that the composing process generates thinking.

THINKING WITH COMPUTER POWER

The computer is a tool with which we can write. It is also a tool that can present learning experiences with which students can interact. Although we recognize, too, the thinking skills that are inherent in engaging students in programming, that is not our focus in this chapter. We demonstrate ways of writing and revising with a word-processing program. We also consider selected software that is recommended for developing thinking abilities.

INTEGRATING THINKING ACROSS THE CURRICULUM

We feel that the best way to engage students in learning is through developing a meaty topic to which they can relate in their own lives. Integrated studies can occur in humanities or core programs at the secondary level, and they readily occur in the self-contained elementary school classroom. Any teacher can plan instruction, however, around a theme that allows for individual interests and abilities. Within the integrated unit of study lie opportunities for students to engage in thinking processes that represent all levels of specificity and provide for varied levels of performance.

REFLECTION: INFUSING THINKING INTO ALL INSTRUCTION

The final chapter provides a review of the philosophy that undergirds the presentation throughout this text. The authors make explicit the perspective of "teaching *for* thinking" and its implications for all teachers.

SUMMARY

Teaching thinking requires comprehensive knowledge of the theory and research related to the complex study of thinking. Although the study is complex, we can clarify the processes involved for ourselves as teachers and for the students we teach, even those in primary grades. We can select teaching strategies and behaviors that will best stimulate student thinking, and we can plan lessons that will engage students in working with the gathering of factual data, processing that data in varied ways, and then making the results public. The most effective learning experiences will focus on broad integrative themes, permitting students consciously to apply varied levels of thinking, making choices as appropriate. Thinking instruction crosses all levels and subject areas so that it affects the lives of all students and teachers. Focusing on the thinking processes lends excitement to both teaching and learning.

CHALLENGE

At the end of each chapter, we include suggestions for getting started with the topic at hand. Try some of these ideas and consider how you can work with your students to stimulate their thinking.

1. Cluster around a word or topic that interests you, for example, holiday, my car, friendship. See how many different clusters of ideas develop.

2. Select a good book that you might read aloud or study with students in your class—for example,

Primary: *The Dead Tree*, Alvin Tresselt
Upper Elementary: *Alice in Wonderland*, Lewis Carroll
Junior High School: *The Human Comedy*, William Saroyan
High School: *The Heart Is a Lonely Hunter*, Carson McCullers

As you read the book, take notes or mark passages as you think about learning activities based on the language or content the author presents. Plan several lessons following the SAFE Demonstration Lesson Plan described in this chapter.

3. Make a list of all the terms that you associate with thinking processes—for example, conclusion, synthesis, schema, creativity. Jot down a few notes about the meaning of these terms. Compare your ideas with others in the class. Volunteer to explore the meaning of one term, beginning with the index of this book. Finally, compile a glossary of terms as you clarify these meanings.

4. Map the thinking activities that occur in your classroom. How will you group them? Work in a small group of four to six persons to compare maps. As each person presents his or her map, ask questions and make suggestions that might make the map more comprehensive.

NOTES

1. Howard Gardner, *Frames of Mind: The Theory of Multiple Intelligence* (New York: Basic Books, 1983).
2. Varied articles in Julie Jensen, ed., *Composing and Comprehending* (Urbana, Ill.: National Council of Teachers of English.
3. Noam Chomsky, *Aspects of the Theory of Syntax* (Cambridge, Mass.: MIT Press, 1965).
4. First graders in Texas, quoted by The Honorable Shirley M. Hufstedler, former United States Secretary of Education, "Viewpoints," *Language Arts* 58 (January 1981): 11–13.
5. Student art in *The Panther Prowl* 6 no. 3 (February 1987), Parkside School, San Bruno, Calif.
6. Gabrielle Rico, *Writing the Natural Way* (Tarcher, 1984).

EXPLORING FURTHER

Belenky, Mary, et al. *Women's Way of Knowing: The Development of Self, Voice, and Mind.* New York: Basic Books, 1986.

Bossone, Richard. *The Fourth R: Reasoning.* New York: City University of New York, 1983.

Costa, Arthur. *Developing Minds.* ASCD, 1985.

Gardner, Howard. *Frames of Mind: The Theory of Multiple Intelligence.* New York: Basic Books, 1983.

Hays, Janice, et al. *The Writer's Mind.* Urbana, Ill.: National Council of Teachers of English, 1983.

Jensen, Julie, ed. *Composing and Comprehending.* Urbana, Ill.: National Council of Teachers of English, 1985.

Marzano, Robert, et al. *Dimensions of Thinking: A Framework for Curriculum and Instruction.* Association for Supervision and Curriculum Development, 1988.

Moffett, James, and Betty Jane Wagner. *Student-Centered Language Arts and Reading: A Handbook for Teachers*, 3d ed. Boston: Houghton Mifflin, 1983.

National Assessment of Educational Progress. *Reading, Thinking, and Writing.* NAEP, 1981.

Purves, Alan, and Olive Niles, eds. *Becoming Readers in a Complex Society.* Yearbook of the National Society for the Study of Education. Chicago: University of Chicago Press, 1984.

Tiedt, Iris M. et al. *Reading, Thinking, and Writing: A Holistic Language and Literacy Program.* Boston: Allyn & Bacon, 1989.

Valuing

'Tis with our judgments as our watches, none go just alike, but each believes his own.

Alexander Pope

We are all ready to be savage in some cause. The difference between a good man and a bad one is the choice of the cause.

William James

Your system of beliefs is the basis for what you are, feel, think, say, and do.

Sharon Ratliffe

One impulse from a vernal wood
May teach you more of man,
Of moral evil and of good,
Than all the sages can.

William Wordsworth

There ain't no sin and there ain't no virtue. There's just stuff people do. It's all part of the same thing. And some of the things folks do is nice, and some ain't nice, but that's as far as any man got a right to say.

John Steinbeck

Deciding

The strongest principle of growth lies in human choice.

George Eliot

Life often presents us with a choice of evils, rather than of goods.

E. C. Colton

The difficulty in life is the choice.

George Moore

Everyone complains of his memory, but no one complains of his judgment.

La Rochefoucauld

When you do a thing because you have determined that it ought to be done, never avoid being seen doing it, even if the opinion of the multitude is going to condemn you.

Tacitus

Not to decide is to decide.

Harvey Cox

I prefer not to.
Herman Melville

CHAPTER 2

Valuing and Deciding

Objectives

After reading this chapter, you will be able to

- *Define values and valuing.*
- *Explain how a person internalizes values.*
- *Structure assignments for helping students sort out values.*
- *Involve students in varied decision-making processes.*
- *Provide students with a classification system for isolating decision-making variables.*
- *Discuss debatable issues concerning teaching values and decision making.*
- *Create assignments that offer students an opportunity to engage in valuing and deciding.*

We live in a world of choices. Now, more than at any other time in history, each of us confronts an incredible array of personal choices. These choices range from relationships, economics, and vocations to grimmer ones involving drugs (legal and illegal), alcohol, tobacco, and sex. How we handle these decisions, in large part, determines not only our relative degree of satisfaction in life but also, in an era of AIDS and herpes, our physical well-being and life expectancy. In this social context, clearly the educational imperative for teachers is to provide students with appropriate processes for informed values clarification and decision making. This chapter explores issues and aspects of valuing and decision making.

Valuing

DEFINING VALUES AND VALUING

In *Values and Our Youth*, Gordon W. Allport defines values as "meanings perceived as related to self."[1] The definition from *Webster's New World*

Dictionary is more comprehensive: "the social principles, goals or standards held or accepted by an individual, class, society, etc." Both of these definitions are useful but neither suggests an important factor—the behavior that arises out of the values. Jon Voight the actor expressed this values dynamic in an interview. In discussing his approach to acting, he said, "I never went in a direction that didn't have some value in it or took a role without extending myself to see those values succeed."[2] This dualistic nature of values—principles held and acted on—focuses the defining of values. Therefore, for our purposes, *values* are "the internalized principles that guide an individual's thinking and behavior." Just as we own them, values own us in terms of affecting what we think and do.

It follows then, that valuing is the activity that arises out of defining values. In a narrow sense, this could imply establishing worth, but let's think of valuing in a broader context. Turning to *Webster's* again, we find: "Valuing—to place a certain estimate of worth on in a scale of values (e.g., to value health above wealth)." This is a satisfactory definition for general purposes, but we seek a broader one. We define *valuing* as assigning significance or importance to an idea, concept, principle, or thing. With these definitions in mind, let us now turn to some important issues concerning values and valuing.

VALUE QUESTIONS

In *Human Values in the Classroom*, Robert and Isabel Hawley assert that "Human values must be taught because they are the key to survival of the species *Homo sapiens*. Teaching human values is teaching survival skills."[3] Today, students do indeed face decisions that literally are matters of life and death. We have experienced two recent examples.

Situation 1: The bridge beckons every spring, and students from the local high school answer the call. One by one, they take their turns climbing over the handrail and standing poised, gathering courage to jump into the lake below. The length of the plunge varies, depending on the winter's rainfall. Sometimes, the distance is only twenty feet or so, but in drier years it can be as much as fifty. The greater the distance, the longer they hesitate before leaping into the turbid water. Once in a while, one will finally decide not to risk the dangerous leap and will crawl back over the handrail to safety as the others jeer.

Situation 2: The following is a high school student's description of the "drug scene":

> Drugs . . . more drugs . . . and if that's not enough, more drugs. Within the last three years of high school, that seems to be the song that everybody's singing.
>
> "Hey, Kristy, what did you do this weekend?" a friend calls out.
>
> "Oh, hi, Susie. I went out with Scott and I got totally loaded. It was absolutely incredible. How about you?"

"Oh, I went out to that party at Matt's. You should have seen . . . "

And then they walk away thinking nothing of it. Drugs are a big problem. Most people, like the two quoted above, don't even think anything about it.[4]

In both of these cases, the participants are dealing with survival. If the bridge leapers and the partiers were to consider the complex value systems impinging on them, they would find themselves confronting not only the value system of their peers but also those of their families and of the larger society. In both cases, of course, they are performing illegal actions. Here are examples of values in conflict. What responsibility do schools have in helping students to confront such perilous value choices? Schools must provide opportunities for students to examine values and practice valuing. Our society is at risk. Recently, both President Reagan and Secretary of Education Bennett have called for our nation's schools to present values education to students.[5]

What have schools done in the past in helping students weigh value issues? Fred Wilhelms questions the traditional role of the schools:

> How much chance have we provided a learner in our schools to dig down into the immanent questions of values, of the significance of life, of the possibilities inherent in his humanity? How much help do we ever offer him to see the great options he has as to how to spend himself? What is there in our program that helps him to hammer out his own personal set of values, make his own commitments, and decide what to *be*?[6]

A thoughtful consideration of these questions suggests that the confrontation of values should be a major curriculum component in every school in the land. Given the present social upheaval in our society, these questions should and must be answered by teachers and administrators.

And, if schools succeed in thrusting values education to the fore, how would our young people benefit? L. Craig Wilson offers this assessment:

> The search for values is healthy in the long run. . . . There are simply a staggering number of visible alternatives to the American tradition from which the young feel free to choose (among the more interesting are the Eastern philosophies and the cult of astrology). The tragedy lies in the despair that accompanies a conclusion that life is, in the final analysis, meaningless. Of course, if this is true, education is equally pointless.[7]

The evidence is that many of our students have concluded just that and are wasting their lives in a meaningless pursuit of pleasure or escape, even into the grave. To do nothing is to abandon them at a time when they are most needy.

Assuming that we achieve general agreement among educators for extensive values exploration, whose value system should be taught? Many would argue for the dominant value system of our society, but that raises the issue of identifying one dominant system. Wilson proposes a reasonable solution:

> A more stable position—one that would reject both the existential void and the law and order panic—stresses valuing as a complicated continuing process, always incomplete but never divorced from the mainstream of moral history. Educational programming would thus focus on reference points in time (e.g., history) and space (e.g., community), which are larger and not totally controllable by individual choice. The idea would be to make all value systems subject to intelligent debate and the kind of dissent that legitimate scholarship guarantees.[8]

What a welcome climate for intellectual discourse, if indeed we could open all value systems to "intelligent debate."

Clearly, teachers who deal with values and valuing issues in their classes have assumed a demanding task, one fraught with difficulty. How are teachers to deal with these issues without imposing their own beliefs on students? We can begin by increasing our own awareness. We can learn what true valuing is. We need to identify effective ways of exploring value issues with our students. We should inform ourselves about which areas of values clarification produce the most confusion in our students. Then, we can start to help our students examine, clarify, and affirm their own value choices through exposing them to a variety of ongoing opportunities for values clarification and assimilation. To accomplish our goals honestly and adequately, we may have to rethink our beliefs about appropriate areas of inquiry subsumed under usual course descriptions. For if we really want our students to think critically and form independent judgments, we need a broad sense of course content. Of course, we have the additional obligation of informing our students' parents about the form and purpose of our efforts.

HELPING STUDENTS WITH VALUES AND VALUING

To incorporate values education into the classroom, we need first to create a climate of trust and acceptance. Our students will not involve themselves fully if they find that they are exposed to ridicule or humiliation by their teachers or classmates. So, even though the interaction may, at times, become intense or confrontational, it should not be permitted to become mindlessly competitive or mean-spirited. We must foster a free flow of divergent points of view to allow our students meaningful interaction. Hawley and Hawley offer a three-step model for a nurturing environment:

> Step 1: Open the door: to encourage a person to think about value-related subjects and to encourage the sharing of those thoughts with others

Step 2: Accept: to accept the thoughts, feelings, beliefs, and ideas of others non-judgmentally and to encourage others to accept those for what they are without criticism

Step 3: Stimulate: to encourage additional thinking so that individuals can move toward a more comprehensive way of valuing[9]

As we deal with value questions in our classrooms, we must realize that value judgments will inevitably occur. For example, the statement "American Indians suffer from alcoholism and a high suicide rate on the reservations" is not a value judgment. But when an observation is included as part of the statement, it creates the possibility of a values conflict: "Isn't it a pity that American Indians suffer from alcoholism and a high suicide rate on the reservations?" Value conflicts lead to contention in support of opposing points of view. We should both anticipate and welcome such contention as a normal and necessary component of inquiry into value systems. Otherwise, we risk not being taken seriously in our efforts. Aylesworth and Reagan suggest an honest approach:

> When we are faced with some extreme stands on moral issues, we depart from the view that all opinions are of equal worth. Although we want learners to become tolerant (this in itself reflects a value), we do not want them to believe that their values make no difference or that any set of values is as good as any other. In short, we are concerned with the "valuing" students do with their knowing. Our concern should be to help learners develop the ability to do something (value intelligently) rather than simply learn a set of rules.[10]

It is possible to separate the content of a value system from the process of valuing. Raths has investigated how people come to hold certain beliefs and to establish certain behavior patterns. He has identified seven subprocesses that go into the process of valuing:

Prizing one's beliefs and behaviors
1. prizing and cherishing
2. publicly affirming, when appropriate

Choosing one's beliefs and behaviors
3. choosing from alternatives
4. choosing after consideration of consequences
5. choosing freely

Acting on one's beliefs
6. acting
7. acting with a pattern, consistency and repetition[11]

You can see from the different steps in this model that these are observable behaviors. Thus, these behaviors can be measured and evaluated. You can evaluate your students' growth in valuing competency by increasing your own awareness of these processes. But, it is important to remember that values assimilation is an organic process for students and teachers. As such, it requires a flexible and modifiable instructional approach.

Simon and others have researched the manner in which teachers have traditionally guided the young in the study of values and valuing. This research allowed them to categorize values instruction into four approaches:

1. Moralizing
2. Laissez-faire
3. Modeling
4. Values-clarification[12]

Their research indicated that the most effective of these modes was values clarification. In other words, a planned and structured program of values instruction produces the greatest gains in students' valuing competency. Fortunately, because of the emphasis on values instruction in the 1970s, there are a number of exemplary programs available. You will find some of them listed under "Exploring Further" at the end of this chapter. Such resources coupled with your own initiative and imagination will help you create a satisfactory program for values education in your classroom.

GENERAL SUGGESTIONS FOR PRESENTING VALUES IN THE CLASSROOM

We can highlight values in our classrooms. For example, we can create a Values Bulletin Board, which focuses on a different values issue each week. Students can bring in relevant newspaper or magazine articles for the board. We can put a Values Quote of the Day on the chalkboard and ask our students to react to it orally or in writing. We could set up a Values Suggestion Box devoted to students' questions and suggestions and occasionally share the contents for class consideration. We might use Values on Video by videotaping appropriate segments of television shows dealing with important issues and have them as springboards for writing and/or class discussion.

To personalize the values instruction more, we could have our students keep a Values Journal in which they regularly record their own thoughts and feelings about the various issues studied or discussed. We could invite Guest Speakers on Values Issues into our classrooms periodically to present differing viewpoints on timely issues. An important aid for teachers is a long list of Values-Clarifying Questions for stimulating discussions. Some sample questions, which could be included, are as follows:

1. What is your stand on birth control pills?
2. How do you feel about grades in school?

3. Should children grade their parents? Their teachers?
4. What do you think about public welfare for the needy?
5. Are you more or less religious now than you were three years ago? Why?
6. Are you likely to marry out of your race? Why or why not?
7. Have you ever stolen anything? Why?
8. Do you have faith in our political system? Why or why not?
9. Should people always do what they like to do?
10. Is it too easy to get a divorce?
11. Is it okay to cheat if it means winning or losing a game?
12. Are people too materialistic these days?[13]

Questions of this sort can be used in large- or small-group contexts. You should generate your own list of questions, with particular attention to timeliness pertaining to current events. It is important to choose open-ended questions that lend themselves to diverse points of view.

Through activities such as those suggested, our classrooms become miniature research centers for values exploration. And, the beauty of it is that we don't have to purchase many expensive materials or machines. Also, much of the curriculum content we are already teaching lends itself to a values-inquiry approach.

SAFE DEMONSTRATION LESSON PLANS

On the next several pages, you will find a series of sample lessons for teaching values and valuing. These lessons are intended to serve as models for ways to integrate values instruction into your classroom.

SAFE Demonstration Lesson Plan 2.1: Values Collage
Grade Levels: 8–12

OBJECTIVES

Students will

1. create a values collage that reflects either their personal values or community values.
2. relate their individual collages to stories and books they have read in class.

BRIEF DESCRIPTION

Students create a values collage. They display the completed collages creating a museum exhibition. Students then study each other's collages noting which values are represented. Students present their individual collages to the group explaining the value orientation.

PROCEDURES

Stimulus

Cut several pictures from magazines. These should represent various elements of our culture (cars, computers, perfume, animals, toys, sporting goods, and the like). Share these with the class and talk about the values they represent. Stress the abstract values rather than the material ones (for example, a football as a symbol of cooperation or fair play).

Next, let students select two or three magazines from a pile you have collected and give each student a large piece of butcher paper. Have a supply of scissors, glue, and various colors of construction paper available.

Activity

Tell students to create an individual collage, one which reflects either their personal values or community values. Encourage them to use their imaginations as they search through the magazines (*Life, Time, Newsweek, People*). Each student should create a collage. They may use the construction paper to make additional elements if necessary. After they have begun cutting and pasting, check that they are all on track. At this point, a sample collage created by you would be instructive. Once you have checked understanding and progress, let them finish. Caution students against critiquing other's work; this is not a contest for the best collage.

Follow-Up

After all have finished, have students display their efforts by taping them to the walls, so that the collages resemble a museum exhibition. Allow students to walk around and study each collage more closely. Number the collages and have them guess which represent group values and which individual ones. After they have guessed for each, have students identify their collages and tell whether they reflect personal or group values. Solicit volunteers to tell about their collages in greater detail. Finally, have students write about the process and what they learned from it.

Evaluation

Give students general feedback about their behavior, creativity, and resourcefulness as you observed those during this activity. Invite another teacher or the principal to visit the "museum of values" and comment on it to your class. Assign individual credit for each collage on the basis of inclusiveness and degree of insight about values you see.

SAFE Demonstration Lesson Plan 2.2: What Will People Say?
Grade Levels: 6–12

OBJECTIVES

Students will

1. express various value positions for a set of witnesses to different events.
2. compare their own valuing positions to those of others, real and fictitious.

BRIEF DESCRIPTION

Students identify values held by families. They witness various situations by reading descriptions distributed by the teacher. After discussing one of the situations, students imagine what different statements participants might make. They then decide the values revealed by each statement. Students write about the situations, act them out, and discuss the value positions presented.

PROCEDURES

Stimulus

Talk with the class about family value systems and parental concerns about what other people will think about their children's behavior. Solicit several examples of times when your students' parents have asked, "What will people say?" Have a handout containing several eyewitness situations ready for distribution. The following is an example of such a situation.

> *Eyewitness Situation:* A bigger boy beats up a smaller boy in a fight on the playground. Earlier, the smaller boy had called the bigger boy a bad name.
> *Witnesses:* A friend of the smaller boy, the bigger boy's girlfriend, a teacher, and the custodian

Your prepared handout should contain three or four situations.

Activity

Pass out the handout and discuss one of the situations. The point is to put words in the mouth of each of the eyewitnesses. Through what each says, the reader should be able to infer a values position. For example, suppose the teacher who saw the fight said, "Johnny deserves it. He's always causing trouble. I hope Billy smears him." These words would certainly reveal a part of the teacher's value position in terms of conflict resolution.

Next, have students put words in the mouths of the witnesses to each situation on the handout by writing in what each witness says. Give them sufficient time to respond to each situation. Stress the importance of having the witnesses say words that express value positions.

After they have completed their writing, have students share their writing by acting out each situation, using their writing as scripts. Present each situation two or three times with different participants and script each time.

Follow-Up

Discuss the various values positions represented in the different situations presented in the dramatizations. Ask students to choose one of the situations and write it twice again, first with words nearest their own value positions and a second time with words farthest from their own positions.

Evaluation

Collect the writings and read them for your own information about their clarity of thought and their thoroughness. Use a 1 to 5 scale and assign a numerical "grade" to each.

SAFE Demonstration Lesson Plan 2.3: On the Other Hand
Grade Levels: 6–12

OBJECTIVES

Students will

1. study an important issue in depth to determine the pros and cons.
2. prepare a defense to encourage support for a position that is the opposite of their own.

BRIEF DESCRIPTION

Students discuss positions taken by well-known historical figures on controversial issues in the past. Students select an issue for intensive study. After researching their topics, they take a stance on the issue, write a summary, and critique each other's papers. Students then write a paper from the opposite viewpoint.

PROCEDURES

Stimulus

Discuss how our nation's history has been affected by those who took unpopular positions on important issues. Such names as Patrick Henry, Thomas Paine, Frederick Douglass, Martin Luther King, Jr., Elizabeth Cady Stanton, George Wallace, Phyllis Schafley, Jane Fonda, and Dr. Timothy Leary can be mentioned as examples of those who took strong stands either for good or ill, depending on one's point of view. After this discussion, brainstorm some contemporary issues that have opposing viewpoints held about them. Try for a fairly extensive and comprehensive list.

Activity

Ask students to select one of the issues for intensive individual study. After they have each made a selection, talk about how to find background information for their topics. Also, post a listing of students and their topics for general information.

Give students time to research their topics thoroughly and to prepare a written position paper that clearly states their personal stand on the issue. This will probably take a week or two. After they have finished their research and writing, have them share some general comments about their findings and the problems they encountered in their work on the issues.

Follow-Up

Pair students to ensure that students with relatively unrelated topics are working together. Have them exchange and read papers and write comments on the author's presentation of information. Give them ten minutes to prepare an argument in which they take the position opposite from the one they took in their position; this should be a five-minute defense of this opposite point of view. At the end of ten minutes, have each member of the pairs present his or her argument orally. When both have finished, have each member write a short evaluation of how effectively this "on-the-other-hand" viewpoint was argued. Collect the papers.

Evaluation

Evaluate the activity both for the quality of the students' involvement in the process and of the product—the research presented in the paper. You might want to give some consideration to the students' evaluations of both the written and oral efforts in your determination of an appropriate mark for each paper.

SAFE Demonstration Lesson Plan 2.4: Letter Perfect
Grade Levels: 6–12

OBJECTIVES
Students will

1. research an issue of importance to their lives.
2. write a letter expressing their concern about the issue to an appropriate elected official.

BRIEF DESCRIPTION
Students discuss a current issue and reach consensus as a class. Collectively, they compose a position paper. Each student then selects a current issue to research. After completing the research, students write letters to officials to express their concern and reasons for specific actions they recommend. Students critique each other's letters before they are mailed.

PROCEDURES

Stimulus
Select a topic, a current social problem, for discussion by the class. Create necessary charts, graphs, and the like on overhead transparencies to help outline the parameters of the problem. An example of such an issue is the use of steroids to improve athletic performance or physical appearance. Younger students might discuss air pollution or pollution of local streams and rivers.

Engage the class in a discussion of the issue. Have some leading questions prepared to help guide the discussion. Use transparencies as needed to provide, for example, statistical data and definitions. Try to get the class to arrive at a general consensus about the issue and its significance. Write a position statement about the issue on the board. Talk about some possible solutions and categorize these on the board under "possible" and "impossible."

Activity
Tell your students that it is important for them as citizens of a democracy to take stands on issues and to make themselves heard. Tell them you are going to give them an opportunity to practice good citizenship. Each student will select an issue to research. After completing the research, each will write a formal letter of concern to an elected official with suggestions for solving the problem.

Give them time to select an issue that interests them; have them analyze the problem and seek solutions. Such questions as these focus their inquiry:

1. Why is this a serious problem?
2. Who suffers most directly from this problem?
3. What are the principal causes of the problem?
4. Is the problem growing worse? Why or why not?
5. What are some possible solutions?
6. Which solution(s) do you prefer?
7. Which elected official could help do something about this problem?

After students have analyzed their problems and devised possible solutions, have them pair up and discuss their findings.

Have each write a letter expressing concern about the issue and offering one or more possible solutions. This letter should be addressed to an elected official who has the power to affect action on their problem. This letter should first be written in rough draft and then carefully revised for both content and mechanics. Tell them it is essential that their writing be "letter perfect" because it is about an important issue and its perfection will reflect sincere concern. (At this point, you might review the elements of a formal letter.)

Group students into response groups and have them critique each other's letters for content and mechanics. Have them revise the letters based on the critiques and any new thoughts they have. Then, have them write their final drafts. Collect these and proofread them carefully. Provide stamped envelopes and have students address these neatly. Now for the ceremony! Take the entire class to a mailbox so that everyone witnesses the mailing of the letters.

Follow-Up

After mailing the letters, return to the classroom and discuss the entire process. What do they think about exercising their power as citizens? How do they feel? Ask them to share any responses they get from the officials to whom they wrote.

Evaluation

The two important areas for evaluation in this activity are the correctness of form and content of the letters and the completion of them, from first draft through addressing and mailing. Assign one grade for work quality based on a scale of correctness and a second grade based on work habits in fulfilling the assignment. The final grade for each student will be derived from these two grades.

Deciding

As Robert Benchley suggests in the following humorous poem, all too often, emotions play a more important role in decision making than does reason:

> I put my hand upon my heart
> and swore that we would never part;
> I wonder what I might have said,
> if I had put it on my head.

Our students frequently are trapped in situations where their feelings can overpower their judgment. Similarly, we adults have experienced both the pleasure and pain of actions based on a rush of feeling. Decision making is not easy, even under the best circumstances. But, as Sharon Ratliffe and Deldee Herman found in their investigation of decision making, adverse conditions often exist: decision making usually involves frustration and conflict, and decision making usually involves risk taking.[14]

TEACHING DECISION MAKING

How can we help our students be better decision makers? Obviously, they are not going to grow in their decision-making capabilities if we do not provide opportunities for deliberate, thoughtful decision making. To do this, we must be willing to schedule time in our classrooms for student involvement in decision making, and we must recognize that merely learning factual knowledge and information will not teach our students decision-making skills.

Teaching for decision making? The teacher might ask these questions first:

1. What responsibility do I have in providing instruction in decision making for my students?
2. If I am to teach decision-making skills, how should I integrate this instruction into my curriculum?
3. What are some specific strategies for teaching about and for experiencing decision making?

Teachers' Responsibility

Just as teachers often accept a high degree of responsibility for the knowledge students gain in their classes about subject area information, so, too, it is important for teachers to accept responsibility for providing instruction in decision making. Such instruction is quite justifiable, for, as Charles Wales, Anne Nardi, and Robert Stager point out: "Most employers want graduates who know how to anticipate consequences and make decisions. Decision-making gives thinking a purpose. Through our decisions, which are based on what we have learned both in and out of school, we determine the course of our lives."[15]

Given the acceptance of responsibility for instruction in decision making by the teacher, the next issue becomes the integration of such instruction into the curriculum. Most teachers feel anxiety about the amount of instructional time they are allotted for teaching the curriculum content they are already expected to teach. Asking them to sacrifice a significant portion of that time for instruction in decision making threatens them. Yet, such instruction is important and necessary. What to do?

Integration into the Curriculum

First, accept the notion that this does not have to become a dilemma. Your students can receive meaningful involvement in decision making in the context of the regular curriculum. The thinking skills required for decision making are vital in all aspects of intellectual activity. What is required is a change in instructional strategies so that much of the same curriculum content provides the basis for instruction in decision making. For example, suppose that you take a short story, which is a regular part of the curriculum, and, instead of teaching it in the usual fashion, you integrate decision-making instruction by creating a problem/solution dynamic out of the story's content. Engage the students in a process of decision making concerning the story's conflict. You are still using the same material but approaching it differently. Through using your imagination and creativity, you will find it possible to integrate decision-making instruction into many areas of your required curriculum.

Specific Strategies

The following are several general strategies that you might employ:

1. Present a hypothetical situation requiring a decision on the *chalkboard* occasionally and have the students brainstorm alternative decisions.
2. Use the *overhead projector* to present a situation and have the students suggest appropriate solutions.
3. Use a recorded *videotape* to present a problem situation, stop it before the solution is presented, and ask your students to suggest a range of solutions. Then, let them compare their ideas with the actual outcome.
4. Have your students maintain a *decision-making journal* in which they describe their own decision-making efforts and those of others that they have witnessed.

5. Create a *decision-maker-of-the-week* award and publicly value examples of effective decision making by your students.

These are only a few possibilities. As your own awareness and ingenuity increase, you will think of others.

FRAMEWORKS FOR DECISION MAKING

Decision making may take various forms. It can be seen as a matter of asking only a simple question or two—What's really at stake? What's the worst thing that can happen?—and then proceeding with a course of action, or it can be framed in a more formal manner. Patricia Kelly and Leila Christenbury offer this set of steps for formalized decision making:

1. Stating the desired goal or condition
2. Stating the obstacles to realizing this goal or condition
3. Identifying the alternatives available for overcoming each obstacle
4. Examining the alternatives in terms of the resources needed to carry them out, the costs available, and the constraints inherent in their use
5. Ranking the alternatives in terms of their possible consequences
6. Choosing the best alternative[16]

Imagine what a service to our students, if we could actually succeed in getting them to weigh their decisions more fully and thoughtfully. Certainly, nothing will make a teenager's life "fail-safe," but much confusion and grief might be avoided if our students had better tools for decision making.

An even more elaborate structure for decision making has been formulated by Wales, Nardi, and Stager, based on four operations:

Define the Situation
   I. State the Goal:
       1. Identify situation problems.
       2. Create goal options.
       3. Select the goal.
  II. Generate Ideas:
       4. Identify goal problems.
       5. Create idea options.
       6. Select ideas.
Define the New Situation
 III. Prepare a Plan:
       7. Identify new situation problems.
       8. Create plan options.
       9. Select a plan.

IV. Take Action:
   10. Identify plan problems.
   11. Create action options.
   12. Select the next action.[17]

To help students internalize a complicated decision-making process, walk them through it by finding a character from a novel who is beset by several problems or by inventing a hypothetical case study involving problems to be solved. Have your students proceed step by step through the process as they seek choices to guide the character's actions. Toad in *Wind in the Willows,* Homer in *The Human Comedy,* or George in *Of Mice and Men* are examples of characters with decisions to make.

Hawley and Hawley present two different frameworks for formal decision making. The first is a four-stage process with the following format:

1. Identify the end goals of the decision and rank them in order of importance to the decision maker.
2. List all available options, including wild, unrealistic ideas.
3. Examine the value of each of the options in terms of its benefits and weaknesses.
4. Match the values of each option with the end goal.[18]

One especially attractive feature of the preceding framework is in Step 2. The listing of "wild, unrealistic" ideas is an excellent suggestion. It allows the possibility of a serendipitous solution not previously considered. Also, it is consistent with familiar approaches to creative problem solving.

Hawley and Hawley's second method requires a graphic layout of the discrete elements involved in making a decision. They call it decision charting. The following is an example:

Decision–Charting[19]

Ranking	End goals	Decision: buying a car Options	Option values
1	Transportation	Economy car	Money, parking
2	Fun	Sports car	Impress others, have fun
4	Feeling of importance	Luxury car	Maintenance, monthly payments!
3	Make money	Station wagon	Haul stuff
5	To impress others	Fix up junked car	Fun to do

This plan has two advantages: (a) It is easy to visualize all the considerations at the same time, and (b) it establishes rankings for the choices.

Students should appreciate its practicality in weighing choices of colleges to attend, dating for a big dance, or how to spend a monetary gift.

Regardless of whether you select one of these frameworks *in toto*, modify one, or create your own, there is a good argument for presenting a formal process to your students. It helps give them a greater sense of power over a crucial part of their lives—making decisions. It seems likely that a sizable number of teenagers makes poor decisions in risky situations for lack of an effective method. From an instructional standpoint, another advantage of giving students practice with formal decision making is the linking that can be done between valuing instruction and decision making. Thus, the teacher extends such lessons beyond the classroom into the students' life beyond the school. This extension of learning may serve to reveal for our students an essential truth about decision making: "Making a decision to do one thing is also a decision not to do something else."[20] There is real power in making decisions thoughtfully and satisfaction when those decisions produce good results.

SAFE DEMONSTRATION LESSON PLANS

The series of model lessons that follow focus on deciding and decision making. When reviewing these lessons, you might consider their applicability for your classroom. You might also think of additional lessons you could generate out of your own materials, experience, and imagination.

SAFE Demonstration Lesson Plan 2.5: Decisions, Decisions! (Classroom Hopscotch)
Grade Levels: 6–12

OBJECTIVES

Students will

1. make a series of decisions in a short period of time.
2. compare their individual decisions against those preferred by a majority of the class.
3. suggest alternative solutions to several hypothetical problems.

BRIEF DESCRIPTION

Students read a number of problem situations and consider several possible solutions. Students make decisions quickly based on limited information. After the decision-making activity, they discuss the difficulty of making decisions under the pressure of time. Students also discuss additional solutions they would suggest for the situations described.

PROCEDURES

Stimulus

Put together a series of problems and possible solutions. Number and type on 3 × 5-inch cards. The number of cards should equal the number of students in the class. Each card should contain a brief description of the basic situation and three possible solutions to the problem. The following is an example:

> #1
> Charles and Max are good friends, and Charles is doing poorly in math class. Charles wants Max to help him cheat on an upcoming test. If Charles doesn't pass it, his parents will ground him, and he won't be able to go skiing with Max and his friends.
> A. Max should refuse to help Charles but should offer to help him study for the test.
> B. Max should help Charles to cheat this time but tell him he never will again.
> C. Max should tell the teacher so that Charles can't cheat because the teacher is watching him too closely.

You could derive some of the problem situations from stories or books used in the class or from problems you have experienced in your classes over the years.

Talk with the class about the difficulty of making effective decisions, especially when under pressure or in a hurry. Ask for examples from the class; share a personal experience of your own. Tell the class that they are going to make a series of quick decisions.

Activity

Have each student number from one to the total number of students in the class. Ask the students to line up around the perimeter of the room. Tape one of the problem situations to each desk in consecutive order. Explain the traffic pattern to students so they will know how to move from desk to desk around the room. Tell them they will have only one minute at each desk to read the problem and decide on a solution. The following is a diagram of traffic flow:

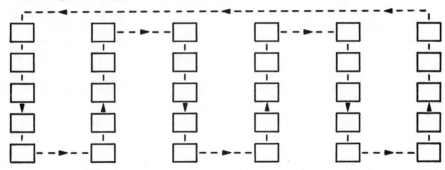

Caution students to be sure they put their decision choices in the right place on their numbered answer sheets because they won't all be starting at number one. Have students return to their desks and wait for your signal to begin the activity.

Give the signal to begin. Use a whistle or clicker to cue the movement from desk to desk. Students will have one minute to select a solution to the problem at each desk, commencing with their own. Students are to read each problem situation rapidly and then mark their choice of the suggested solutions on their answer sheets. After they have finished with each problem, they will continue around the room until their last answer brings them back to the desk nearest their starting point. Have them return to their own seats.

Talk with students about this experience. How did they feel about being under the pressure of the one-minute limit? Were they generally satisfied with their decisions? Did they have better solutions to suggest than those offered as choices?

Follow-Up

Tabulate the number of responses for each solution to each separate situation on the chalkboard. Let students compare their individual choices against the majority choices of the group. Discuss some of the solutions that got many votes and some that got only a few. Look for patterns or trends in the tabulation responses.

Next have students choose any three to five situations (depending on the time available) and ask them to suggest one additional solution for each situation in writing. After they have finished writing their suggestions, collect these and their answer sheets.

Evaluation

Evaluate the answer sheets for completeness. Give one point for each response on the sheet. This rewards the deciding that occurred. Assign grades for the suggestions they wrote by judging the reasonableness and practicability of each.

NOTES

The basic hopscotch activity described works well in other classroom procedures including testing, reviewing previous learning, and writing assignments. Experiment with it.

SAFE Demonstration Lesson Plan 2.6: What Would You Do If . . . ?
Grade Levels: 6–12

OBJECTIVES

Students will

1. decide on the best solution for each of a series of hypothetical situations.
2. create some hypothetical situations of their own.
3. write possible solutions for three situations from those created by the class.

BRIEF DESCRIPTION

Students consider a number of "what if" situations. They discuss possible responses or solutions for each problem situation. Working in small groups, they reach consensus on the best solution for each situation. The class then tabulates their solutions to compare variations in their responses. They discuss differences and what values are represented.

PROCEDURES

Stimulus

Prepare a list of hypothetical "What would you do if . . . ?" situations. Duplicate the list so every student has a copy. Select one of the situations from the list and brainstorm possible solutions with the class. Some sample situations are as follows: What would you do if

a friend and you went into a store and your friend started shoplifting?
someone you know drove down your street, smashed into your neighbor's car, and drove away without stopping?
you went to a friend's home for dinner and you didn't like any of the food that was served?

Activity

Group the class into threes and give them time to discuss each situation and reach consensus on a "best" solution. Tabulate the solutions on the board for comparison of decisions. Have them vote on the solutions to see which choices gain the greatest support. If there is a divergence between their choices and apparent community values, discuss this disparity.

Follow-Up

Have students make up some hypothetical situations of their own. These should be written so you can collect them. Read a number of these aloud and have students write individual solutions for any three. Collect these solutions.

Evaluation

Assign grades based on each student's participation in the group effort and on the quality of the written solutions from each student. Use a primary traits evaluation based on each of the hypothetical situations having the following elements: a brief description of a problem situation and a solution that is legal and possible. Award equal points for each element—for example, ten for the description of the situation and ten for the solution.

SAFE Demonstration Lesson Plan 2.7: I Would If I Could
Grade Levels: 2–12

OBJECTIVES

Students will

1. share some of their hopes, wishes, dreams, and fantasies.
2. identify the barriers that prevent the fulfillment of those hopes, wishes, and so on.
3. select an achievable hope, wish, dream, or fantasy and accomplish or fulfill it.
4. evaluate the value of the experience.

BRIEF DESCRIPTION

Students discuss their fantasies and the various reasons that these fantasies cannot be realized. They then identify one fantasy that they could possibly achieve given help or changed circumstances. Each student plans to achieve a fantasy and report on the procedures and results.

PROCEDURES

This activity can be oral for younger students. Adapt the choices to fit the age level of the students.

Stimulus

Talk with your students about the role of hopes, wishes, fantasies, and dreams in our lives. Mention the fact that some of these, when acted out or fulfilled, can lead to great accomplishment, but others can lead to unhappiness or tragedy. Share some examples of famous persons who have fulfilled their dreams. Discuss the constraints that keep people from achieving their dreams or fulfilling their fantasies. These might be physical, financial, legal, religious, moral, or psychological. For example, you might wish you could swim the English Channel, but your physical condition, lack of ability, or financial burden might forbid it. Share one of your own dreams or fantasies with the class and ask them to identify the constraints.

Activity

Ask your students to make individual lists of "I would if I could" statements. These should be based on their own particular hopes, dreams, wishes, or fantasies. They should be structured as follows:

1. I would take a vacation to New Zealand if I could, but I can't, so I won't.
2. I would write a best-selling novel if I could, but I can't, so I won't.
3. I would bake a perfect pumpkin pie if I could, but I can't, so I won't.
4. I would go skydiving if I could, but I can't, so I won't.
5. I would discover a cure for cancer if I could, but I can't, so I won't.

After each student has a list of ten or twelve items, give them a chance to discuss their lists in small groups. They should talk about the appeal and the constraints of the listed items. When this discussion is completed, tell them it is possible for them to empower themselves by trying to achieve one of their "I woulds." Have them select one that seems more readily attainable than the others. Qualify their selection by requiring that it not be illegal, excessively dangerous, expensive, or too time consuming. Also, you could require that it be witnessed and certified by a responsible witness such as a parent, teacher, or adult friend. An example of this selection from the list already given would be Number 3. It is now changed as follows:

3. I would bake a perfect pumpkin pie if I could, *and I can, so I will.*

After each student has selected one of the "I woulds" to accomplish, tell students they must accomplish their "I would" objective within the next two weeks. Tell them, also, that the classroom can serve as a forum for their performance of their "I would" if they choose and if it involves an activity appropriate to the classroom. For example, the pumpkin pie could be served to the class for their evaluation.

Follow-Up

At the end of the two weeks, have students write about their experience. They should explain what they undertook and what they accomplished. Before they write, tell them this was an experiment in making and carrying out a decision. Tell them to talk about the decision making and execution as part of their written reports. Their reports should also include their witness' certification.

Evaluation

Assign grades on this assignment based on your analysis of the students' participation and your evaluation of the written reports. Because the emphasis was on deciding to take an action, each student who took one should receive full credit, regardless of whether the action produced totally satisfactory results. The written reports should be evaluated for how fully the action taken and results are described.

SAFE Demonstration Lesson Plan 2.8: Lessons for Life
Grade Levels: 4–12

OBJECTIVES

Students will

1. generate a list of "life skills" that should be taught in school.
2. decide on which of these skills is most crucial and defend its importance in a short speech.

BRIEF DESCRIPTION

Students consider a list of things they should teach in school. They then make a list of their own. After sharing their lists, students prioritize them based on the importance of each item. They write a speech that they might present to the school board to convince the board to include the recommended item in the curriculum. Students present the speeches to a mock board meeting.

PROCEDURES

Stimulus

Dr. Carl Sagan has chosen the following topics as things he wishes "they would teach in school":

1. Baloney detection.
2. Pick a difficult thing and learn it well.
3. Don't be afraid to ask "dumb" questions.
4. Listen carefully.
5. Everybody makes mistakes.
6. Know your planet.
7. Science and technology.

8. Nuclear war.
9. Don't spend your life watching TV.
10. Culture.
11. Politics.
12. Compassion.[21]

Share this list with your students and discuss possible reasons why Sagan included each of the topics on his list. Ask them which of these topics is most surprising for its inclusion and which is most predictable. Then, tell your students you want them to think about a similar list of their own.

Activity

Have each student compose his or her own list of topics that each would like to see taught at school. Encourage them to think carefully and imaginatively in making their choices. Here are two examples of students' lists which show insight and variety:

Laura's List:
1. Why we should all learn to live together.
2. To learn from experience.
3. To learn to be non-prejudiced.
4. To be a good listener.
5. To handle rejection.
6. To like ourselves.
7. How to achieve our goals.
8. How to enjoy the arts.
9. How to respect others.
10. How to get along with your family.
11. How to save money.
12. What your priorities are.[22]

Jeremy's List:
1. How to talk your way out of a fight.
2. How to dress properly.
3. How to drink properly from a glass.
4. How to roll an "R" in Spanish.
5. It's not the end of the world if you don't get an "A."
6. What exactly goes on in our nation's capitol.
7. How to dance.
8. What responsibility means for an adult.
9. How to cheat the IRS out of money.
10. A more efficient study method for history.

11. More about space exploration.
12. How to buy an automobile without getting a lemon.[23]

As you can see, these lists offer a wide range of topics. Your students will mention many different topics. After they have written out their lists, have some of them read their lists aloud to get a sense of the things they chose. Then, ask them to prioritize their lists by renumbering their topics according to their estimate of the relative importance of each.

Follow-Up

Have students select one of their topics to argue for in a speech to the school board. Tell them they don't actually have to deliver the speech, but they are to pretend that they are going to at the next board meeting. Have them each write a three- to five-minute argument telling why the topic they selected should be taught at school. After they have finished writing, you might have the students role play a mock board meeting at which the students read their speeches to the "board."

Evaluation

In grading this activity, assign separate grades for the students' lists and their speeches. Have the students brainstorm a set of criteria for evaluating the speeches. Use this list for a scoring rubric—for example,

5   Clearly stated topic; persuasive argumentation; strong conclusion
4   Same as for a 5, but not as convincing
3   Major elements present, but thin in argumentation
2   Major element(s) missing; weak argumentation
1   Evasion of topic; no real sense of direction

SUMMARY

Despite all the other forces that influence how students live their lives, teachers do have a vital role to play in helping students learn about values and decision making. For powerful and compelling reasons, teachers must use instructional time in allowing students to compare and clarify values and to engage in a study of decision making, including participation in deciding for themselves their position on important issues. Actually, the teacher may play several roles—catalyst, facilitator, devil's advocate, provocateur—in working with students in these areas of inquiry. The thinking skills students gain through their involvement in valuing and deciding are truly "survival skills," for, as José Ortega y Gasset has said, "Life is a constant process of deciding what we are going to do."

CHALLENGE

Take a few minutes, no more than five, to list as many values as you can think of, either personal or community values. After you have finished listing, categorize the items on your list by placing a *C* in front of those that are community values and a *P* in front of the personal ones. Next, select three values from each category and think about how those values are manifested in your life and in your community. Are there specific behaviors or features that reflect those values? Are the personal values affirmed both privately and publicly? Write an imaginary conversation with yourself in which you argue the pros and cons of one of your personal values. After you have finished, decide how you could present a lesson featuring personal values to your class.

NOTES

1. Gordon W. Allport, *Values and Our Youth* (New York: Holt, 1960).
2. Herb Gluck, "What Hollywood Taught Jon Voight," *Parade* (3 May 1987): 18–19.
3. Robert C. Hawley, and Isabel L. Hawley, *Human Values in the Classroom* (New York: Hart, 1975), 13.
4. From a composition on drug abuse, Gilroy High School, Gilroy, Calif., 1987. Used with permission.
5. *San Jose Mercury-News*, 11 April and 15 April 1987. San Jose, Calif.
6. Fred T. Wilhelms, "Priorities in Change Efforts," in *Curriculum: Quest for Relevance*, ed. William Van Til (New York: Houghton Mifflin, 1971), 171.
7. L. Craig Wilson, *The Open Access Curriculum* (Boston: Allyn and Bacon, 1971), 44.
8. Wilson, *The Open Access Curriculum*, 45.
9. Hawley and Hawley, *Human Values*, 148–149.
10. Thomas G. Aylesworth, and Gerald M. Reagan, *Teaching for Thinking* (Garden City, N.Y.: Doubleday, 1969), 111–112.
11. Sidney B. Simon, Leland W. Howe, and Howard Kirschenbaum, *Values Clarification* (New York: Hart, 1978), 18–19.
12. Simon et al., *Values Clarification*, 15–18.
13. Simon et al., *Values Clarification*, 142–157. Adapted from lists presented herein.
14. Sharon A. Ratliffe, and Deldee M. Herman, *Adventures in the Looking-Glass* (Skokie, Ill.: National Textbook, 1976), 150.
15. Charles E. Wales, Anne H. Nardi, and Robert A. Stager, "Decision-Making: A New Paradigm for Education," *Educational Leadership* 43, no. 8 (May 1986): 37–41.
16. Patricia Kelly, and Leila Christenbury, "Thinking Skills." From a handout at the NCTE Conference, Philadelphia, 1985.
17. Wales et al., "Decision-Making."
18. Hawley and Hawley, *Human Values*, 212.
19. Hawley and Hawley, *Human Values*, 213–214.
20. Ratliffe and Herman, *Adventures in the Looking-Glass*, 154.
21. Carl Sagan, "Twelve Things I Wish They Taught at School," *Literary Cavalcade* 37, no. 6 (March 1985): 3–5.
22. From a student's list of "Twelve Things I Wish They Taught at School," Gilroy High School, Gilroy, Calif., 1986. Used with permission.
23. From another student's list for same activity as Note 22. Used with permission.

EXPLORING FURTHER

Abramowitz, Jack, and Warren J. Halliburton. *Searching for Values.* Globe Book Company, Inc., 1973.

Hawley, Robert C., and Isabel L. Hawley. *Human Values in the Classroom.* Hart Publishing Company, 1975.

Perlstein, Marcia H., ed. *Flowers Can Even Bloom in Schools.* Westinghouse Learning Press, 1974.

Raths, Louis E., Sidney Simon, and Merrill Harmin. *Values and Teaching: Working with Values in the Classroom.* Columbus, Ohio: Merrill, 1966.

Ratliffe, Sharon A., and Deldee M. Herman. *Adventures in the Looking-Glass.* Skokie, Ill.: National Textbook, 1976.

Simon, Sidney B., Leland W. Howe, and Howard Kirschenbaum. *Values Clarification*. New York: Hart, 1978.

Smuin, Stephen. *Turn-Ons!: 185 Strategies for the Secondary Classroom*. Wadsworth, Calif.: Fearon Pitman, 1978.

Ubbelohde, Carl, and Jack R. Fraenkel, eds. *Values of the American Heritage: Challenges, Case Studies, and Teaching Strategies*. National Council for the Social Studies, 1976.

Wales, Charles E., and Anne H. Nardi. *Successful Decision Making*. West Virginia University Center for Guided Design, 1984.

Wales, Charles E., and Robert A. Stager. *Guided Design*. West Virginia University Center for Guided Design, 1977.

Wilson, L. Craig. *The Open Access Curriculum*. Boston: Allyn & Bacon, 1971.

We explore and we retrench, we investigate and we stabilize. Step by step we expand our awareness and understanding both of ourselves and of the complex environment we live in.
Desmond Morris

Thinking in its lower grades is comparable to paper money, and in its higher forms it is a kind of poetry.
Havelock Ellis

Mind is the great lever of all things: Human thought is the process by which human ends are ultimately answered.
Daniel Webster

Men should be judged, not by the tint of skin, the gods they serve, the vintage that they drink, nor by the way they fight, or love, or sin, but by the quality of thought they think.
Adela Florence Cory Nicolson

CHAPTER **3**

Models of Thinking

Objectives

After reading this chapter, you will be able to

- *Develop lessons that follow levels of thinking described by Bloom.*
- *Use questions to help students probe more deeply into topics.*
- *Design lessons based on the Questioning Circles model.*
- *Guide students to search for greater meaning in a literature selection.*

The recent emphasis in education on teaching thinking skills has led philosophers, psychologists, and curriculum experts to create what amounts to a warehouse full of thinking models, taxonomies, frameworks for higher-order thinking skills, and theories for teaching thinking. And yet Benjamin Bloom's taxonomy, created in the mid-1950s, continues to be the most widely used method for classifying thinking skills.

Robert H. Ennis, a philosopher, argues that Bloom's taxonomy is too vague and does not include criteria for judging the outcome of an activity. He does admit, however, that the taxonomy reminds us that there is much more that schools should be doing other than simply teaching memorization. Ennis prefers the term *critical thinking* to *higher-order thinking skills* such as those outlined by Bloom. He defines critical thinking as "... reflective and reasonable thinking that is focused on deciding what to believe or do."[1] Ennis' most recent skill clusters (1985) include clarifying issues and terms, identifying components of arguments, judging the credibility of evidence, using inductive and deductive reasoning, handling argument fallacies, and making value judgments.[2]

More recently, Robert J. Sternberg, a psychologist, created a triarchic model of intelligence, which includes skills involved in knowledge acquisition, performance, and metacognitive, self-monitoring skills. Sternberg's theory sketches a process whereby skills can be taught and tested as purposeful tasks.[3]

Edys S. Quellmalz combines both Ennis' and Sternberg's frameworks along with the classes of tasks and methods of inquiry developed by curriculum experts into a general framework of analysis, comparison, inference, and evaluation.[4] She summarizes components of the problem-solving process, thus

1. identifying the problem (essential elements and terms).
2. identifying appropriate information, content, and procedural schemata.
3. connecting and using information to solve the problem.
4. evaluating the success of the solution.

Note that this process is not unlike the scientific or discovery methods discussed in Chapter 4. Quellmalz identifies the thinking skills used during problem solving as

1. clarification.
   a. identifying or formulating a question
   b. analyzing major components
   c. defining important terms
2. judging the credibility of support, source, and observations.
3. inference.
   a. deduction
   b. induction
   c. value judgments
   d. fallacies
4. evaluation of adequacy of solution based on criteria.

We can apply the problem-solving strategies and thinking skills to subject matter in any classroom. Students in a history class, for example, might discuss an event—the Boston Tea Party, the assassination of John Kennedy, a presidential election. They would analyze, compare, infer, and evaluate as they discussed the event, following these steps:

1. Analysis of the elements of the event—data collection
2. Comparison of the social, political, economic, cultural, and geographic features; identification of causes and effects—data processing
3. Making predictions, hypotheses, and conclusions based on data gathered—further processing
4. Evaluation of the credibility of arguments, decisions, and reports; evaluation of the significance of the event[5]

Arthur Costa analyzed and reported on various thinking models in the literature on thinking.[6] Of those summarized by Costa, perhaps the best known is also the oldest, that published by Bloom and others in

1956. According to Costa, it is best to adopt a familiar model as a guide in materials selection, staff development, and defining thinking. Once one has adopted a description of human intellectual functioning, teaching methodologies, curriculum sequences, learning activities, and assessment procedures can be developed that will go beyond superficial learning.[7]

This chapter explores two very different models showing how each can be used to develop lessons to fit a variety of classroom situations. Benjamin Bloom's six levels of thinking will be illustrated with several lessons for a junior high school core class unit called "Kids Are Talking" ("The Events of Our Lives"), a lesson focusing on a study of African tribes, and a lesson based on *The Good Earth*.

The second thinking model for lessons in this chapter is "The Questioning Circle," from *Questioning, A Path to Critical Thinking* by Leila Christenbury and Patricia P. Kelly.[8] These lessons illustrate how effective Christenbury and Kelly's framework is for studying a work of literature, *The Diary of Anne Frank*.

Bloom's Taxonomy

Benjamin Bloom's *Taxonomy of Educational Objectives*, which first appeared over thirty years ago and was widely referred to in university education classes, is perhaps even more popular today. As a model for teachers to use in planning lessons, it offers a sensible yet flexible categorization of thinking descriptions.

DEFINING THE TAXONOMY

Bloom defined six levels of thinking, which he labeled knowledge, comprehension, application, analysis, synthesis, and evaluation. Knowledge represents the basic level and evaluation the most complex. These levels, condensed, are defined as follows:

> *Knowledge:* The analogy of the mind as a file where specifics, universals, methods, and processes are stored and retrieved when needed illustrates the knowledge level; involves the process of relating and remembering.
>
> *Comprehension:* Translation, interpretation, and extrapolation in a narrow or unilateral sense.
>
> *Application:* The use of abstractions in particular or concrete instances, for example, general ideas, rules or procedures, generalized methods, technical principles, ideas, and theories which can be applied in other situations.

Analysis: The breakdown of elements, relationships, and organizational principles into parts in order to clarify communication, organization, and effects, as well as their bases.

Synthesis: Putting together of parts, or elements to form a whole, a new pattern or structure not seen before.

Evaluation: Judgments made in terms of external or internal evidence, quantitative or qualitative judgments of material or methods using criteria.[9]

APPLYING BLOOM'S TAXONOMY

An exciting nontext-oriented unit is one that involves the actual lives of students. This idea is applicable to all grade levels because students at each grade level are limited to the events of their lifetimes. Therefore, a third grader will usually have no more than nine years with which to be concerned, whereas a twelfth grader will have about sixteen or seventeen years to research.

Each of the three lessons in this section are keyed to one of the levels of Bloom's taxonomy. The objectives for each lesson are described in terms of expected thinking behaviors appropriate for the given level. However, and this is the crucial aspect of using Bloom's taxonomy, each lesson also illustrates how within a level there are many degrees of difficulty. In fact, a particular activity at the "knowledge" level may very well be more difficult than one at the "analysis" level. What binds each of these lessons together therefore is the type of thinking expected from it rather than the difficulty of a particular task. The following lessons were all field tested in a seventh-grade core (language arts, social studies) class with students whose lives began in 1971 or 1972 and extended at the time of the unit up to 1985.

The three lessons that follow illustrate the use of Bloom's taxonomy at the knowledge, application, and synthesis levels. The unit plan includes all six levels of the taxonomy, and an outline at the end of this section suggests activities for Bloom's other three levels—comprehension, analysis, and evaluation. The activities in the unit proposed here involve "I-Search," a personalized approach to research developed by Ken McCrorie;[10] "sample-search," a method for selecting topics to be researched, developed by the author; and "We-Search," a group method for doing research developed by the author. I-Search is an alternative to the research project that involves discovery about a certain topic as well as discovery about how to do research. Students are active participants, not limited by a preestablished thesis. Not only do students learn library skills, but they also learn how to do interviews and how to analyze information. The nature of research including the irrelevancy and difficulty of much of the material, conflicting viewpoints, and chance discoveries become inherent in the search. Much like a diary, students write about their experiences as they unfold incorporating metacognitive awareness into the entire process.

The culminating projects of this unit are twofold. One exciting product is a class scrapbook, which chronicles all the events of the students' lives together in a magazine format. The other culminating project is a videotape done in the style of a television news program. Three SAFE Demonstration Lesson Plans for both projects follow.

SAFE DEMONSTRATION LESSON PLANS

SAFE Demonstration Lesson Plan 3.1: The Events of Our Lives
Grade Levels: 3–12

OBJECTIVES

Students will

1. recall the events of their lives in a brainstorming activity.
2. sort the events recalled into at least ten different categories.
3. define the events recalled and categorized through a sample-search exercise.

BRIEF DESCRIPTION

This illustrates a unit on "The Events of Our Lives" and establishes a knowledge base through a combination of recalling and simple encyclopedic researching. The objectives of this lesson all qualify as "knowledge-level" thinking, and yet there are varying degrees of difficulty between the different activities; for example, simply recalling the events in a brainstorming activity is not nearly as difficult as searching through sources in a library and defining an event.

PROCEDURES

Stimulus

Tell the class that the happenings during their lifetimes will be the focus for this unit of study. There may be events surrounding the lives of famous people, events concerning government or politics, events relating to the arts, or to any other aspect of world-worthy news.

Spend an entire period brainstorming various events with the class. Write everything named on the board. (Have a volunteer copy everything on a piece of paper so copies can be made.)

Activity

Distribute copies of the previous day's brainstorming events. Together with the class, decide how the list can be categorized into no more than ten categories. (One class listed the following: important U.S. events, space, fads, sports, political events, famous people, disasters, firsts, kidnappings/disappearances, inventions.) Organize the class into small groups of three to five and have them decide which events go with each category. Prepare the "Sample-Search Activity Form" to be used in the library by each student.

Student Directions for I-Search Topic Selection

1. Pick ten events (one from each category).
2. In the library and from family, friends, teachers, and others, try to find out the five Ws and one H for each. (Use the forms provided.) Use encyclopedias, card catalogs to locate books, almanacs, atlases, and your own knowledge.

NAME: _____   PAGE _____

Category: _____	Category: _____	Category: _____
Item: _____	Item: _____	Item: _____
Who? _____	Who? _____	Who? _____
What? _____	What? _____	What? _____
When? _____	When? _____	When? _____
Where? _____	Where? _____	Where? _____
Why? _____	Why? _____	Why? _____
How? _____	How? _____	How? _____

Category: _____	Category: _____
Item: _____	Item: _____
Who? _____	Who? _____
What? _____	What? _____
When? _____	When? _____
Where? _____	Where? _____
Why? _____	Why? _____
How? _____	How? _____

Sample–Search Activity Form

3. Select any five of your choices on which you would like to do a complete I-Search. Indicate these five by circling them.
4. You will be assigned one, two, or three of your *five* choices on which to actually do an I-Search. (We will avoid duplications.)
5. Spend two or three class periods in the library. As students complete their "sample-search," confer individually with each to reach agreement on the topic(s) they will later research.

Follow-Up

During the next two weeks, students will be involved in an individual I-Search on each of their topic(s). Refer to "Applying Bloom's Taxonomy" in this chapter for an explanation of the I-Search procedure.

Evaluation

Evaluate each student's sample-search page during the individual conference. The small groups of three to five students can be reconvened in order to share and respond to each other's I-Search topics.

SAFE Demonstration Lesson Plan 3.2: Making a Scrapbook
Grade Levels: 3–12

OBJECTIVES

Students will

1. sequence all of their collected data from the I-search into one continuum.
2. organize their collected data in a logical way.
3. work as We-Search teams to tie loose ends together where information is incomplete.
4. illustrate selected findings in a class scrapbook.

BRIEF DESCRIPTION

This lesson illustrates Bloom's taxonomy and involves students in application. In between these two lessons, the I-Search procedure can provide for comprehension of the events. The students are now ready to do learning activities involving application, analysis, synthesis, and evaluation.

To create a scrapbook of the most memorable events of their lives, the class will need to work together in cooperative learning groups. Each group will be assigned one or two categories to pull together into a coherent part of the whole-class project. Where not enough information was gathered earlier on some topics, We-Search may be necessary to fill the gaps.

A Sample Scrapbook

First woman to run for Vice President

PROCEDURES

Stimulus

Have students meet together to share their I-Search reports. (An I-Search report is an informal diary of a student's quest for information on a topic. It should reflect successes as well as failures or frustrations. If done properly, it should contain entertaining and informative writing.) Ask each group to select one group representative to read his or her report to the whole class.

Activity

List all the I-Search topics on the board with their dates and have the class sequence them chronologically. (This would be a good time to make a time line with narrow butcher paper that extends across the front of the classroom above the chalkboard. On it not only the I-Search events would appear but also the birthdates of each of the students in the class. This would make a nice class project for a small group of students who complete their regular work ahead of the others.)

Have the class groups draw for the ten categories established earlier. (If there are five groups, each group draws two categories.) Prepare box lids (photocopy-paper boxes are perfect) for each category and label them. Place each I-Search report in its appropriate box to be used as resources by the various groups.

Have each group study the collected data for each of their two categories in order to plan their two sections for the class scrapbook project. If a group finds any events incompletely covered or if there are other events not researched yet that the group feels are essential to their topic, students are to work as a We-Search team to tie up loose ends. (A few more days in the library may be necessary.)

Students are now ready to begin assembling their scrapbook sections. A dividing page should be designed and created for each section. Pictures from old magazines, memorabilia, charts, graphs, and original drawings can be included. Summaries of each event selected for representation in the scrapbook and/or combined presentations of the various categories can now be written. (One class used large 12 × 18-inch pages of construction paper for its scrapbook, which allowed plenty of room for pictures, charts, graphs, and so forth.)

Follow-Up

Enlist the services of an artistic student to design a cover for the scrapbook and then have one of the groups assemble the sections. Have everyone in class autograph the back cover.

Evaluation

Evaluate each section of the scrapbook and determine how many points to award each group. If individual contributions are clearly known, extra points can be awarded to certain students. Display the scrapbook at an open house for parents, in the office, or at the district office.

SAFE Demonstration Lesson Plan 3.3: Kids Are Talking
Grade Levels: 3–12

OBJECTIVES

Students will

1. plan a videotaped program.
2. compose a script for a videotaped program.
3. design and construct sets, props, and costumes for a videotaped program.
4. create scenes from the events of their lives for videotaping.

BRIEF DESCRIPTION

This lesson illustrates the synthesis level. See the outline, "The Events of Our Lives: A Guide" (page 73) for suggested activities for the levels of Bloom's taxonomy that are not included in these lessons.

Students synthesize all the information accumulated about the events of their lives. In addition, students learn firsthand the technical skills of videotaping, acting in front of a camera, and all the creative crafts necessary in television production.

PROCEDURES

Stimulus

Videotape and show the class a news broadcast complete with anchors, weather forecaster, sportscaster, and advertisements. Have the class analyze the program in order to make a list of all its components.

Challenge the class to select events from their studies that could be scripted, acted out, and transformed into a student news program spanning their lifetimes.

Activity

Organize the class into specialty groups such as script writers, actors (anchor girl and anchor boy, roving reporters, advertisers, and so forth), art committee (to make props, prepare title and credits), filming crew (depending on the age of group, this can include prompters and camera persons, and any other groups on which the class decides).

Establish a shooting schedule, trying to film one or two segments during each class period. (A segment entails an event, an advertisement, or a filming of the credits.)

Follow-Up

Arrange several showings of the completed videotape for other classes, parents, school administrators, and/or board members. Have students make posters to hang in the cafeteria, library, and office, which advertise the coming event.

Evaluation

Prepare rating sheets for students in other classes to fill out after seeing the videotape and discuss openly in class all feedback received from viewers. Then ask students to write an evaluation of the project to be shared orally together. Finally, note the excitement and *esprit de corps* that doing a project of this range brings to the class.

Rating Sheet for "Kids Are Talking" Video

1. Which segment of the video did you like best? Why?
2. Can you think of any events that should have been included?
3. Which events do you think should not have been included?
4. Give your opinion of the technical aspects of this video.

Unit Planning Using Bloom's Taxonomy

Bloom's taxonomy is useful as you plan a unit of study. The outlines and lessons that follow illustrate both its use for planning objectives of a unit as well as activities. The first example represents an outline of objectives for studying African tribes; it is followed by a lesson that uses the objectives of comprehension, analysis, and synthesis. The second outline and lesson show how the activities for a unit based on *The Good Earth* use the taxonomy.

A UNIT ON AFRICAN TRIBES

The objectives for a preplanned unit on African tribes need not be cast in stone because many objectives will be enhanced by the input of the students as learning unfolds. If you intend to teach thinking, however, it is helpful to have a list of these objectives clearly in mind when first initiating a unit.

THE EVENTS OF OUR LIVES: A GUIDE

Knowledge
1. Recalling the events of our lives in a brainstorming activity
2. Labeling/naming the events
3. Listing the events
4. Sorting the events into ten categories
5. Defining the events in a sample-search

Comprehension
1. Locating the events/persons in library sources
2. Restating in own words (I-Search method) the information found
3. Describing the events (I-Search)
4. Reporting the events (I-Search)
5. Explaining the events (I-Search)

Application
1. Sequencing all the data into a continuum
2. Organizing all the data in a systematic way
3. Illustrating the findings in a class scrapbook or collection

Analysis
1. Examining the events for reclassification into new categories
2. Classifying the events into new groups
3. Writing comparisons/contrasts about items within a group
4. Researching more deeply where necessary
5. Interpreting the meaning of these events

Synthesis
1. Planning a videotape
2. Composing a script
3. Designing and constructing sets, props, and costumes
4. Creating scenes from the events of our lives for videotape

Evaluation
1. Prioritizing the events
2. Judging the events (I-Search conclusion)
3. Evaluating the events (I-Search conclusion)
4. Rating the events as a class
5. Predicting the long-term effect of the events

African Tribes: Objectives

1. *Knowledge:* Students will list many of the tribes of Africa and cluster them into the geographic areas of Africa.
2. *Comprehension:* Students will identify the ten basic elements of a particular tribe: food, shelter, clothing, family structure, government, geographic setting, weapons and tools, religion, leisure, and language.
3. *Application:* Students will illustrate the tribe on a poster, dramatize a folk tale of the tribe, or construct an artifact or mask appropriate to the tribe.
4. *Analysis:* Students will research the tribe using filmstrips, books, encyclopedias, and other resources.
5. *Synthesis:* Students will create a publication or booklet worthy as a library resource for other students.
6. *Evaluation:* Students will decide whether the tribe was better off before nationalism and whether it will endure.

SAFE DEMONSTRATION LESSON PLAN

The following sample lesson from a unit on African tribes was used in a seventh-grade core class; however, it could be adapted for use in grades five, six, or eight. The subject matter could be American Indians or on a more global scale, the basic cultures of man.

SAFE Demonstration Lesson Plan 3.4: We-Search on African Tribes
Grade Levels: 5–8

OBJECTIVES

Students will

1. identify the basic characteristics of a particular tribe's culture: food, shelter, clothing, family structure, government, geographic setting, weapons and tools, religion, leisure, and language.
2. research one tribe using filmstrips, books, encyclopedias, and other resources.
3. create a publication or booklet worthy as a library resource for other students.

BRIEF DESCRIPTION

This lesson begins with cooperative research, We-Search, to locate descriptions of ten basic elements of a community group. The research culminates in the writing, illustrating, and publishing of a booklet by each group. If the teacher has a computer and a printer in the classroom, a word-processing program together with a graphics program will greatly enhance the excitement of this project.

PROCEDURES

Stimulus

Locate a copy of *Ashanti to Zulu: African Traditions* by Margaret Musgrove.[11] Read the book aloud to the class, showing the beautiful illustrations as you go. This book provides in pictorial form the symbols, animals, artifacts, costumes, and food of one African tribe for each letter of the alphabet. In addition, the author includes an outline map showing the locations of each tribe. A book of this kind offers a wonderful starting place for a class embarking on a quest of information on African tribes. In addition, it demonstrates one way of organizing the unit, an easy way to let the groups of students choose a tribe for their special study.

Make copies of the outline map from the book to distribute to each cooperative learning group of five students. This map shows each tribe and its location, so it will facilitate group selections of tribes to research.

Activity

Once the cooperative learning groups have each chosen a tribe, they will We-Search and bring essential materials from the library into class. Or, each small group can be scheduled for a period in the library to check out resources.

We-Search groups of five spend several class periods in a circle exploring the various books from the library, taking notes. They are guided in their quest for information by a list of ten basic needs: food, clothing, shelter, family structure, government, geographic setting, weapons and tools, religion, leisure, and language. Each student in the five-member group will be responsible for two of the basic needs, thereby assuring coverage of all ten needs. (NOTE: *National Geographic* magazine provides one of the richest sources of information for this project. If the teacher is fortunate to have duplicate copies of back issues, students might even be able to cut out pictures to be used later as illustrations in the completed booklets.)

Follow-Up

Schedule each group for two-period blocks of time at the computer. (This works especially well for a core class or in an elementary self-contained classroom.) Students often work in pairs at the keyboard so that one can edit as the other composes. Those not at the computer can still offer advice and work quietly on further research, illustrations, or graphic plans for the completed pages.

After all groups have had at least two double periods at the computer or ample time to type and print their text and to make graphic titles and cover sheets for their booklets, students can cut, paste, and lay out the pages of their projects.

Evaluation

Evaluate each completed document on the following criteria: coverage of the ten basic needs, authenticity of the writing by the students, organization, and creativity of the layout design.

Sample Rubric

5   full coverage of the ten basic needs, authentic writing by students, well-organized, and creatively laid out

3   average coverage of the ten basic needs, some authentic writing by students, some evidence of organization, and creative layout design

1   poor coverage of the ten basic needs, little if any authentic writing by students, little or no evidence of organization or design

Give students a copy of the booklet published by their group to share at home with their families, display additional copies of all the tribe booklets together at an open house, in the school library, and at the district's central office.

The "Students' Tribe Booklets," on the opposite page, are examples of student work on this project.

A UNIT ON *THE GOOD EARTH*

There is not much difference between a planned activity and a planned objective for a unit, as the following list of activities shows. SAFE Demonstration Lesson Plan 3.5 engages students in comprehension, analysis, synthesis, and evaluation. It gives students an opportunity to bring together their experiences of reading *The Good Earth* to form a new whole and to judge the value of this classic book for a given purpose. Additional lessons on application and synthesis appear in Chapter 10.

The Good Earth: Activities

1. *Knowledge:* Students will track the oral reading of *The Good Earth* by the teacher in order to learn about China's peasant society through the life of Wang Lung.
2. *Comprehension:* Students will cluster to gain an understanding of the life cycles represented as a theme in *The Good Earth*.

The Masai people do many things during their spare time. For instance many of their warriors hunt for their family needs such as clothing, food, shelter, and other essential needs. The women take great pride in preparing the food which the warriors have brought home. Many of the younger women help clean and make clothing for the family. The Masai children love to play many games. Many of the Masai children do not have an education, so they have a lot of spare time to play many games and have fun. The young boys look foward to becoming a young warrior, but before the young boys become (men) warriors they must take a bravery test and kill a lion. Many young boys can't wait for that special moment. One more thing the Masai people love to have are special celebrations, such as dancing and jumping up and down. When they celebrate these things such as jumping high up and down, in the backround drums and other instruments play as one Masai dancer leads the other dancer to join him. These are just a few of the games and activities they do in their spare time.

   SHELTER

The Bushman live in small straw houses. The woman knows best how she likes her house so the women do the building. They lay some branches together like an arch and then pile the grass around the branches and over them. It takes a half hour to build the house. The new scherm would be cool and shady inside in the daytime. At night it gives protection from the chill in the air after the sun has set. On the bottom of the house there is red sand. The wife, husband, the childern, and the grandpa live in the one house they build. When they move they leave their house, but destroy it and they're on their way again. Then when they find another place to live they start all over again.

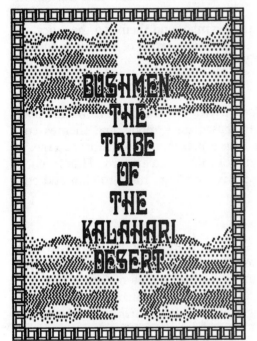

Students' Tribe Booklets

3. *Application:* Students will plant beans, the life-saving food for Wang Lung's family, and will write a daily log on the beans' growth (see Chapter 10).
4. *Analysis:* Students will examine the many times in the story that the symbols of earth and the color red appear and will compare and contrast male and female roles as depicted in *The Good Earth.*
5. *Synthesis:* Students will create mandalas, which represent the essence of *The Good Earth,* and will plan a slide show with taped music and narration based on pictures from *National Geographic* magazines (see Chapter 10).
6. *Evaluation:* Students will rank the many characters in *The Good Earth* from good to evil.

SAFE Demonstration Lesson Plan 3.5: Making a Mandala
Grade Levels: 7–10

OBJECTIVES

Students will

1. identify the most important symbols and themes in a work of literature.
2. judge the importance of each symbol and theme to the story.
3. rank characters from best to worst in terms of human goodness.
4. create a mandala.

BRIEF DESCRIPTION

After students have read *The Good Earth,* the teacher reviews the book by developing clusters and charts based on symbols and themes contained in the story. Creating mandalas is presented to students as a means for recreating *The Good Earth* symbolically in an art form. Finally, cooperative learning groups of three to five students meet to plan and construct a group mandala.

Stimulus

Initially, the following clusters and charts are made on the board with input from the class; later, they are transferred to large sheets of butcher paper to be displayed in the room for a longer period of time.

At the board, cluster ideas with the class around the words *earth* and *red,* symbols repeated throughout *The Good Earth,* as in the figure, "Clustering Ideas."

Chart with the class the theme *cycles,* which occurs in many forms in *The Good Earth,* as in the figure, "Cycles in *The Good Earth.*"

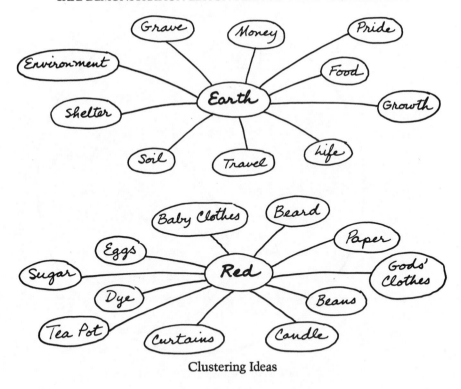

Clustering Ideas

THE GOOD EARTH

Cycles

A Man's Life Cycle: Birth ⟶ Marriage ⟶ Children ⟶
⟶ Their Marriage ⟶ Grandchildren ⟶ Death

A Plant's Life Cycle: Seed Is Planted ⟶ Growth ⟶
⟶ Harvest ⟶ Seed Is Planted ⟶

Profit Cycle: Crop Sold For Silver → More Land Is
Bought → More Land Is Planted → Harvest Yields
More Crops → More Silver ⟶ More Land ⟶

Cycles in *The Good Earth*

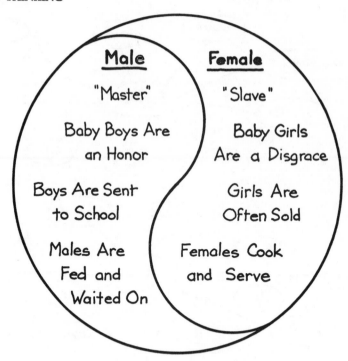

Yin–Yang Based on *The Good Earth*

Using a yin–yang symbol as background, list with the class the characteristics of males (yang) and females (yin) in the society of Wang Lung, as in the figure, "Yin–Yang Based on *The Good Earth*."

Explain to the class what a mandala is (in Oriental art and religion, any of various designs symbolic of the universe). Show the class examples of mandalas like those in the figure, "Mandalas."

Activity

Divide the class into cooperative learning groups of three to five. Allow a class period during which each group plans a mandala to symbolize *The Good Earth*. They may use ideas from the clusters and charts, which should now be displayed in the room, or they may come up with other ideas. Suggest that a mandala can visually represent the most important ideas from the book.

Follow-Up

Allow another class period during which cooperative learning groups again meet to construct their planned mandalas. Provide construction paper and felt pens if possible.

Mandalas

Evaluation

Have each group show its mandala to the class to see if other students can grasp clearly the symbolic meaning of each mandala.

Arrange a bulletin board display of all the mandalas as a celebration of *The Good Earth*. Attach first-, second-, and third-prize ribbons to the three judged to be the best.

Have each student write a descriptive essay of the mandala their group created in which they explain the meaning behind each of the symbols used.

The Questioning Circle

One of the newer models for thinking instruction provided by Christenbury and Kelly is the Questioning Circle.[12] Their schema safeguards students and teachers from the rigidity of hierarchical or sequential models. These authors believe that orderly progression of thought patterns rarely occurs during a discussion of literature or events. They feel furthermore that there is no evidence to support the concept that one cognitive level— for example, evaluation—is superior to another.[13] We pointed this out also in our introductory discussion of thinking, noting the recursive nature of the thinking process.

Christenbury and Kelly depict the processes using the Venn diagram with three overlapping circles,[14] as shown in the figure "The Questioning Circle." Circle 1 represents the subject (a literature text, a science experiment, an ethnic group). Circle 2 represents the individual (personal experiences, values, ideas). Circle 3 represents the world (other literature, facts, external knowledge). Obviously, these discrete components impinge on each other, overlapping in areas a, b, and c to produce more complex thinking. The most integrative thinking occurs when all three circles overlap, bringing the subject matter, personal reality, and the world, or external reality, together as in the central area of the diagram or core.[15]

According to Christenbury and Kelly, this system of overlapping circles more nearly represents the individual's experiences, values, and ideas. The third circle represents the world and other literature or external reality.[16] According to Christenbury and Kelly, this system of overlapping circles more nearly represents the reality of the questioning process than do sequential and hierarchical schemata.[17] They contend "... that conceptualizing the questioning process in the form of these three circles is useful. While each circle represents a different domain of cognition, the circles overlap, as does knowledge, and are not ordered. Furthermore,

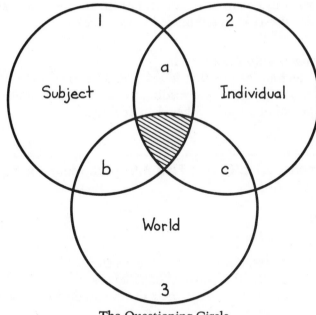

The Questioning Circle

in the one area where all three circles overlap lies the union of the subject being explored, the individual's response and experience, and the experience of others. The intersection of the three circles, which we term *dense,* contains the most significant (higher-order) questions. . . ."[18]

The very nature of overlapping circles allows the questioning strategy of the teacher to start anywhere with a dense question, a shaded question, or a white question and to revolve in a nonordered fashion that remains logical and flexible.[19] When using their model for literature, Christenbury and Kelly advocate posing the *dense* question early as a basis for an ongoing discussion instead of as a culminating question that very often frustrates students by repeating ground already covered.[20]

Use of the Questioning Circle in this section shows how it adapts to a work of literature as a whole, *The Diary of Anne Frank.* In these lessons, the questions can be used as a stimulus or as an evaluation of some of the key themes of the diary.

A UNIT ON *THE DIARY OF ANNE FRANK*

A poignant way to acquaint eighth, ninth, and tenth graders with World War II is through the writings of Anne Frank who was aged thirteen, fourteen, and fifteen when she wrote *The Diary of Anne Frank.* Otto Frank, his wife, and two daughters; a family of three called Van Daan; and a Dutch dentist, Henrik Dussel, live hidden from the Nazis in the attic of an Amsterdam business establishment for two years from July 1942 to August 1944 as chronicled in this book.

SAFE Demonstration Lesson Plans

The four lessons that follow could be used at the beginning, in the middle, or at the end of reading the book. They are designed to address the book holistically rather than analytically.

SAFE Demonstration Lesson Plan 3.6: Going into Hiding
Grade Levels: 6–10

OBJECTIVES

Students will

1. recall information from a story.
2. describe personal experiences.
3. imagine what their own attitude would be like if they lived in hiding.
4. speculate about whether such a situation could happen anywhere today.
5. conclude what the policy was toward Jews in Amsterdam at the time.
6. decide what they would do if their own family were forced to flee an enemy.

BRIEF DESCRIPTION

Shortly after beginning the reading of *The Diary of Anne Frank*, this lesson can provide a strong focus on its historical significance.

The Questioning Circle technique anchors the study and reading of *The Diary of Anne Frank*. Questioning engages students in thinking on several levels but in no particular order. This discussion sets the stage for future discussions and activities.

PROCEDURES

Stimulus

Pose as the all-encompassing question, "Could a situation such as the one that sent the Franks into hiding for two years happen anywhere on earth today?" (This represents a *dense* question and helps center the discussion that follows.)

Activity

Once the class has read the diary entries leading up to and including the arrival at the Secret Annex, set aside a class period for the following discussion based on the Questioning Circle. There is no particular order established for these questions. Feel free to move back and forth between *white* and *shaded* questions. And don't forget to restate the *dense* question periodically.

White Questions

TEXT: Why does the Frank family go into hiding?

READER: Have you ever been cut off from friends due to illness, quarantine, moving, or for other reasons? Describe what it felt like.

WORLD: What was the policy in Amsterdam toward Jews at this time?

Shaded Questions

TEXT/READER: If you had to go into hiding, who would you most resemble in attitude: Anne, Margot, or Peter?

TEXT/WORLD: Are we meant to believe that there were other Jews in hiding during this period? What evidence is given?

READER/WORLD: If your family were forced to flee Naziism, would you willingly go into hiding?

Dense Question

TEXT/READER/WORLD: Could a situation such as that which sent the Franks into hiding for two years happen anywhere on earth today?

Follow-Up

Furnish copies of all the questions from the activity section for the students. Have students write a brief essay on the dense question posed above. Allow them to address the white and shaded questions as a means for giving substance to their papers.

Evaluation

Form student-response teams of three to five and have each author read his or her essay to obtain feedback. Have students comment especially on ideas that were not brought up in the oral discussion. Next, reconvene the entire class and have a reporter from each response group tell the class about any "new" ideas expressed in the individual papers. Finally, have students revise and rewrite their essays and submit them for a grade. Use the following rubric for scoring:

Sample Rubric

5   gives a clear response to the dense question and includes references to some of the white and shaded questions

3   responds adequately to the dense question, but gives very little attention to the white or shaded questions; or responds thoroughly to the white or shaded questions, but gives little attention to the dense question

1   responds weakly to all three types of questions

SAFE Demonstration Lesson Plan 3.7: Writing a Diary
Grade Levels: 8–10

OBJECTIVES

Students will

1. recall ways in which several of the inhabitants of the Secret Annex spend their time.
2. tell how each would spend time were he or she to suddenly find him or herself isolated or imprisoned.
3. cite examples of people who are forced to live in isolation (prisoners, exiles).
4. imitate Anne's diary in a long-term diary-writing assignment.
5. analyze Anne's diary for its chief characteristics.
6. compare their own diary-writing attempts to Anne's, based on its chief characteristics.
7. imagine a slice of life today that if chronicled in diary form would be of interest to future readers or audiences.
8. list all the qualities of Anne's diary that make it valuable reading about World War II as well as about a young girl's life.

BRIEF DESCRIPTION

This is a good lesson to start very soon after beginning the reading of *The Diary of Anne Frank*. Because it entails the actual writing of a diary by students, they gain an immediate appreciation of Anne's diary.

Students keep a daily diary and compare it to Anne Frank's. The joys, frustrations, and other emotions so graphically portrayed by Anne make an interesting model for adolescents who, for the first time in many cases, discover how universal the problems of growing up are.

PROCEDURES

Stimulus

Discuss the following dense question: "What characteristics of Anne's diary make it especially authentic to you and to the world?"

Activity

As soon as they begin reading *The Diary of Anne Frank*, ask students to obtain a "diary" for themselves. (This can be a small notebook.) Begin setting aside ten minutes of each period following the silent or oral reading of *The Diary of Anne Frank* to write dated diary entries. Have students name their diaries as Anne names hers "Kitty." Put students at ease by promising that diaries will be kept confidential and only graded for evidence of entries. Continue the diary exercise for as long as students maintain an interest. (Some will want to write extra entries on the weekends.)

Follow-Up

After diary writing has been maintained for at least two weeks, set aside a class period for the Questioning Circle. The questions that follow may be used in any order, but they are labeled white, shaded, and dense.

White Questions

TEXT: How do some of the inhabitants of the Secret Annex spend their time?

READER: If you were forced into hiding or found yourself in a situation like the inhabitants of the Secret Annex, how would you spend your time?

WORLD: Cite several examples of people who are forced to live in isolation.

Shaded Questions

TEXT/READER: Have you ever kept a diary for a particular period of time? (Describe the situation and diary length as compared to Anne's.)

TEXT/WORLD: Why has Anne's diary become a classic work of literature?

READER/WORLD: Can you imagine a slice of your life today that you could chronicle in a diary that would be of interest to future generations?

Dense Question

TEXT/READER/WORLD: What characteristics of Anne's diary make it especially memorable to you and to the world?

Evaluation

Brainstorm a list of the qualities of Anne's diary that make it valuable reading about World War II. Brainstorm another list of qualities that make the book interesting (valid) to a teenager. Next ask students to take another look at their own diaries and decide whether they contain enough authentic qualities. Finally, have students write articles for the school newspaper that address the dense question posed earlier.

SAFE Demonstration Lesson Plan 3.8: The Qualities of Courage
Grade Levels: 8–10

OBJECTIVES

Students will

1. cite instances of courage by inhabitants of the Secret Annex and their protectors.
2. recall instances of personal courage.
3. describe other examples of courage in the world.
4. speculate on whether they would have been willing to risk hiding Jews in World War II Europe.
5. report other examples of courage they have experienced.
6. decide which qualities in Anne are her most memorable traits of courage.
7. evaluate Anne's outlook on the world in terms of true courage.

BRIEF DESCRIPTION

The Diary of Anne Frank is the outpouring of a brave young girl who wrote, "In spite of everything, I still believe that people are really good at heart." This kind of utterance, which permeates the diary, has given Anne Frank a lasting place in history as a young woman of courage. This lesson gives students an opportunity to explore the theme of bravery in the person of Anne and uses varied media to focus on the value: courage. It relates personal experiences and moments of courage as represented by Anne to a worldview of the trait.

PROCEDURES

Stimulus

Write the following dictionary definition of courage on the board: "the ability to face difficulty or danger with firmness and without fear." Read aloud to the class the following passage from *The Diary of Anne Frank:*

"In spite of everything, I still believe that people are really good at heart." Discuss whether this statement represents hope and tolerance. Then discuss the dense question: Does this statement represent fairly your understanding and the world's view of what true courage involves? Finally, set aside a class period for the Questioning Circle. Use the following questions in whatever order seems appropriate.

White Questions

TEXT: Cite instances of courage by members of the Secret Annex and their protectors.

READER: When have you had to be unusually brave due to circumstances beyond your control?

WORLD: Can you think of any other examples of courage in which people had to find inner strength to continue or to stay alive?

Shaded Questions

TEXT/READER: If you had been living in Amsterdam during World War II, would you have been willing to risk your life to hide Jews? Why or why not?

READER/WORLD: What qualities of courage have you observed in your lifetime by members of the human race?

TEXT/WORLD: What qualities in Anne are her most memorable traits of courage (patience, a sense of humor, persistence, honesty, and so forth)?

Dense Question

TEXT/READER/WORLD: Do the hope and tolerance expressed repeatedly by Anne in the diary and epitomized in her statement, "In spite of everything, I still believe that people are really good at heart," represent fairly your understanding and the worldview of what true courage involves?

Activity

Ask students to spend one week looking for examples of courage in the various media (for example, newspapers, television, magazines) and to bring them in to share with the class and for a bulletin board display.

Have students write a short piece about courage. They might include references to *The Diary of Anne Frank*, to news stories about courage, or to personal experiences. One eighth-grade student wrote the following:

Courage
KONG HSU

Courage in the dictionary is "the quality of mind or spirit enabling one to meet danger or opposition with fearlessness, calmness, and firmness."

We learned about different types of courage from *The Diary of Anne Frank* and our class discussion. We learned of long-term courage and short-term courage. Anne Frank went through two years of hardship. Such courage as hers is not met by many individuals—living a life in which every day is dangerous. I also think Anne Frank showed great courage by expressing all her feelings and writing them in her diary. She was able to express her romantic feelings so clearly while many people find it hard to put such things into words. Anne Frank clearly displayed long-term courage.

Follow-Up

Have students share their news stories in front of the class. Engage students in a discussion of the difference between long-term and short-term, or momentary, courage. Form response groups of three to five students for reading and sharing of short written pieces on courage.

Evaluation

Evaluate the writings about courage with the following rubric:

Sample Rubric

5   gives a clear response to the dense question posed in this lesson and differentiates between long-term and short-term courage
3   responds adequately to the dense question, but gives very little attention to the difference between long-term and short-term courage
1   responds weakly to both the dense question and to the idea of long-term versus short-term courage

---

SAFE Demonstration Lesson Plan 3.9: Happy Hanukkah!
Grade Levels: 8–10

OBJECTIVES

Students will

1. recall the references to Hanukkah in *The Diary of Anne Frank*.
2. describe religious observances that they have observed or experienced.

3. research the meaning and practices behind Hanukkah.
4. emulate a Hanukkah celebration.
5. decide whether and, if so, how religious celebrations bring people closer together.

BRIEF DESCRIPTION

Students become involved in an actual celebration of Hanukkah. Besides lighting the candles of a menorah for eight days, they draw names and have a gift exchange. However, the gifts must all be handmade or food they have prepared themselves in keeping with the spirit of the Secret Annex in *The Diary of Anne Frank.*

PROCEDURES

This lesson is especially appropriate if taught close to the actual time of Hanukkah; however, it can be effective at any time of the year. Hanukkah is the Jewish Feast of Lights, or Feast of Dedication. Hanukkah begins on the twenty-fifth day of the Jewish month of Kislev, which falls in December. It lasts eight days. At sundown on each day, a new candle is lighted. The feast dates back to 165 B.C. when Judas Maccabaeus honored the re-dedication of the Jewish Temple in Jerusalem.

Stimulus

Bring a menorah and candles to class. Close the drapes and turn off the lights to darken the room. Have a volunteer light the center candle and the first candle on the left. Then read aloud to the class a short story from *The Power of Light* by Isaac Bashevis Singer.[21] These short stories are each about some aspect of Hanukkah and will acquaint the students with many of the practices of Hanukkah, such as the traditional serving of potato pancakes, the game of dreidel, and so forth. Each day for eight consecutive days, have a different volunteer light an extra candle allowing them to burn down for the rest of the period.

Activity

Prepare a drawing by writing down each student's and the teacher's names on little pieces of paper. Hold the drawing, which may include the teacher, and instruct students to prepare a handmade, baked, or other original gift for their recipients by the final day of the Hanukkah celebration. (In other words, no one is to buy a gift.) Explain that the inhabitants of the Secret Annex had to use their own resources in coming up with gifts for each other.

On the final day of Hanukkah in class, exchange the gifts in the following way: A volunteer begins by giving his or her gift to his or her recipient. The recipient opens the gift and shows it to the rest of the class and then takes his or her turn giving his or her gift also. And so the chain of gift giving continues until everyone has shared. It is amazing how many resourceful ideas can come out of this exercise. In one class, there were items such as foil bracelets accompanied by the following rhyme:

ANNA EHRLICH

Three bracelets
Just for you
And really!
They're sterling silver too.

paper tree ornaments; a very special sandwich; a box of cookies; a raft, made out of ice cream sticks, that floated; and an original poem:

Happy Hanukkah

JAMINE ERGAS

We light a candle every day
"Happy Hanukkah," is what I say.

Hanukkah is a joyous time,
A time for laughter,
A time for rhyme.

Let's all celebrate
In the memory of Anne
And try to relate to her life
If we can.

So once again I say,
"Happy Hanukkah and happy day!"

Plan a party for the final day of the celebration. (The mother of a Jewish girl in one class sent delicious potato pancakes as her daughter's contribution to the party.) Entertainment would make this day a very special one.

Finally, set aside a class period after the celebration has been completed for the Questioning Circle. Use the following questions in whatever order seems appropriate.

White Questions

TEXT: What references to Hanukkah are made in *The Diary of Anne Frank?*

READER: Have you ever observed a religious rite similar to Hanukkah? If so, describe it.

WORLD: What is the meaning behind Hanukkah?

Shaded Questions

TEXT/READER: If you have never experienced Hanukkah before, what was it like for you?

TEXT/WORLD: From the stories you heard read about Hanukkah and from the references to it in *The Diary of Anne Frank*, what are the most common practices that go along with it?

READER/WORLD: In what way do religious celebrations or rituals of any kind serve to bring people closer together?

Dense Question

TEXT/READER/WORLD: How did our classroom celebration of Hanukkah and your understanding of it in *The Diary of Anne Frank* create a bond of friendship and good feeling as well as a tolerance for religious differences?

Follow-Up

Have students write a short piece about the Hanukkah celebration. Invite them to include their own personal role in the gift-giving ritual, their emotions felt, and their understanding of any of the questions discussed during the Questioning Circle as in the following example by one student.

Hanukkah

JONI LOFTIN

I feel that celebrating Hanukkah was a good experience for all of us. It was also an excellent experience to mix Christmas and Hanukkah together by giving gifts. Although Hanukkah is not really a gift giving holiday, I think it brought the class closer together.

I wouldn't hold back being friends with someone of the Jewish religion. I am Christian, and I liked celebrating Hanukkah. I have nothing against it.

During the celebration, I got a chance to think more about Anne Frank, her courage, and her life. I don't think I'd be able to survive like she did and as long as she did, not being able to make a sound or go outside. I especially wouldn't be able to survive without a phone. I really enjoyed this experience.

Evaluation

Judge this lesson on the basis of tone in the writings of students. If they have truly learned to think differently about diversity in this world, this attitude will be obvious in their writings.

SUMMARY

This chapter illustrates how effective Bloom's taxonomy is when the teacher uses it to plan objectives and activities for units of instruction. The involvement of students in tasks that are applicable to the real world goes hand in hand with planning. Students need to know that the projects they do in class will have meaning in their lives.

Another model illustrated in this chapter, the Questioning Circle, provides the teacher of literature with a guide for extending the thinking of students well beyond the classroom walls.

CHALLENGE

1. Using Bloom's taxonomy, outline the objectives for a unit of study that includes all six levels.
2. Using Bloom's taxonomy, design activities at each of the six levels for a unit of study.
3. Compose white, shaded, and dense questions, which could be used in a class, for one chapter of a book.
4. Compose white, shaded, and dense questions, based on the reading of a novel as a whole, for a particular lesson.

NOTES

1. Robert H. Ennis, "A Logical Basis for Measuring Thinking Skills," *Educational Leadership* (5 Oct. 1985): 45.
2. Ennis, "A Logical Basis for Measuring Thinking Skills," 46.
3. Nelson Quinby, "On Testing and Teaching Intelligence: A Conversation with Robert Sternberg," *Educational Leadership* (Oct. 1985): 50–53.
4. Edys S. Quellmalz, "Needed: Better Methods for Testing Higher-Order Thinking Skills," *Educational Leadership* (Oct. 1985): 31.
5. Quellmalz, "Needed: Better Methods," 31.
6. Arthur L. Costa, ed., "Toward a Model of Human Intellectual Functioning," in *Developing Minds: A Resource Book for Teaching Thinking* (Association for Supervision and Curriculum Development, 1985).
7. Costa, *Developing Minds*, 62.
8. Leila Christenbury, and Patricia P. Kelly, *Questioning a Path to Critical Thinking*, ERIC/RCS and NCTE, 1983.
9. Benjamin S. Bloom, et al., *Taxonomy of Educational Objectives, Handbook I: Cognitive Domain* (New York: David McKay, 1956).
10. Ken McCrorie, *Searching Writing* (Upper Montclair, N.J.: Hayden Book and Boynton-Cook, 1980).
11. Margaret Musgrove, *From Ashanti to Zulu: African Traditions* (Dial Press, 1976).
12. Christenbury and Kelly, *Questioning a Path to Critical Thinking*.
13. Ibid., p. 5.
14. Ibid., p. 14.
15. Ibid., p. 12–13.
16. Ibid., p. 12–13.
17. Ibid., p. 12.

18. Ibid., p. 13.
19. Ibid., p. 13.
20. Ibid., p. 17.
21. Isaac Bashevis Singer, *The Power of Light* (New York: Avon Books, 1982).

EXPLORING FURTHER

Bell, M., and N. Steinaker. *The Experiential Taxonomy: A New Approach to Teaching and Learning.* New York: Academic Press, 1979.

Dewey, J. *How We Think: A Restatement of the Relation of Reflective Thinking to the Educative Process.* Boston: D. C. Heath, 1933.

Joyce, Bruce, and Marsha Weil. *Models of Teaching.* Englewood Cliffs, N.J.: Prentice-Hall, 1980.

Krathwohl, D., B. S. Bloom, and B. B. Masia. *Taxonomy of Educational Objectives: Handbook II: Affective Domain.* New York: David McKay, 1964.

Lipman, M., A. M. Sharp, and F. S. Oscanyon. *Thinking in the Classroom,* 2d ed. Philadelphia: Temple University Press, 1980.

Presseisen, Barbara Z. "Thinking Skills: Meanings, Models, Materials." In *Developing Minds: A Resource Book for Teaching Thinking,* edited by Arthur L. Costa. Association for Supervision and Curriculum Development, 1985.

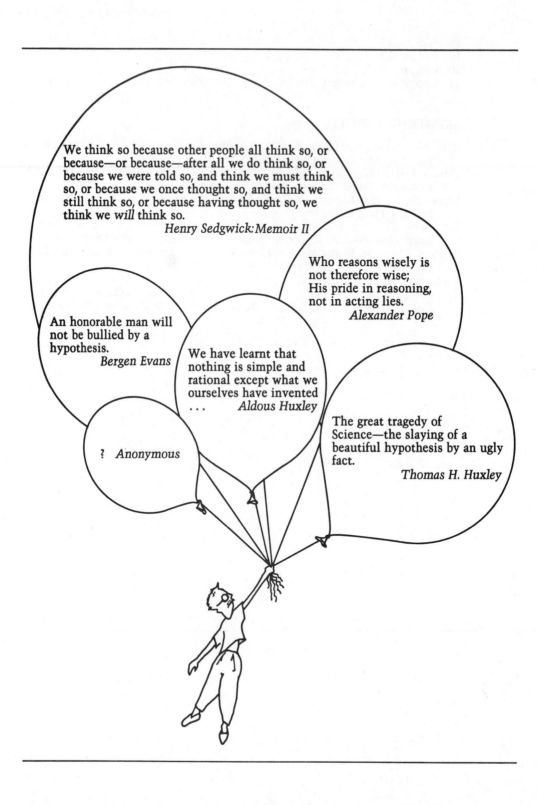

CHAPTER 4

Discovery Methods

Objectives

After reading this chapter, you will be able to

- *Identify two major forms of inductive reasoning.*
- *Discuss the advantages and shortcomings of the scientific method.*
- *Structure syllogisms for deductive reasoning.*
- *Analyze syllogisms for validity.*
- *Write exercises for teaching inductive and deductive reasoning.*
- *Identify two kinds of informal reasoning: "burr sticking" and creative thinking.*
- *Create assignments that require informal reasoning processes.*

In one "Peanuts" cartoon strip, Charlie Brown goes to "Doctor" Lucy for psychiatric counseling. He asks her two questions: "What can you do when you don't fit in?" and "What can you do when life seems to be passing you by?" Whereupon, Lucy tells Charlie to follow her, and after they have ascended a nearby hill, she leads him through a process of clear, logical reasoning. First, she points out how big the world is and how much room there is for everybody. Then, she asks him if he has seen any other worlds. He answers, "No." She asks, "As far as you know this is the only world there is . . . Right?" He says, "Right." She looks at him skeptically and asks, "There are no other worlds for you to live in . . . Right?" Again, he agrees. She continues, "You were born to live in this world . . . Right?" "Right," he concedes. "WELL, LIVE IN IT, THEN!" she shouts, as he does a backflip in astonishment. In the final frame, she stands over the crestfallen Charlie and demands, "Five cents, please." Obviously, Lucy thinks she has provided appropriate therapy.

Like Lucy, we can help our students develop a greater understanding of their world through increasing their logical thinking skills. To assist them effectively, we must give them activities and exercises that will involve them in systematic thinking processes, and we must be patient and encouraging as they struggle to grow inductive and deductive thinking capabilities. They will grow. We can have confidence in that, for humans are by their very nature thinkers. So, our task is to expand both the quantity and the quality of our students' thinking. This chapter explores both formal and informal processes of reasoning.

Formal Reasoning

The techniques of formal reasoning are tools for thinking, and, as such, they are subject to both correct and incorrect usage.

Just as an unskilled carpenter might use too large a hammer and do unnecessary damage, so, too, might one's misapplication of the tools of formal reasoning lead to error or abuse. Used skillfully, these processes allow us to separate truth from falsehood, to separate fact from mere opinion, and to distinguish half-truths and distortions of truth. By acquiring greater skill in the processes of formal inquiry, we become more perceptive, less gullible, and more confident. These are important attributes for us to exhibit as teachers and for us to nurture in our students. Because we use inductive reasoning more frequently than deductive in our daily lives, we will discuss it first.

INDUCTIVE REASONING

We use inductive reasoning more frequently because it proceeds from the gathering of specific facts or instances to an inferential generalization. We use induction to decide what manner of dress is appropriate for the day's weather or business affairs. We test the waters of our various relationships by examining the words and behaviors of others. We make economic decisions about the purchase of goods and services based on our inductive analysis of cost, quality, and quantity. Our generalizations guide our actions in each of these situations, and we live with the consequences of our choices; sometimes happily, sometimes to our regret.

There are two major forms of inductive reasoning. One approach involves drawing a general conclusion after gathering numerous bits of data; the other, more restrictive in nature, requires the setting up and testing of hypotheses. Because these two approaches are not mutually exclusive, they are often combined, especially in tightly controlled research studies in the physical sciences.

Approach Number One: Gathering Evidence

Questioning leads us as we assemble facts, examine them, and draw conclusions. Generally, the soundness of our conclusions is related directly to the quality of our questions. If we shop for a new car and base our choice only on such factors as the appearance, the feel of a kicked tire, and the highest speed indicated on the speedometer, we may find ourselves the unhappy owners of a vehicle that doesn't meet our needs.

Similarly, we often hear students generalizing about their peers, their teachers, music, movies, television, food, and many other aspects of their lives in grossly unsophisticated terms. Because they usually have failed to pursue a systematic process of inquiry, their generalizations are often subject to collapse when we ask for supporting facts or evidence. Even under the best of circumstances, students need to know that "there are comparatively few generalizations which always hold true."

Our students should learn to test not only their own generalizations but also other people's to determine if they are true or valid. The easiest test to apply is that of the "sweeping generalization." If the speaker uses such words as *all, always,* or *never,* can such usage be fully justified? Because these words imply that there are no exceptions, they must be used with care. The best way to guard against being misled by sweeping generalizations is to demand more precise information from the speaker. Does *all* really mean *all* or *most?* Does *most* mean *nearly all* or just *over half?* Such clarifying questions can discourage unqualified generalizing.

Another important consideration is the authority for the evidence that supports a generalization. Both qualitative and quantitative factors come into play when we are testing the validity of general statements. So, our students must ask questions about the credentials or qualifications of the researcher as well as questions about the number of instances (the n) on which the conclusion is based. For example, if a student asserts that his mother read in a magazine that high school students today are worse readers than were any previous generation, two important questions are who was the author of the information about student-reading abilities and what are the author's qualifications for making such an assertion. Then, we need to determine what statistical data led to that conclusion. In other words, how many of today's students were compared with students from previous generations? Beyond that, we still need to know how representative were the samples studied: Were they a wide cross section of students from a number of states over a wide range of generations? Only when we have accustomed our students to rigid examination of generalizations in this manner will we see real improvement in the quality of their analysis of inductive reasoning.

Terms such as *average, normal, typical,* and *usual* also present obstacles to clear thinking. What is really meant by such a phrase as "the average student"? Average in what sense? In age? In socioeconomic level? In academic ability? In mode of dress? In participation in cocurricular activities? Terms such as *average, normal, typical,* and *usual* suggest the individual's membership in a large grouping of similar individuals. But, how large, in fact, are such groupings? In citing the *average,* the speaker should inform us whether *average* refers to the arithmetical mean, the simple mean, the median, or the mode.

The common form of research we require of students is the gathering of evidence for writing reports, reference papers, and essay questions or preparing for speeches or debates. Unfortunately, however, we may not provide adequate opportunities for extensive inductive reasoning activity during the regular classroom routine. If our students are to improve in their application of this reasoning, they must be given frequent opportunities to question, weigh, examine, and decide from available sources of evidence. As educators, if we are really serious about educating students for citizenship in a democracy, we should consider truly making the teaching of thinking the center of our instructional activity.

Still another important area of teacher behavior for enhancing thinking is patience. We must learn to be patient, to wait longer for student responses to our questions, so that thinking can occur. In the box is a problem that requires students to work through a process of inductive reasoning to a solution. As you read it, visualize your own classroom and

---

Which is whose?

This is a problem in inductive thinking. Four people live on the same street and each owns a different pet. You are to study the facts provided, and then decide which pet each person owns.

1. Bart, Connie, Wayne, and Pam live on the same street.
2. They own a rabbit, a donkey, a monkey, and a dog, but not in that order.
3. The owner of the monkey lives next to Wayne.
4. Connie does not talk to the owner of the dog.
5. Bart and the dog's owner are college classmates.
6. Pam's best friend owns the monkey.
7. Connie would never own a rabbit or a monkey.
8. Pam and the rabbit's owner want to open a bagel bakery.
9. There are twelve houses on the street.
10. Wayne lives in a white house; Bart lives in a green one.

Which pet does each person own?

a. Bart owns the _____.

b. Pam owns the _____.

c. Connie owns the _____.

d. Wayne owns the _____.

---

your behavior as a teacher while presenting this activity. Would you allow your students, even the slowest of them, enough thinking time to complete this task successfully? Would you avoid interrupting them or trying to "help" them unnecessarily?

After your students have completed this activity, how would you discuss it with them? You could have them tell the kinds of questions they asked. You could ask them how they structured their approach to solving the problem. You could find out how they decided which questions to ask. You could ask which of the facts were unnecessary. You could ask which specific facts convinced them that they had found the correct solution. It is important to have students spend time thinking about their own thinking activity, for, as someone once said, "We learn neither by thinking nor by doing, but by thinking about what we are doing."

SAFE demonstration lesson plans.   On the next few pages, there are a series of sample lessons for stimulating inductive reasoning. You may wish either to use the lessons as outlined or to modify them as appropriate for your own classroom. Remember, these are intended to serve as examples of the kinds of inductive thinking assignments you can bring into your classroom on a continuing basis. Ideally, as your students gain proficiency with these experiences, they will begin to apply the systematic thinking behaviors required for these activities in their other learning tasks.

> Is ice cream good because you like it, or do you like it because it is good?

> Both!?

SAFE Demonstration Lesson Plan 4.1: So, What Happened?
Grade Levels: 9–12

OBJECTIVES

Students will

1. analyze a list of details excerpted from a story that they have not read.
2. infer the ending of the story from their analysis of the details.
3. write their reasons for choosing the ending they chose.

BRIEF DESCRIPTION

Students read a list of details selected from "The Lottery" by Shirley Jackson. After analyzing these details, they infer how the story ends. Then, they write their reasons for their inferences.

PROCEDURES

Duplicate copies of the following list of details from "The Lottery." If they have already read "The Lottery," you will need details from a different story.

Selected details from "The Lottery" by Shirley Jackson

1. The date is June 27.
2. The village has only 300 people.
3. The lottery starts at 10:00 A.M. and lasts less than two hours.
4. Everyone in the village is included in the lottery.
5. Many stones are piled in a corner of the village square.
6. Much of the ritual of the lottery has been forgotten or discarded.
7. Attendance is checked to ensure that every inhabitant of the village is present or has a representative there for the drawing.
8. Only the men or boys over the age of sixteen do the drawing for families.
9. No one is permitted to look at the piece of paper he or she has drawn until after everyone has had a chance to draw one.
10. Some of the other nearby villages no longer hold the lottery each June.
11. When everyone has finally drawn, Bill Hutchinson discovers that he has the winning "ticket." Bill has a wife, Tessie, and three children.
12. Tessie argues that the drawing wasn't fair because the director of the lottery made Bill draw too quickly.
13. Next, five new slips of paper are put in the box, one slip for each member of the Hutchinson family, and the rest of the slips are discarded.
14. Each of the Hutchinsons draws a slip from the box.
15. After each family member has drawn a slip of paper, the slips are opened, and Tessie has the one with the black spot.
16. Again, Tessie argues that the drawing was not fair.
17. All the villagers join in giving Tessie her prize.

Stimulus

Ask students if they have ever known how a story or movie would end before the ending. Talk with them about the kinds of clues or details that enabled them to guess the ending(s) correctly. List some of their responses on the board.

Activity

Pass out duplicated copies of the list of details from "The Lottery" to each student. Ask them to analyze these details carefully, and then guess how the story ends. Have them write their reasons for selecting the ending they did.

Follow-Up

Have students pair up and discuss their endings and the rationales for them. Each pair of students should decide which one of the pair has made a sounder guess. Ask some students to share their guesses and rationales with the entire class.

Read the author's ending for the story, or the entire story if time permits.

Evaluation

Collect the students' papers and evaluate the quality of thinking implicit in their rationales. Write a short comment on each paper about your assessment of the thinking that took place. Be positive.

SAFE Demonstration Lesson Plan 4.2: What Next?
Grade Levels: 4–10

OBJECTIVES

Students will

1. infer the last elements in a series of sequences.
2. explain how they inferred their answers for completing the sequences.
3. create three sequences of their own.

BRIEF DESCRIPTION

Students use inductive reasoning to complete the last elements in a series of sequences. After completing the sequences, they write explanations of the reasoning that led to their choices. Then, they create three sequences of their own.

PROCEDURES

On a ditto master, create a series of varied sequences: for example, numbers, shapes, words. Each sequence should have the final element omitted:

3, 8, 18, 38, 78, _____

bay, cay, day, gay, hay, _____

Stimulus

Do a couple of sequences with the entire class using an overhead transparency. Talk with them about the reasoning involved. Then pass out duplicated copies of the sequences you created. Ask them to complete each sequence.

Activity

Have students write a brief explanation for each of their choices. Go over each sequence with the entire class. Have each student who responds give both choice and the explanation for that choice. This not only allows the rest of the class to compare their responses and explanations but also helps them become aware of the thinking processes that took place.

Follow-Up

Have each student create a series of three sequences with the final element missing in each sequence. Have them exchange papers and complete each other's sequences. Ask them to rank the sequences in order of difficulty and give reasons for their rankings.

Evaluation

Examine the completed sequences to determine which of the sequences were troublesome and to judge the quality of their explanations.

Here I pause for one moment
to exhort the reader never to pay any
attention to his understanding when it stands
in opposition to any other faculty of his mind.
The mere understanding, however useful and
indispensable, is the meanest faculty in the human
mind and the most to be distrusted; and yet the
great majority of people trust to nothing else—
which may do for ordinary life, but not
for philosophical purposes.

Thomas De Quincey,

"On the Knocking at the Gate"

in *Macbeth*

SAFE Demonstration Lesson Plan 4.3: Let the Buyer Beware!
Grade Levels: 7–10

OBJECTIVES

Students will

1. evaluate a series of advertisements for their intellectual and emotional appeal.
2. assign a rank order to the advertisements and give reasons for their rankings.
3. create an advertisement for a product of their choice.

BRIEF DESCRIPTION

Students establish their own critical criteria to evaluate a series of advertisements for a product in common use. Then, they rank each of the advertisements and give reasons for their rankings. Finally, they create an advertisement of their own.

PROCEDURES

Select a number of advertisements for a common product such as shaving cream, perfume, motorcycles, or cake mix. Mount each of the advertisements on stiff paper or cardboard and number each on the back. Then, videotape several commercials from television. Tape some you consider effective and some you consider poorly done.

Stimulus

Play the videotape of the commercials, taking time to discuss the relative strengths or weaknesses of each one. Then look at a couple of magazine advertisements with the class and discuss their merits. Distribute the advertisements you mounted to the class.

Activity

Ask students to evaluate the merits of each advertisement in terms of its intellectual and emotional appeal. Tell them to assign a rank order to the advertisements, number one being their first choice, two their second choice, and so on.

Follow-Up

List the numbers from the back of each advertisement on the board and tabulate the score of each by totaling the entire class's ranking scores. Discuss the results of the tabulation. Determine what factors weighed heaviest in the rankings. After discussing the implications of those factors with the students, work with them to create an evaluation scale or set of factors that are vital to a successful advertisement.

Evaluation

Have each student select a product and create an advertisement for it. Use the evaluation scale to judge the merits of each advertisement. Display the finished advertisements in the classroom.

SAFE Demonstration Lesson Plan 4.4: Walk on By
Grade Levels: 3–10

OBJECTIVES

Students will

1. demonstrate how a person's emotional state affects the way he or she walks.
2. discover why nonverbal behavior offers important cues for understanding other people.

BRIEF DESCRIPTION

Students brainstorm a list of emotions that may be inferred from the body language of people in various stressful or emotionally charged situations. Then, volunteers demonstrate the body language of people as reflected in their manner of walking. Next, the students use inductive reasoning to identify behavioral clues that are important to members of the helping and dramatic professions.

PROCEDURES

Videotape characters from television shows walking in various tense or humorous contexts. Select instances where the character's emotional state is quite obvious in the person's manner of walking and some instances where it is not so obvious.

Stimulus

Play the videotape of the people walking with the volume turned off. Pause after each walker to allow the students to infer what emotion is projected through the body language. List these emotions on the board.

Activity

Have students singly, in pairs or triads pantomime walking contexts. The following are some examples:

- Walking into the nurse's office as if very sick
- Walking into the principal's office as if in serious trouble
- Walking up to a teacher and receiving an all *F* report card
- Walking up to a teacher and receiving an all *A* report card

- Walking through a cemetery on a dark night
- Walking through a cow pasture
- Walking through an alligator-infested swamp
- Walking as though plotting to get even with someone
- Walking as if you were a penguin
- Walking out to an airplane to take your first parachute jump

Follow-Up

Have students suggest some of their own walking contexts and act them out.

Discuss the behavioral clues revealed by the ways people walk. Identify which clues are easiest to read and which are more difficult. Discuss why these clues are important to a doctor, a teacher, a police officer, or a professional actor.

Evaluation

Have students vote on their three favorite walks from the pantomimes. See if other students can recreate them from memory.

SAFE Demonstration Lesson Plan 4.5: What Are You Looking At? Grade Levels: 3–10

OBJECTIVES

Students will

1. categorize the shows presented on prime-time television by types.
2. draw some generalizations concerning the logic of scheduling by local and network television executives.

BRIEF DESCRIPTION

Students examine prime-time television schedules for each night of the week in order to categorize the shows by types and by frequency. Then, students analyze their survey information and develop some generalizations about why and when various shows are offered. Next, students suggest what changes they would make if they were in charge of scheduling shows for prime-time viewing.

PROCEDURES

Duplicate prime-time television schedules for each night of the week. Pass out a copy of the duplicated schedules to each student.

Stimulus

Select one night's schedule and survey it with the class. Identify the various categories in which the shows can be grouped (for example, police shows, situation comedies, and public affairs).

Activity

Have students categorize the schedules for each night of the week into the groupings previously identified. Have them tally the totals for each type of show and the total hours for each type of show for the week. Then have them develop some generalizations based on their data. Some questions to guide them are: What shows are offered most frequently? Based on the variety and frequency of the types of shows, what assumptions can be made about the preferences of the viewers? What determines on which day and at what time a show is aired?

Share the students' conclusions by collectively composing generalizations. Write these on the board. Finally, have them modify the week's schedule according to their own personal preferences.

Follow-Up

Have students pair up to compare their modifications of the week's schedules. Then ask each member of the pairs to write a reaction to what they like best and what they like least about their partner's suggested schedule.

Evaluation

Have each student watch a show of a type that he or she rarely or never watches. Have students write a review of that show in which they discuss its strongest and weakest points.

Approach Number Two: Testing Hypotheses

This second type of formal reasoning involves much greater control of the conditions under which research evidence is assembled and analyzed. Often called the *scientific method*, it is commonly used in the experimental sciences. The steps include:

1. The experimenter formulates a question or hypothesis that is answerable in terms of its truth or falsity or in yes/no. For example, an agricultural researcher might ask if blue-eyed cows produce more milk than do brown-eyed ones.
2. Then, the researcher sets up a controlled experiment to determine the truth or falsity of the hypothesis.

If the researcher is successful in controlling all the variables involved in the study and if the conclusion derived from the data cannot be explained in any other way, then, the hypothesis is fairly tested.

We can guide our students in experimental research in our own classrooms. If animals or plants are a part of the class, students can set up various experiments involving them. They can also do experiments with fluids, solids, manipulatives (for example, cuisenaire rods), numbers, and words. In encouraging them to undertake such investigations, we must also make them aware of the limitations of their conclusions and caution them against research involving human subjects.

The following are suggestions for research studies, which students could undertake in the classroom:

- Determining whether beans grow better in soil mixed with sand or soil mixed with compost
- Determining whether mice gain more weight on a vegetarian diet or on an all-meat diet
- Determining which twelve adjectives appear most frequently in our daily newspaper
- Determining whether a story was written by a woman or a man, based on certain elements of style or content
- Determining how often numbers appear in certain patterns in the statistics of the professional or baseball leagues
- Determining the frequency of simple, compound, and complex sentences in the works of two major American writers

A cautionary statement about the scientific method is in order. Often, when this mode of research is mentioned, the speaker seems to imply that it constitutes the *only* legitimate or valuable research. It is important to remember that this method is a construct of the human mind and not an inherent part of nature. As with most such constructs, the method has its own deficiencies and limitations. The assembling of evidence and testing of hypotheses are the core of the method. The limitations of this type of experimental research arise out of the difficulty of identifying and controlling the variables involved and out of trying to extrapolate conclusions from that research, which extend beyond the specific context under which the research occurred. Thus, we can help our students understand these limitations by having them qualify their conclusions with such phrases as "in this case" or "under these conditions, this result ensued."

DEDUCTIVE REASONING

In deductive reasoning, there is a change of direction. The reasoning moves from a general truth to a specific conclusion. Sherlock Holmes is famous as the great exemplar of deductive reasoning. He makes astute general observations and then draws a conclusion, often to Dr. Watson's mystification. In *A Study in Scarlet*, for example, Holmes traces his deductive process for Watson:

> I had already determined in my own mind that the man who had walked into the house with Drebber, was none other than the man who had driven the cab. The marks in the road showed me that the horse had wandered on in a way which would have been impossible had there been any one in charge of it. Where, then, could the driver be, unless he were inside the house? Again, it is absurd to suppose that any sane man would carry out a deliberate crime under the very eyes, as it were, of a third person, who was sure to betray him. Lastly, supposing one man wished to dog another through London, what better means could he adopt than to turn cab-driver. All these considerations led me to the irresistible conclusion that Jefferson Hope was to be found among the jarveys of the metropolis.

After Holmes goes on to explain how he located the villain among the city's cab drivers, he assures Watson that ". . . the whole thing is a chain of logical sequences without a break or flaw." Dr. Watson exclaims, "It is wonderful!" and insists that Holmes's merits should be publicly recognized.

Syllogism, the tool of deductive reasoning, consists of a major premise (MP), a minor premise (mp), and a conclusion (C). These are structured as follows:

MP: All National Football League players are under forty years of age.

mp: He is a National Football League player.

C: Therefore, he is under forty years of age.

As you can see from this example, deductive reasoning is reasoning by inference.

We can teach our students the syllogistic method of reasoning. Once they have learned how to structure their own syllogisms, they can examine them for validity. Because the conclusion to a syllogism evolves out of the relationship between the two premises, it should be considered valid as long as those premises are true or assumed to be true. For example,

MP: Everyone who lives on that street is named Jones.

mp: He lives on that street.

C: Therefore, his name is Jones.

As you can see, the major premise in this example serves as the generalization for which the minor premise is a particular instance. Assuming that the premises are true, we can then judge this to be a valid syllogism.

In analyzing the validity of syllogisms, we must also recognize some essential conditions. The first of these conditions involves the precision of the vocabulary in the syllogism. The terminology of both premises must be precise and consistent. Thus, words such as *average, usual, normal, typical,* and *regular* lead to difficulty because they are imprecise or ambiguous. How does one establish whether someone or something is "typical" or "average"? Consider this syllogism:

MP: When it rains more than usual, we have a flood.
mp: It has rained more than usual.
C: Therefore, we will have a flood.

How does one determine what "usual" means? It could mean more rain in quantity in a certain time period or continuous rainfall over a certain period of time without consideration of the volume of that rainfall. The wording of this syllogism is simply not precise enough.

Consistency of definition is also very important in creating syllogisms. For example, there are some problem terms in this syllogism:

MP: When unemployment reaches a critical point, a recession occurs.
mp: Unemployment is now at a critical point.
C: Therefore, we will have a recession.

What is meant by "critical point" and "recession" in this example? "Critical point" could refer to a specific number of unemployed workers, but it could also mean a general feeling held by investors. "Recession" also suggests various meanings. Unless there is general agreement about the meaning of the words in the premises, the conclusion will not be accepted.

Another important consideration in creating syllogisms is that a qualification in either of the premises must be repeated in the conclusion. Any use of *all, each, every, none, always,* or other terms allowing for no exceptions must be retained in the conclusion. Also, conditional terms such as *few, some, many, often,* and *seldom* must be repeated in the conclusion, if they appear in either of the premises:

MP: Some of the students in the class cheated on the test.
mp: Those who cheated will receive a failing grade.
C: Therefore, some of the students will receive failing grades.

It is important for our students to understand that the omission of qualifying terms often leads to invalid or unsupportable conclusions, the fallacy of the "sweeping generalization." Given the massive attempts by advertisers, office seekers, and various organizations to urge us to some course of action or to persuade us to purchase a certain service or product, we render a valuable service to our students when we alert them to the hazards of the sweeping generalization, as in this example:

MP: Any organization that opposes child abuse deserves our financial support.

mp: This organization opposes child abuse.

C: This organization deserves our financial support.

A number of people in San Francisco were surprised to learn that an organization that solicited donations by phone to oppose child abuse actually passed on only a small amount of each dollar (less than 15 percent) to the child-abuse center it named in the phone solicitations. Clearly, that organization did not deserve support.

Still another consideration in syllogistic reasoning is the "begging the question" fallacy. This fallacious reasoning occurs when the conclusion to a syllogism is identical with one of the premises:

MP: Skydiving is a high-risk sport because of the danger involved.

mp: He is a skydiver.

C: Therefore, he practices a high-risk, dangerous sport.

Because the conclusion merely restates the same point as the major premise, the argument goes nowhere. This circular argumentation invariably occurs in a syllogism that makes the same assertion in a premise and the conclusion.

You can help your students get started with syllogistic reasoning by giving them sample syllogisms that have one of the three elements missing. By analyzing the information in the other two elements, they should be able to supply the missing one. The following are examples:

1. MP: Some of the graduates of the class are going to attend a technical school.

   mp: He is a graduate of the class.

   C:

2. MP: Only dogs that had had their distemper shots were permitted in the park.

   mp:

   C: Therefore, his dog was not permitted in the park.

3. MP:

   mp: He bought crunchy peanut butter at the health-food store.

   C: Therefore, he eats expensive peanut butter.

Analyzing the syllogisms in an exercise of this type gives your students valuable practice in such skills as grasping part-whole and whole-part relationships, identifying underlying assumptions, and dealing with ambiguities. Each of these skills is important for students as they develop greater sophistication in deductive thinking processes.

SAFE Demonstration Lesson Plans

On the next few pages, there are five lessons that focus on deductive reasoning. As you examine them, consider how you could adapt each lesson for use in your own classroom. You might also consider any other activities that the lessons suggest to you for use in your classes.

SAFE Demonstration Lesson Plan 4.6: Street Talk
Grade Levels: 3–10

OBJECTIVES

Students will

1. identify the purpose of each in a series of international traffic-control signs.
2. infer what correct and incorrect driving behaviors are implied by each sign.
3. create a new sign to monitor some aspect of behavior related to traffic control.

BRIEF DESCRIPTION

Students examine a series of street signs used for traffic control. They identify each sign's meaning for motorists. Then, they infer what correct and incorrect driving behaviors created the need for each sign. Next, they suggest a new street sign of their own creation and give a rationale for its need.

PROCEDURES

Make a series of traffic signs such as used internationally for traffic control. (Available in DMV driver's handbook.)

Stimulus

Discuss with students the purpose of the rules in such games as tag, dodge ball, hopscotch, and badminton.

Activity

Display each of the signs sequentially. Ask students to identify each sign's meaning and to state at least one specific driving behavior implied by each sign. It will help the students if you ask them to consider what driving behavior or behaviors made each sign necessary.

Have students share their inferences for each of the signs in pairs or small groups. Then seek large-group consensus on each of the signs.

Follow-Up

Ask each student to create a new sign that could be used as an international symbol for traffic control. EXAMPLE.   A picture of a skier with an *X* over it to indicate no skiing on a hill.

Evaluation

Collect the handout sheets and examine the students' responses for each of the symbols. Check to see if their responses do give an appropriate inference from each symbol. Return the papers and collectively do three or four syllogisms to fit different symbols.

SAFE Demonstration Lesson Plan 4.7: You're Telling Me!
Grade Levels: 4–12

OBJECTIVES

Students will

1. infer specific facts or details suggested by newspaper headlines.
2. write syllogisms based on generalizing from the headlines.

BRIEF DESCRIPTION

Students read a series of newspaper headlines and infer some of the facts or details behind the headlines. Then, they write syllogisms based on the headlines, inferring the minor premise and conclusion. EXAMPLE.   "Legal Whirlwind Swirls Around Helpless Woman," *San Jose Mercury*, 23 June 1986:

MP: A helpless woman cannot receive needed assistance because of legal problems related to her condition.
mp: The legal problems cannot be resolved.
C: Therefore, the woman must remain in her helpless condition.

PROCEDURES

Select several newspaper headlines on a variety of subjects. Attach the headlines to a sheet of blank paper, leaving several spaces between the headlines. Duplicate copies of this master for each member of the class.

Stimulus

Discuss with the class the use of each headline as a generalization. Display some headlines using an overhead projector and ask students to suggest specific facts or details suggested by the headlines. Convert two or three of these suggestions into syllogisms.

Activity

Pass out the duplicated sheets containing the headlines you have selected and ask students to write one or two underlying particulars or specifics for each headline. Then ask them to write a syllogism for each of two different headlines.

Next share some of the major specifics or details from the stories accompanying the headlines. Ask students to compare their inferential guesses with the actual specifics from the stories. What kinds of inferences did they make? How accurately were they able to infer the facts or details of the stories? How valid were the syllogisms they wrote?

Follow-Up

Have each student select his or her best syllogism and rewrite it on a separate sheet of paper to be handed in.

Evaluation

Collect these syllogisms and analyze them for their validity. Write a brief comment on each paper noting the quality and imaginativeness of the syllogisms.

SAFE Demonstration Lesson Plan 4.8: By Design
Grade Levels: 3–12

OBJECTIVES

Students will

1. evaluate the logic of the packaging design for a variety of products.
2. design packaging containers of their own and provide a rationale for their designs.

BRIEF DESCRIPTION

Students will consider the logic of the packaging for a variety of common products. They will make judgments about the form and function of that packaging. Then, they will create packaging designs of their own and provide a supporting rationale for them. Finally, they will select the best designs from the class and tell why these designs are superior.

PROCEDURES

Bring to class a variety of commercial-product packages such as an egg carton, a L'Eggs container, a TV dinner tray, and a tictac box.

Stimulus

Discuss the logic of each of the sample packages with the class. What is the primary function of each package? What other functions does each serve? What are the advantages of this form of packaging? The disadvantages? Does anyone have a suggestion for a different or better way to package one of the products?

Activity

After you have spent some time discussing the packages you have brought to class, give students the task of creating a package design of their own. The following are some possible design problems:

- Designing an automobile that will protect the passengers from collisions, fire, and flood
- Designing a container that will increase the sales of your company's brand of cottage cheese
- Designing an efficient carrying kit for a teenager's cosmetics and junk food
- Designing a case for shipping live dogs or cats by the postal service.

Follow-Up

After students have completed one or more of the design problems, have them get into small groups and discuss their ideas. Ask them to focus on the kinds of deductive processes they applied in deciding on their designs. What assumptions did they make about the product to be packaged? What limitations did they impose? What were their considerations regarding appearance, cost, and availability of materials?

Evaluation

Within each group, have students select the design idea that they consider superior. Share these ideas with the entire class. Then collect each student's design and comment on the most positive and negative aspect of each.

SAFE Demonstration Lesson Plan 4.9: What Did You Mean by THAT?
Grade Levels: 4–10

OBJECTIVES

Students will

1. analyze a series of invented words and provide definitions.
2. use a series of invented words in sentences.
3. invent some words of their own and provide definitions.
4. use their invented words in syllogisms.

BRIEF DESCRIPTION

Students are given a list of invented words to analyze and define. These words are made up by combining common prefixes, roots, and suffixes. Then, students use each of the invented words in a sentence. Next, students create and define several words of their own. Finally, they use their invented words in syllogisms.

PROCEDURES

Prepare a list of invented words for students to define. These words should combine common prefixes, roots, and suffixes. EXAMPLES. Prelunarly, pseudoaquaphiliac, semidactylic, neonecrophobianess. This activity fits well with a language study focusing on root words and affixes.

Stimulus

Write a couple of the invented words on the board and ask students to provide definitions for each of the component parts of the words. Then ask them to suggest appropriate definitions for the entire word.

Activity

Hand out the lists of words and give students time to analyze and define each word. Then ask them to write a sentence using each word. Next ask students to invent three to five words of their own, with their own definitions. (You will find it useful to provide them with a list of common prefixes, roots, and suffixes.)

Follow-Up

Ask students to write syllogisms in which they incorporate two or three of their invented words.

Evaluation

Collect the students' words and compile a class dictionary. Have several copies of the dictionary in the classroom so students can refer to them, and place several copies in the school library to share with other students.

SAFE Demonstration Lesson Plan 4.10: Words of the Wise?
Grade Levels: 9–12

OBJECTIVES

Students will

1. read a series of quotations centered around a common theme.
2. analyze the inherent logic of the quotations.
3. write syllogisms derived from five of the quotations.

BRIEF DESCRIPTION

After analyzing a series of quotations centered on a common theme, students select five of the quotations and write a syllogism for each. Next, they share their syllogisms and vote on each to indicate their relative degree of agreement or disagreement with the logic therein.

PROCEDURES

Select a series of quotations on a common theme and duplicate them or print them individually on 5 × 7-inch cards. For example, here are quotations on generational conflict:

Your old men shall dream dreams, your young men shall see visions.
    JOB 2:28, BIBLE

Say what thou wilt, the young are happy never. Give me bless'd age, beyond the fire and fever, past the delight that shatters, hope that stings, and eager flutt'ring of life's ignorant wings.
    SIR WILLIAM WATSON

Crabbed age and youth cannot live together. Youth is full of pleasure, age is full of care.
    WILLIAM SHAKESPEARE

When we are young we long to tread a way none trod before.
    WILLIAM BUTLER YEATS

You who are old, and have fought the fight, and have won or lost or left the fight, weight us not down with fears of the world as we run!
    CALE Y. RICE

A young man who has not wept is a savage, and the old man who will not laugh is a fool.
    GEORGE SANTAYANA

Youth is a blunder; manhood a struggle; old age a regret.
    BENJAMIN DISRAELI

Our youth we can have but today, we may always find time to grow old.
    GEORGE BERKELEY

Youth is life as yet untouched by tragedy.
    ALBERT N. WHITEHEAD

In sorrow he learned this truth: one may return to the place of his birth, he cannot go back to his youth.
    JOHN BURROUGHS

Stimulus

Show the class one of the quotations and discuss the logic behind it. Ask them to infer what behaviors might inspire or provoke such a statement. Working as a group, create a syllogism from the quotation and test its validity.

Activity

Present the quotations to students either on duplicated sheets or by posting them on 5 × 7-inch cards in front of the class. Have each student select any five to turn into syllogisms. Give them time to write the syllogisms. Share some of them after they have finished and analyze the logic of each.

Follow-Up

Ask students to engage in value voting on their levels of agreement with each of the syllogisms. They might vote on a three-point scale to show their relative agreement. Then have them vote on the original quotations, using the same scale. Compare the results. Note any significant differences in the total score for each quotation and the syllogism derived from it. Discuss the scoring results.

Evaluation

Collect each student's five syllogisms and evaluate for both correctness of form and logical validity. Return their efforts with appropriate comments.

Informal Reasoning

If you make people think they're thinking, they'll love you. If you really make them think, they'll hate you.
   DON MARQUIS: THE SUN DIAL

In his study on the American high school, John Goodlad contends that "most teachers simply do not know how to teach for higher levels of thinking." He goes on to charge that teachers are even actively discouraged from trying to teach for such skills. With the advent of the required teaching of critical thinking skills now a reality in many states, perhaps the next few years will see a substantive change in the thinking activities offered to students. We have examined the primary formal methods of discovery in the preceding sections of this chapter. Now, let us turn our attention to some "informal" methods, or less formal if you prefer.

BURR STICKING

Ken Macrorie suggests an interesting method for encouraging thinking in an article for *Media and Methods*. He uses the metaphor of burrs sticking to one's clothing as a means of describing a method for increasing student thinking. He freed his students to do their own thinking by giving up the assignment of topics based on the literature he asked them to read. Instead, he let them find their own topics for writing by encouraging them to respond to the people, relationships, ideas, and events that stuck to them as they read. Because the topics that attracted their interest were generally related in some way to their own lives or experiences, they became more actively involved. Consequently, thinking did occur—higher-level thinking than they had previously demonstrated. They wrote better, and their writing was more interesting to read. And, as they struggled with the literature on their own terms, they explored many of the aspects of character, plot, theme, and style, which Macrorie ordinarily would have pointed out to them in a lecture.

We have had a similar experience in stimulating student thinking through the medium of reading notes. We require them to take a certain number of pages of reading notes for each story or book assigned. In these notes, they may ask questions about events, characters, or vocabulary. They may offer opinions about the logic or believability of plot developments. They may express agreement or disagreement with actions taken by the characters or with rhetorical decisions by the author. They are not permitted, however, merely to summarize the plot or incidents within it unless they use a brief summarizing statement as a springboard for an expression of their own thinking about some aspect of the story. As a result of using this approach, we have found that our students are able to discuss literature in greater depth and more interestingly in their oral discussions and their written responses.

There is a strong similarity between the method employed by Macrorie and the one we have found. Both approaches require the instructor to step aside, to get out of the students' way so they can engage in thinking based on their own involvement with the materials they are studying. For the teacher who wonders whether all of the important elements of the literature will be "covered" by this approach, we can report that our experience has been much the same as Macrorie's. Students usually touch on most of the essential things that were to be studied anyhow, and they display more ownership of the material. As Macrorie says, "Thinking isn't forced, isn't accompanied by ten required steps. Like most other acts of value, consequence, or pleasure, it's carried out by Self Two—spontaneously, instantaneously, instinctively—as well as Self One—carefully, directly, rationally. Because it's a personal act, thinking must find initiative in a thinker, not a teacher, who may provide a challenge or model, but never the impetus."

The following reading notes were taken by a student on the book *Give Me One Good Reason* by Norma Klein. It is a novel about a "liberated" woman who wants to have a child but does not want a husband or father for the child.

p. 9   She smokes a pipe to help her stop smoking. I wonder if she inhales the pipe smoke. I'll bet she doesn't smoke the pipe in public.

p. 12   What does she mean by "exemplary couple"? I think she probably means they would look good together and other people would be jealous of them.

p. 17   She says she sees herself as being a "terribly good parent." I wonder if her parents were good parents. She sounds sort of conceited to me. She is proud that she has handled every important adult decision that has come her way. She's 32 and unmarried. I wonder what some of her adult decisions were.

p. 21   She is surprised when her mother is upset about Matthew sailing to England so soon. She wonders if her mother thinks she has lost her last chance for marriage. She thought her parents realized that marriage wasn't important for her. I wonder if my parents would be surprised if I told them I never intend to get married.

As you can see, the reading notes are directly related to the characters, events, ideas, and incidents that attract the student's attention. The major advantages of assigning reading notes on literature are the following: First, it keeps the teacher from getting between the student and the reading experience, allowing the student a direct interaction with the literature. Second, it allows the teacher to see how the student perceives the material. Thus, more of the responsibility for learning falls on the student, where it properly belongs. Thinking is more likely to happen during such learning activities that are not teacher-dominated.

LATERAL THINKING

Another approach to structuring thinking in a less formal way is through what Edward de Bono calls *lateral thinking*. This creative approach to problem solving encourages the thinker to step away from the usual perceptions of or approaches to a problem to arrive at a creative solution. This approach is based on de Bono's notion that vertical or hierarchical thinking often leads one to impose needless restrictions that, instead of leading to a solution, only compound the problem. Thus, if one thinks oneself into a hole, vertical thinking only leads to a deeper hole. For example, suppose a school is having difficulty with students' littering the campus. So, according to the usual mode of vertical thinking, a system of punishments is undertaken as a means of solving the problem. As a result of the punishment system, littering does diminish slightly, but more students now leave the campus to shop at fast-food restaurants or convenience stores and the rate of tardiness increases dramatically. What would have been a more creative solution for the problem? One possibility would be the creation of a Litter Lottery that rewards students who are seen disposing of litter properly by giving them the opportunity to win prizes in a lottery. Another possibility is to give the entire student body and school staff a reward if the litter level is maintained at or below a certain point. The reward might be a trip to an amusement park or beach for the entire school on a school day.

De Bono differentiates lateral thinking from vertical thinking, the "traditional type of thinking," by delineating these differences:

1. Vertical thinking is sequential and linear; lateral thinking is divergent and serendipitous.
2. Vertical thinking selects only relevant information; lateral thinking may seek out irrelevant information.
3. Vertical thinking requires being right at each stage of the path to a solution (logic or mathematics); lateral thinking may necessitate being wrong at some stage in order to find a correct solution.

De Bono believes that the exclusive emphasis on vertical thinking in the past makes it necessary to teach lateral thinking now. He says both kinds of thinking are required for effective thinking, and they are complementary. Lateral thinking is generative of solutions, whereas vertical thinking is selective. An activity for demonstrating this would be to have your students rename familiar objects (desks, chairs, chalk, and doors, for example) and give reasons for the new names they chose. The following is an example of another problem solved by lateral thinking:

> Suppose you are in an audience of one hundred people and you want to find out who is the tallest person in the group. You can ask the entire audience to stand to see who is tallest. Or, you can ask how many are taller than a certain height, say six feet, and then ask how many are a greater height and so on until you find the tallest. Using lateral thinking, you can ask who thinks he or she is the tallest and then ask if anyone is taller than that person. This approach leads to a quick solution to the problem.

Suggestions for other problems for practicing lateral thinking in your own classroom are as follows:

- Students who learn how to do a new kind of math problem get bored while waiting for the rest of the class to learn how.

- Some students need to review the uses of colons and commas, but most of the class already knows this material.
- Students do not like to use the restrooms during brunch and the passing periods because they are smoky and crowded.
- Students who ride the school buses complain about the rowdiness and vulgarity on the buses.
- Students want to use bigger, more difficult words in their writing, but sometimes they do not know how to spell these words.

Although lateral thinking is included under informal approaches to reasoning in this chapter, de Bono does favor a formalized program of thinking instruction for our schools. He believes such instruction for one hour every week throughout the educational system would be sufficient to bring about the needed attitude of lateral thinking in our students.

It is not possible in the space limitations of this chapter to elaborate all the processes and aspects of lateral thinking. If you wish additional information, you may want to consult the books by de Bono that are cited at the end of this chapter.

SUMMARY

The discovery or inquiry method of thinking is closely associated with the scientific method. The scientific method and the logic that is subsumed within it suggest ways of engaging students in conducting experimental research studies even in primary grade classrooms. Discovery methods involve students in asking questions and creating possible solutions that they can test.

Such methods are not limited to science classes but can be applied to theories about historical or sociological problems as well as to studies of values and attitudes. Student inquiry leads to the creation of knowledge, and that lends a sense of excitement to their learning and a greater appreciation for inquiry conducted by others, scholars in the field.

CHALLENGE

1. Develop a method for involving your own students with an area of subject matter in a way that will require them to engage in burr-sticking thinking.

2. Ask your students about their own thinking/learning processes. How did they learn to ride a bike, tie their shoes, or read a book? Then make an agreement with them to learn how to do something as a group that no one in the class presently knows how to do. It could be a physical skill or a cognitive piece of information—for example, the syntax of six sentences in Swahili. Share the learning experience and talk about how

different class members were able to achieve success and about the implications for teaching and learning.

EXPLORING FURTHER

Altick, Richard D. *Preface to Critical Reading,* 3rd edition. Holt, 1956.

Carroll, Lewis. *Symbolic Logic and The Game of Logic.* Dover, 1958.

de Bono, Edward. *Lateral Thinking: Creativity Step by Step.* New York: Harper, 1970.

de Bono, Edward. *New Think.* New York: Avon, 1971.

Hooper, Judith and Teresi, Dick. *The Three-Pound Universe.* New York: Macmillan, 1986.

Wheatley, Jon. *Prolegomena to Philosophy.* Belmont, Calif.: Wadsworth, 1970.

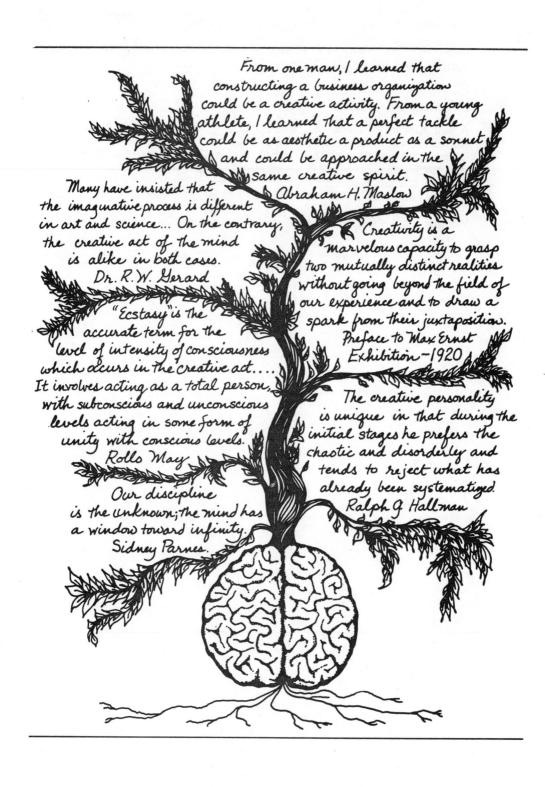

From one man, I learned that constructing a business organization could be a creative activity. From a young athlete, I learned that a perfect tackle could be as aesthetic a product as a sonnet, and could be approached in the same creative spirit.
Abraham H. Maslow

Many have insisted that the imaginative process is different in art and science... On the contrary, the creative act of the mind is alike in both cases.
Dr. R. W. Gerard

"Ecstasy" is the accurate term for the level of intensity of consciousness which occurs in the creative act.... It involves acting as a total person, with subconscious and unconscious levels acting in some form of unity with conscious levels.
Rollo May

Creativity is a marvelous capacity to grasp two mutually distinct realities without going beyond the field of our experience and to draw a spark from their juxtaposition.
Preface to Max Ernst Exhibition - 1920

The creative personality is unique in that during the initial stages he prefers the chaotic and disorderly and tends to reject what has already been systematized.
Ralph G Hallman

Our discipline is the unknown; the mind has a window toward infinity.
Sidney Parnes.

CHAPTER 5

Whole-Brain Thinking

Objectives

After reading this chapter, you will be able to

- *Discuss current brain research.*
- *Outline the relationship of whole-brain thinking to education.*
- *Plan teaching strategies that enhance balanced thinking.*

> Education enables individuals to come into full possession of
> all their powers.   JOHN DEWEY

Although knowledge of the physical structure of the brain is being enhanced daily, more is unknown than is known about the brain. It is estimated that the average brain with its 10 billion individual nerve cells can
make interconnections that total 10 with 800 zeros following it. Compare this number with the number of atoms in the Universe, which is
estimated to be 10 with 100 zeros after it.[1] To help students increase their
learning capabilities and make as many interconnections as possible, we
need to be familiar with brain research, understand its implications for
education, and facilitate learning that encourages students to explore
their potential.

The figure that follows is a graphic representation of the concepts
discussed in this chapter. The figure illustrates a mapping technique that
enhances whole-brain thinking by allowing for organization in a free-
flowing visual manner. The direction of the chapter starts at the bottom
with research, the basis of learning, and moves upward to the implications of brain research for education and to a variety of teaching strategies
that make for effective education.

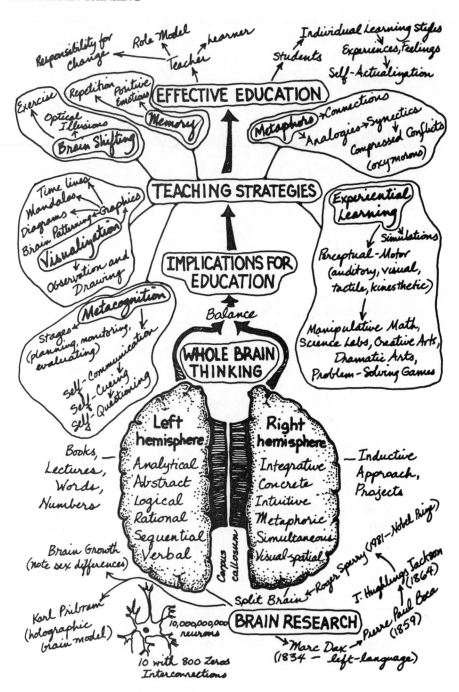

Brain Research: Theory into Practice

Brain research has clarified our understanding of problem-solving skills and physical and mental abilities. In becoming familiar with the research, we can better understand ourselves and how students learn. We talk in terms of right/left hemisphericity to emphasize the dichotomy between the different kinds of thinking that occur in two sides of the brain. However, it is important to note that current researchers are discovering that functions and modes previously attributed to one side or the other may be found in some degree in the opposite side as well. Furthermore, they are looking not just at hemisphericity but at multiple divisions, in all directions. It is most appropriate therefore to aim for whole-brain thinking, a balanced approach using both sides of the brain.

In *The Amazing Brain*, Robert Ornstein and Richard Thompson present a clear explanation of the human brain's anatomy, mechanisms, and processes. They trace the history of split-brain research beginning in 1834, with the work of Marc Dax, a French physician who was denied recognition for his carefully documented evidence of a strong association between damage to the left hemisphere and loss of language. Twenty-five years later, French neurologist Pierre Paul Boca documented cases of speech loss related to damage in a certain portion of the left frontal lobe. In 1864 British neurologist J. Hughlings Jackson concluded that the left hemisphere is the location of the "factory of expression." Since that time, many other neurologists, neurosurgeons, and psychiatrists have established that the two cerebral hemispheres of human beings process two different modes of thought.[2]

Roger W. Sperry's split-brain surgery, which won him the Nobel Prize in 1981, showed the specialized functions of the two cerebral hemispheres. Sperry found that the left brain deals with information sequentially, analytically, and linearly while the right brain thinks conceptually, intuitively, and inductively, with the connector, the corpus callosum, allowing the two halves to communicate. If, for instance, a person with a severed corpus callosum held a pencil in the right hand but did not see it, he or she could verbally describe it in a normal fashion; however, if the pencil was in the left hand, he or she could not describe it at all. The explanation is as follows:

1. The left hand informs the right hemisphere.
2. There is no communication to the left (verbal) hemisphere due to the severed corpus callosum.
3. The right hemisphere has limited speech capacity.
4. Therefore, the person is unable to describe the pencil.

Recent research with normal people confirms much of the neurological explorations done with pathological and surgical cases. The evidence comes from various sources—tests of vision, eye movements, reaction time, ear preference, and electrical signs of brain asymmetry.[3] A new conception of human knowledge, consciousness, and intelligence has developed from the split- and whole-brain studies.

MEMORY + EXPERIENCE = LEARNING

The holographic brain model indicates that "holonomic knowing" is the best, most efficient and natural way to obtain information. Karl Pribram of Stanford University devised the model of the holographic brain, which provides insight into two of the brain's mysteries: the fusion of memories and current experience into learning and the resistance of that learning to damage. Pribram's model is, as Marilyn Ferguson states, " . . . an all-encompassing model that is generating considerable excitement among those intrigued by the mysteries of human consciousness. His holographic model marries brain research to theoretical physics. . . . "[4]

A hologram is a three-dimensional image, which results from a process using lasers. Light is sent to a photographic plate from two sources, the object and a reference beam deflected by a mirror from the object and onto the special holographic plate that records the fragments of the shattered rays when they collide. If the plate were broken, the whole three-dimensional image is still reconstructed in each particle when the laser is passed through it.[5]

The findings of this search for reality and the brain/mind/consciousness connection relates to the ancient Eastern philosophers' concept expressed in a Buddhist sutra:

> In the heaven of Indra there is said to be a network of pearls so arranged that if you look at one you see all others reflected in it. In the same way, each object in the world is not merely itself, but involves every other object, and, in fact, is every other object.[6]

If this model proves to be a truth about human functioning, then memory is stored throughout, and every part of all is all of everything. Thus, learning is resistant to injury, and memory capacity is infinite. Pribram's approach proves that there are more ways of knowing than we in our limited explorations have dreamed. It tells us that, although we have focused on the rational mind of the left hemisphere and have been trying to promote the metaphorical mind of the right hemisphere, we must now move toward a holistic approach. Development of both spheres is essential to the full development of the human capacity with each sphere an integral part of the other.

BRAIN RESEARCH SPECIFIC TO STUDENT GROWTH

Research on brain growth and integration cycles leads us to confirm the importance of being aware of discoveries in the development, organization, and operation of young people's brains. As teachers, we have a responsibility for assimilating this knowledge and transforming it into practice.

For example, the growth period is especially important for girls ages ten to twelve years and should be looked at by educators. Girls' brain growth is three times that of boys' at that stage. Paul MacLean's research reports that the rear right hemisphere of the neocortex is an area of much growth, evening out a previous weight differential between the two hemispheres, leaving girls with a more symmetrical neocortex. At this point in their development, many more girls may be able to handle advanced problem solving in science and mathematics than current educational curricula promote. Our sequence provides for such work during the boys' major growth spurt, ages fourteen to sixteen years, which is often three years too late for girls to make the best use of brain-development patterns.

Herman Epstein discovered that brain growth between the ages of two and sixteen occurs in four four-year cycles in which periods of rapid growth are followed by the slower integration of that growth into the cognitive system. This pattern closely resembles Piaget's growth stages, information that can also be useful in assessing children's competencies at various developmental levels.[7]

IMPLICATIONS OF BRAIN RESEARCH FOR EDUCATION

Knowing that the brain hemispheres process information differently makes it imperative that we expand our concept of education. In Western culture and education, the left hemisphere is most often the focus of attention. It is considered more systematic and technological, putting things in sequential order and keeping things sensible and organized. On the other hand, the right hemisphere—the conceptual, intuitive side that enjoys play, metaphor, and imagery—has been neglected in our educational system. We need to focus on varied intellectual processes, seeking a balance between right- and left-brain thinking.

Because words and images communicate more clearly together than either could alone, we know that the complementary workings of both sides of the brain engage students in higher cognitive processes. We must remember that learning is a process that occurs in students' minds and that how information is presented is key to the issue. The techniques you use now and those included in this book can be enhanced and be more effective when understood within the context of both hemispheres. Because much education is left-brain oriented and because we know that effective thinking requires both hemispheres' ways of processing information, we will now explore techniques to draw upon right-hemisphere capabilities that complement left-brain processes.

Students who are predominantly left-brained may appear to be learning well through the traditional methods of books, lectures, words, and numbers. The less verbal are forced to try to learn in this same manner although it is difficult for them to work to their full potential. Both verbal and less verbal students, on the other hand, are losing out on developing their right-hemisphere thinking because we do not tend to teach for this kind of thinking. We're losing in both cases.

We must balance book and lecture instruction with other techniques that tap the right hemisphere. Instead of the usual lecture format of telling students information and then testing, we could use visualization to arouse the students' interest. We could use the inductive approach so that when students are introduced to a concept in the book they are stimulated to think and have more interest and better understanding. We can use pictures, drawings, and diagrams to help them comprehend. We can integrate learning through projects that help students apply concepts, instead of using written tests all the time. We can teach thinking skills most effectively in conjunction with content objectives, or at times we may choose to focus directly on thinking instruction in short lessons. Units developed on the basis of whole-brain thinking require more thinking preparation at the beginning, but once the methodology becomes familiar, the advantages to students and to teachers are rewarding. With comprehension and motivation improved, both teaching and learning become more enjoyable and stimulating.

Because it has been demonstrated that creativity and genius are the result of integrating experience, knowledge, and intuition, it is essential that we as educators attempt to balance the development of the whole brain. We can teach students to use all parts of the brain and to shift consciously from one brain style to another to meet each demand.

SUMMARY OF RESEARCH

1. The two hemispheres of the brain perform different functions. The left side is systematic, analytical, verbal; the right side is conceptual, integrative, visual/spatial.
2. The multiple divisions of the brain necessitate our teaching to the whole brain using a balanced approach to meet the learning needs of all students.
3. Information on brain-growth patterns is useful in determining children's competencies at various developmental stages.
4. We can teach students to use their whole brain by incorporating different teaching strategies that trigger various parts of the brain.

As depicted in the figure on page 128, studies of brain research have significant implications for teaching. They are the foundation upon which our educational philosophy is built. In the next section, we examine specific strategies that promote whole-brain thinking.

Teaching Strategies That Implement the Research

Research confirms what teachers have always observed: Students learn in different ways. Presenting lessons both visually and verbally allows students to make connections between what they already understand and what they are to learn. Engaging all senses in a learning experience lets students choose the most comfortable style of learning.

Keep in mind that using these ideas does not take time away from the curriculum because they illustrate how concepts are taught; it is the process, rather than the product. By using different approaches in each step of teaching any subject—introduction, explanation, review, and evaluation—we help students develop a variety of thinking styles, feel comfortable in using their strength to learn and to achieve by developing any deficient skills. In this section we present teaching strategies that enhance the right-hemisphere thinking processes and complement the more commonly used left-brain thinking mode. The figure on page 135 highlights the concepts and activities.

VISUAL THINKING

Many ideas are better understood through visual strategies that integrate information in a way some students find easier to comprehend and remember. For the highly visual learner, success in school could depend on opportunities to use this mode of learning. For the verbal student, development of this ability offers an alternate way to learn and to express ideas. Visual thinking, a basic way of obtaining, processing, and presenting information, is a part of every subject.

Observation

One way of collecting and interpreting data is through visual observation. Students observe in science class as they experiment, in home economics class as they create a pattern, in math class as they do geometry. One of the best ways to get students to observe is to have them draw what they see because drawing requires scrutinizing the details and seeing the overall spatial relationships.

In *Drawing on the Right Side of the Brain,* Betty Edwards explains that when adults draw, the left hemisphere may define and label what is to be drawn, thereby interfering with the right hemisphere's ability to see the real object. Her presentation of experiencing the shift from left- to right-brain dominance outlines the inherent abilities of the artistic potential of the right hemisphere.[8] In a second book, *Drawing on the Artist*

Within, Edwards explores the nature of the creative process and shows us how to enhance creative potential through new ways of perceiving and through the use of problem-solving skills.

Give art the status it deserves as a way of expressing thinking. Enrich your curriculum by including thinking expressed through art: scientific drawings, art culture in history, writing complemented with a picture "worth a thousand words." Emphasize the process of seeing versus the final product of a drawing to encourage students to appreciate the experience.

Help students to distinguish between labeling and describing. Verbal description is present in poetry. In science, students describe their subject so as to recognize the structures. In the social sciences, we use photo essays and films to provide the visual representation lost in the text. We can turn off the sound track so students can deduce information to strengthen visual thinking.

We can integrate visual representation into our lessons by presenting ideas graphically and having the students use diagrams, charts, drawings, constructions, mandalas, graphs, maps, and mind maps. Visual representations are helpful in solving math and logic problems. Time lines can be used in a variety of ways: In prewriting, they can develop a character's life; in a self-concept activity, students can show their life story to date; in a decision-making class, students can determine the decisions they will be making for the next twenty-five years.

Mapping

Mapping helps students organize ideas in a graphic form, allowing them to move freely from one idea to another, thinking flexibly without worrying about linear organization. Because our brain does not deal with words in lists, networks of words and ideas must be juggled and interlinked in order to communicate.

One way to do mapping is called *clustering,* the least structured of the forms. The main idea is centrally placed and other ideas are arranged around it (see the figure, "Clustering"). Gabrielle Rico, in *Writing the Natural Way,* points out that in the prewriting stage of composing, the ideas must flow freely and not be held back by the sequential demands of the left hemisphere. The resulting writings are of a higher level of fluency, coherence, description, and syntax.[9]

Tony Buzan, in *Use Both Sides of Your Brain,* presents what he calls *brain patterns* in which all words are connected to another idea to give the pattern a structure. The figure (page 128) showing the structure of this chapter is an example of this graphic form. Buzan suggests that this format can be used for note taking, reviewing information, planning, and solving problems. Arrows, colors, geometric shapes, and codes, can be

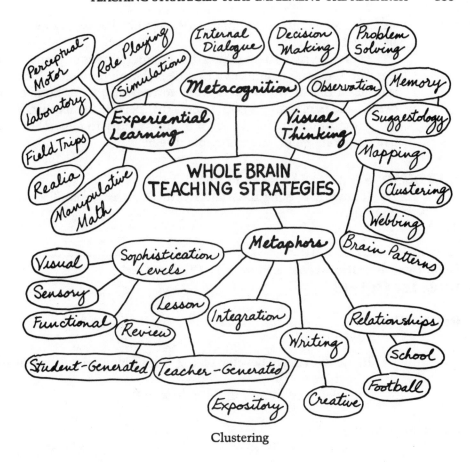

Clustering

used to connect ideas.[10] Because brain patterns are an individual form of representing ideas, the criteria for evaluating them should be based on the appropriateness for the maker, not a set of abstract rules.

Memory

Provide students with strategies for remembering. It has been demonstrated that relaxed states are very effective in learning, for storing information, and for accessing information when needed. Building on the work of Georgi Lozanov who demonstrated a rapid acceleration of learning in children with the suggestology approach, researchers are currently documenting the acceleration of students in such programs. It is important to note that this approach is based on a warm, comfortable, and colorful environment; relaxed students; multiple learning modality techniques; and the use of specific music and vocal sounds—all lending themselves to create a highly suggestive situation in which the students are able to assimilate the information readily and enjoyably with no resistance to learning.[11]

There are many techniques for improving memory and expanding learning. One mnemonic device is the peg-word method, which involves learning a list of words (pegs) that correspond to the numbers one to twenty and using images of the items that need remembering. Visual imagery, attention, repetition, belief in one's ability to remember, and positive emotions all help memory performance.

SAFE DEMONSTRATION LESSON PLANS

The following lessons illustrate instruction that promotes whole-brain thinking.

SAFE Demonstration Lesson Plan 5.1: Thinking Art
Grade Levels: 1–12

OBJECTIVES

Students will

1. use drawing to develop seeing, imagining, and creating in any subject area.
2. understand humor in their drawings.

BRIEF DESCRIPTION

These exercises promote right-brain drawing, allowing students to develop a more confident attitude about their drawing abilities and to enjoy the fun of imagining.

PROCEDURES

Younger students usually just draw, letting their hand move as their picture gives them ideas for more pictures. The rule they appear to follow is "Do it and see what happens." After about the fourth grade, the "rule" children appear to follow is "Don't do it unless you can do it right." Their pictures, often word-bound, do not allow pictures to emerge from pictures (right brain). Students often "decide" they are not artists because they cannot draw a horse like the class artist. We must change this attitude.

Stimulus

Allow students to draw anything they wish for five minutes. As with writing, many students will not be able to think about what to draw.

ASK: Did you have a hard time deciding what to draw? Why do you think it was difficult? Easy? Why do we become uneasy about our drawings as we get older?

SAY: Today you are going to experience drawing as it should be—a free-flowing, enjoyable activity.

Activity

Exercise 1: Nonstop Drawing

Give students large sheets of paper and direct them to draw whatever they wish following only two rules: First, once their hand starts to move, they cannot stop; second, they cannot lift their pencil off the paper. They can go back and forth anywhere on the paper without stopping or lifting their hand. Allow about two minutes.

Next, direct students to do the same thing, except they must immediately draw what you call out for them to draw at intervals. For example, if students are drawing a car and you call out "horse," they cannot finish the car; they must turn the drawing of the car into a horse or move the hand elsewhere on the paper to draw the horse. This procedure gets students out of their "rut." Start with simple commands such as basketball, tennis racket, grapes, or the back of a cat's head and then progressively get more complicated. Students may even close their eyes to draw a dog or open their eyes and draw themselves on the back of an elephant.

Exercise 2: Nonstop Writing

Tell students to write nonstop, connecting all their words in a giant snake, without worry about spelling, punctuation, or content. They may write a letter to the man on the moon, to their right brain, to their grandmother on the space shuttle. The important thing is that they experience writing as a flowing process. No one needs to read it. The essence is that words bring images and images bring pictures.

Exercise 3: Words

All words flash images in our minds. Students should select three words from a word bag, a list on the board, or self-generated lists. They take turns telling the class to imagine a picture including three words such as *butterfly*, *doughnut*, and *Paris*. A class member might draw a butterfly carrying a doughnut past the Eiffel Tower located beneath the Atlantic Ocean. This process strengthens visualization and fantasy.

Follow-Up

Display the drawings for all to enjoy, and students can share their nonstop writing with a peer.

Evaluation

Humor is the art form, enjoyment and freedom the goal. Appreciate the students' responses to "Tell me about your drawing." Note the students' appreciation of the humor in their drawings and their understanding that mistakes are okay and are true opportunities for growth.

SAFE Demonstration Lesson Plan 5.2: Mandalas
Grade Levels: 1–12

OBJECTIVES

Students will

1. represent ideas through symbols.
2. create a mandala.

BRIEF DESCRIPTION

Students represent a concept through a mandala, using symbols, creative graphics within a circle, and various art materials.

PROCEDURES

The mandala is an ancient artistic and symbolic expression with a series of images in a circular pattern representing the harmony, wholeness, and continuity of life or of a person. The circle shape of the mandala is a universal shape that helps us focus into the center of our being. Since its creation in Tibet over 2000 years ago, the mandala has been made by many cultures. Discussion of symbolism is important in this activity.

Stimulus

Create and share a mandala with students, asking them what they think is being said through the visual images and colors. Students should contribute many ideas without judgment from you. After responses, tell them what you were intending through this visual presentation. Discuss your use of symbols. Generate ideas for symbols representing topics of interest to students.

Activity

Explain the background of the mandala as an art form and the fact that there are no rules for constructing a mandala, other than that the shape is a circle. This is important because the representative image of the central concept should be in the center of a circle. Students can begin by clustering around their own names as they identify things that are important to them.

The students' first mandala should represent themselves because telling about themselves in a new fashion ensures familiarity with the subject so that the process is not totally new. Constructing a mandala also reinforces self-esteem in students. Students should discuss the variety of ways they can present their ideas in a circle (halves, quarters, pie-shaped sections, concentric circles, diagonal lines), whatever is appropriate to express pictorially the levels or depth of the concept. A variety of art materials can be used (magazine pictures, drawings, cut paper, photographs, tissue paper, realia, paint, colored pencils, felt markers). Give students ample time to work on their mandalas.

Follow-Up

Students share their mandalas by highlighting some facets of their work, explaining the image and the reason for the choice, the selection of art materials to express the concept, and the form it takes within the circle.

Students may prepare a written description of their mandala, including the above elements and other highlights of their composition. Post the visual expressions with the written explanations where all can enjoy them.

Evaluation

Younger students may tell you what they especially like about their mandala: "Tell me two things you think are special about your mandala." Older students may self-evaluate based on specific criteria, or you may evaluate the work. Criteria should be shared with the students before they begin the project. Consider giving five to ten points for each of the following:

- Overall representation of concept
- Appropriate presentation within the circle
- Completeness of expression
- Variety of art media
- Thought shown in total presentation
- Neatness
- Aesthetic quality

For a first mandala, you may simply wish to evaluate students on their effort in pulling together their thoughts about themselves in a visual presentation. Thus, students might all receive an A, Excellent, or twenty-five points for turning in a finished mandala, as required.

NOTES

Mandalas can be used in any subject area as a visual means to present an important concept. In the study of government, the three branches of our democratic system can be shown in a circle divided into three parts. The creative energy and thinking necessary to present the information in such a format far outweighs the knowledge gained through preparing a chart.

The mandala is an effective way to share a book with guidelines specifying inclusion of plot and characters. Additional writing could include the ideas you would want shared which are difficult to express in this art form.

Following the writing or reading of a poem or story, a mandala may be used in place of a filmstrip, slides, poster, or any other visual aid normally created.

SAFE Demonstration Lesson Plan 5.3: Mnemonics
Grade Levels: 4-12

OBJECTIVE

Students will learn a technique for remembering a specific list of information.

BRIEF DESCRIPTION

Students create visual images to remember lists of words and information in any subject area.

PROCEDURES

Visualization has been used as a memory strategy since the ancient Greeks. Having students create visual images to remember a list of words strengthens their ability to visualize and provides them with a memory strategy they can apply in other areas. Although we often object to the degree of emphasis on memorization in our classes, there are times when the need for a memory strategy would be helpful. Memory, an essential part of learning, requires both sides of the brain.

Stimulus

Give students a list of twelve words to memorize in two minutes. Then, they list as many of those words as they can. After checking the results, students compare their scores. Ask several students to share methods they used to help themselves remember.

Discuss the technique of connecting words in the form of a visual image. EXAMPLE. If three of the words are *clock, gloves,* and *eggs,* the visual image may be a clock with gloves on the tips of the hands and an egg placed next to the outer edge of each number.

Give students two minutes to study a second longer list in the same fashion. Check for improved scores. Sharing their visual images will aid students in learning from each other.

Activity

Tell students they can create visual images to help them remember the information in any subject area. As homework, have students select another subject area or topic. They are to record images on paper, making the images vivid to help themselves remember concepts from the selected area of study. After trying the imaging process, they should write a paragraph describing the thinking process they experienced and how well the procedure worked.

Follow-Up

Students discuss and display the visual presentations with accompanying written information the next day.

Evaluation

Repeat this activity periodically. Compare pretest and posttest results for objective evaluation of student progress. Chart students' progress in learning to memorize given new material.

METAPHOR

Metaphors project similarities between things otherwise unlike, stimulating discovery of new relationships. The game of football and the institution of the school seem very different, yet in many ways the two have parallel structures. Rules, discipline, and competition prevail. It takes hard work to succeed in each. The students form the class, while the players form the team. The teacher coaches, and the manager directs as the principal oversees. The superintendent governs from the top as does the owner, and the Board of Education sets the policies as does the commission. We might say therefore that school is a football game, a metaphor that students can readily understand.

Metaphors provide the connection between previous learnings and new concepts. Although teachers often use metaphors in teaching, we usually don't teach metaphorical thinking explicitly. To enable our students to think creatively, we can discuss metaphors, asking students to generate similarities and differences between concepts they are studying and what they already know.

One way to introduce metaphors to students is to have them play with questions such as "Which weighs more, zero or one?" Emphasize that the answer is not important, only the reasons for the answer. The question of zero and one can be introduced as a math lesson, a writing lesson, or a health lesson in terms of nutrition and weight. Generate other questions to stimulate thinking; for example, which is taller, blue or green? Or, how is a cloud like a sheep?

There are different levels of sophistication in metaphors. First, there are the visual connections (milk is white, and water is clear). Other sensory connections come next (they smell different or water is thinner than milk). Functional metaphors are more difficult and more useful (they are both drinks and are good for people to drink). We can help students progress toward sophistication by guiding their thinking through thoughtful, caring questions: How do people use them? What good do they do? In what other ways are they alike?

In evaluating students' abilities in all right-hemisphere processes, we should not judge proficiency but assess what students need to help them improve. With this attitude, students develop their thinking skills. The process of making the connection is more important than the specific content of the lesson. We should always respond to the students' connections, positively searching as their guide to help them clarify their thoughts. Metaphorical thinking is not only effective but also fun. We need the ability to play with ideas and concepts in order to brainstorm to solve problems and to be creative.

SAFE Demonstration Lesson Plan 5.4:
From Analogies to Compressed Conflicts
Grade Levels: 4–12

OBJECTIVES

Students will

1. think in divergent ways.
2. create direct analogies, personal analogies, and compressed conflicts.

BRIEF DESCRIPTION

Students think in unusual ways, answering questions that have no one right answer; the appropriateness of the answer comes with the reasoning behind the answer.

PROCEDURES

A direct analogy is a similarity in some respects between things that are otherwise not alike. A personal analogy is a similarity in some respects between a person and a thing. A compressed conflict is a phrase where words that do not usually go together are put together to form a creative description.

Stimulus

In a class discussion, ask students questions such as:

1. Which description do you prefer—rough yellow or rough purple? Why? What pictures do you see with each description?
2. What fruit do you like? Why? What fruit is like you? Why? What difference do you see in the two questions?

Activity

Introduce students to direct analogy, personal analogy, and compressed conflicts with this worksheet, which includes questions and fill-in sentences such as the following:

Direct analogy: Which weighs more—nine or ten? Why?

A football is like a _____

because _____.

Personal analogy: What number acts like you? Why?
Become the spring in the seat of a big old chair. Describe yourself. How do you look? How do you feel? How do you act? What would you like to do?

Compressed conflict: Pleasing pain is _____

because _____.

An example of disciplined freedom is _____

because _____.

Create your own compressed conflict and explain one example of it.

Follow-Up

After students have had enough practice with thinking on these levels, they use these strategies in writing experiences such as the ones described in the metaphorical and synectics lessons that follow. Students should share, share, share!

Evaluation

Observe the participation and the level of understanding and risk taking of individual students. Give positive feedback and encouraging comments to further thinking in this vein.

NOTE

Compressed conflict is sometimes called an oxymoron (pl. oxymora).

SAFE Demonstration Lesson Plan 5.5: Metaphorical Feathers
Grade Levels: 1–12

OBJECTIVES

Students will

1. create varied metaphors.
2. write a poem using a metaphor as the stimulus.

BRIEF DESCRIPTION

Students write a poem making connections between the subject and the students' prior knowledge. Guidelines and appropriate expectations are built into the lesson.

PROCEDURES

A metaphor is a figure of speech in which one thing is likened to another in an implied comparison. Metaphorical thinking is fun and effective in the creative play of ideas.

Stimulus

Each student plays with a feather, "discovering" its qualities. As a class, use a mapping technique to record the students' responses to their experience with the feather. On chart paper, record the poetic responses of students. For younger students, a one-line poem could be "A feather is softer than a violet's petal." For older students, the poem could be a compilation of the many similarities and differences between a feather and an analogue.

Activity

Have students create a poem on a topic from any subject area. Use the following patterns to assist students.

Example for Primary Students

My name is (a noun) ——————————————————————.

It sounds like ——————————————————————————.

It tastes like ———————————————————————————.

It smells like ———————————————————————————.

It looks like ————————————————————————————.

It feels like ————————————————————————————.

It reminds me of ——————————————————————————.

My name is like ——————————————————————————.

Example for Older Students

As a _____.

I feel _____.

I think _____.

I am _____.

A good word to describe me is _____.

I wish _____.

I must _____.

I will _____.

Students may use the given pattern to structure their poem or reorganize the ideas synthesizing the elements into a metaphorical presentation. Some students may choose to create poetic riddles, further synthesizing the descriptors to create a personification.

Follow-Up

Direct students to create a poster picturing the subject and highlighting the poem. Older students may compile their riddles into a class book.

Evaluation

Comment positively on the metaphorical connectors. Ask questions to encourage deeper thinking and structuring of the metaphor. Observe the thinking behind the connections.

SAFE Demonstration Lesson Plan 5.6: Synectics
Grade Levels: 4–12

OBJECTIVES

Students will

1. generate analogies and compressed conflicts.
2. create a lively descriptive piece of writing.
3. produce an appropriate art form to accompany the written piece for publication.

BRIEF DESCRIPTION

Students follow a given format to create a descriptive piece of writing, produce an appropriate art form, and compare their "before synectics" piece with their piece using synectics.

PROCEDURES

Synectics, which is derived from Greek, means the joining together of different and apparently irrelevant elements. Applied to learning, synectics involves the use of metaphor to develop original ideas. It is a strategy that you can use to improve creativity.

Stimulus

Students write three sentences on a topic of their choice. Collect these and set them aside until later for comparison purposes.

Activity

Using the format that follows, model the process of using synectics to create a class writing. Sample answers are given for better understanding of the process. Choose any subject familiar to students as you work collectively, recording ideas on the board as students suggest them.

Synectics

1. Subject _Clouds_

2. Your subject is most like:

What animals?	What foods?	Make one choice from your lists.
Samoyed	marshmallows	animal _panda_
Kitten	whipped cream	food _whipped cream_
bunny	mashed potatoes	Which of these is most like your subject? (topic)
mice	milk	
panda	scallops	
hamster	eggs	

3. Close your eyes and become the food and/or animal. How did you feel, look, and act as the subject? Write at least twenty responses.

panda soft	playful	sits on top
cuddly	calm	wisps
bulbous	whipped cream floating	whipped
shaped	fluffy	crowning glory
opposing colors	fancy	snowy mountain
heavy	decorated	melting
layy	creamy	moustache above lips

4. From your list above, put two or three words together to create at least ten phrases that describe your nature subject.

softly whipped	shaped moustaches
creamy cuddly	layily melting
playfully bulbous	calm snowy mountain
heavily decorated	fancy crowning glory
fluffy opposing colors	floating wisps on top

5. Combining these ideas, express your thoughts on your subject.

> *Clouds*
>
> *Clouds – fancy, softly whipped*
> *crowning glories above us.*
> *Playfully bulbous, they float calmly*
> *past the snowy mountain peak.*
> *Like fluffy-shaped moustaches,*
> *they heavily decorate the dom ed sky*
> *until they lazily melt*
> *into wisps amidst sunshine.*

Have students follow the process on their own. They can write a prosaic or poetic piece, using the ideas generated.

To publish their work artistically, have students select an appropriate art form to accompany their synectics piece of writing. Students may select from such projects as slides, filmstrips, posters, mobiles, and books to highlight their writing.

Follow-Up

In a group-, peer-, or self-editing situation, students can use the following questions to consider improvements for their writing:

1. Is there a central idea?
2. Does the piece of writing present a good overall description?
3. Are there evidences of analogies having been made?
4. Are there some compressed conflicts (words put together that usually do not go together)?
5. Does the overall effect appear natural or forced?

Students then revise their writing, addressing these questions. Students share their works in small groups.

Evaluation

Students self-evaluate, comparing the sentences they wrote at the beginning of the lesson—"before synectics" and writing done "after synectics."

EXPERIENTIAL LEARNING

Another way to reach the right hemisphere's preference for seeing the whole is through experiential learning. Theoretical knowledge is complemented with direct experience, giving students a chance to look at the subject holistically. It is especially important for students who have difficulty with verbal processes because direct experiences let them use the strengths of their individual learning style. Laboratory experiences, field trips, realia, manipulative math materials, simulations, and role playing enable students to stretch their learning and develop thinking strategies not required in textbook learning. Experiential learning gives students a context for learning that stimulates more personal involvement, especially with young children who must explore with their senses and manipulate their surroundings.

Simulation is a technique that allows students to experience a subject in an analogous situation. Commercial games are available, which is a good way to learn how to set the experience. Later, developing one's own simulations that relate to instruction is more satisfying. Role playing creates experiences where students take the part of other people and try to act as those people would in given situations. Television game shows where students answer questions, which demonstrate knowledge of literary characters, or trials dramatizing historical events are meaningful approaches.

Auditory, visual, tactile, and kinesthetic senses provide another channel for students to understand more completely. To answer our request for multisensory learning, a program includes perceptual motor experiences for the development of kinesthetic, tactile, auditory, visual, and graphic thinking; manipulative math; experientially based science; music and movement; art with variety in media; dramatic arts; and problem-solving and logical thinking games. Although not solely a right-hemisphere process, music seems to be heard with the right hemisphere. The work of Georgi Lozanov, a Bulgarian physicist, includes the use of music while students relax in a method called "suggestology." It affirms that students learn more material in less time when barriers are eliminated and an optimal environment is created.

These strategies complement the traditional verbal approaches so that the instructional program, like the integrated brain, can make use of a full range of skills and talents.

SAFE Demonstration Lesson Plan 5.7: Shifting Gears
Grade Levels: 4–12

OBJECTIVES

Students will

1. be aware of how they think.
2. experience how it feels to shift between hemispheres.

BRIEF DESCRIPTION

Students shift between the brain hemispheres when given an optical illusion and see beyond the obvious first answers in geometric designs.

PROCEDURES

We can make better use of our mind by exercising both sides of our brain and relating the two. We can think of our brain as a muscle and the more we flex it, the stronger it becomes. What happens in any situation is that one side is more active than the other and that shifts occur because of perceptual or activity changes. When trying to strengthen the skill of moving from one side to the other, it is important to be aware of what is happening. Optical illusion exercises show students how brain-shifting works. However, because the process occurs spontaneously, it cannot be considered a willful movement.

Prepare the figures presented in this lesson on transparencies to present to the students during the lesson.

Stimulus

Show the first figure.

ASK: What do you see? (Answer: Two profiles; a vase.) Are you able to see two images?

SAY: Our brain allows us to see one image at a time and we can move back and forth to either image. Feel the shift as you do this.

SAY: Today you are going to allow your brain to see beyond the obvious first answer and shift between the two hemispheres.

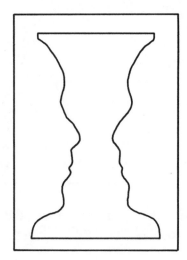

Activity

Present the following figure. Have students work in pairs to determine the number of squares they see in the figure.

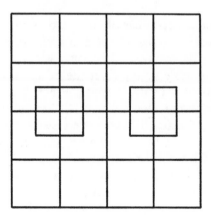

A left brain answer would be twenty-four or twenty-seven. To see the total of forty squares, students must view the figure with their right brain, noting the obvious twenty-four squares, the three encompassing squares, nine boxes created by four squares, and four boxes of nine squares. Those who can picture these other boxes have made the perceptual shift from the left to the right brain.

Activity

Give students the following figure to determine the number of triangles they see. ANSWER. Twenty-seven.

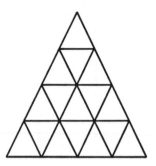

Partners report their answers to the class and share how they got their answers. Students should discuss how they feel when they make the shift.

Follow-Up

Students should search for other optical illusions and puzzling figures with which to challenge their friends. Some students will be able to create their own pictures.

Evaluation

Observe the students' abilities to perceive the images and to express their reaction to shifting between hemispheres.

SAFE Demonstration Lesson Plan 5.8: A Storm Within
Grade Levels: 7–12

OBJECTIVES

Students will

1. brainstorm ideas.
2. use a step-by-step problem-solving procedure.

BRIEF DESCRIPTION

Following a structured format, students individually problem solve using brainstorming and discuss their reaction to the process.

PROCEDURES

Brainstorming involves four hemispheric shifts. In the first step of writing out the problem, the left brain goes through the process of defining and verbalizing, allowing us to feel focused. The right brain then takes over in the actual beginning phase of brainstorming as ideas flow forth in an unrelated and haphazard way. In a relaxed situation, thinking seems effortless. Both spheres of the brain come into play during the evaluation process. The left brain judges and applies the responses to reality. The right brain focuses on appealing intuitive ideas. During the integration phase, the left and right brain see the solution holistically and specifically.

Stimulus

Pose one of the following problems to the students and ask: "What procedure would you use to solve this problem?"

EXAMPLES: What should be the theme for the upcoming dance?
How will you solve a conflict between two of your friends?
What can you do to bring up a grade in science?

SAY: Brainstorming involves the generation of ideas as you experienced it in groups, but we are applying it here individually to your own thinking process.

Activity

Have students select a problem and follow these steps as you guide them.

1. Write out the problem concisely.
2. Visualize the most desirable outcome to the problem.
3. Write out the problem again, this time in view of your visualization. The problem statement might change.
4. Break down the situation into manageable parts.
5. Analyze each subsection to determine the need for more information.
6. In a comfortable position and with pen in hand, now pose the problem to yourself again. Write any answers that come to mind, allowing them to flow quickly, not passing judgment on any idea.

After students have done this for a while, have them look at their notes and write the first thought that comes to mind. Then have them start over again, perhaps along the same path or taking a different route. Continue doing this for ten to fifteen minutes, stopping and starting again at five-minute intervals. Have the students look at their responses and evaluate their ideas, being aware of their left- and right-brain influences.

Allow the students to write a solution or express their position on the problem at this point of the activity. Some may have a solution, others may be on their way to a solution, and others may still be confused.

Follow-Up

Have the students think about the experience and respond to these questions:

1. How did you feel when you were brainstorming? Did you feel relaxed?
2. Did you feel any different between the time you wrote out the problem and when you started the actual brainstorming?
3. Did you see the ideas with words or in pictures?
4. Did you have a sense of timelessness or vagueness about the problem?
5. Did the ideas come from many directions or in an orderly way?
6. Did any one idea excite you?
7. Did you feel the shift back to the left brain when you did the evaluation?

8. In coming to the solution, did you feel a sense of integration between the two hemispheres?

Prepare a copy of these steps for your students to use individually when you pose another situation or problem and have them do the exercise again. The more exercise the brain gets, the better it works, and the more aware students will be in feeling the shifts.

Evaluation

Observe students' involvement and participation in the activity and their answers to the follow-up questions.

SAFE Demonstration Lesson Plan 5.9: Good Graph!
Grade Levels: 2–12

OBJECTIVES

Students will

1. conduct a survey.
2. report data on an attractive graph.

BRIEF DESCRIPTION

Students conduct a survey on a topic of their choice and visually present their findings in a creative graph.

PROCEDURES

Graphing shows relationships in a visual representation that adds a dimension to the processing of information. Viewing graphs enables students to remember information better. Creating them allows students to apply graphing skills in the synthesizing of information.

Stimulus

Have students raise their hand for the month of their birthday as you call out the months. Ask the following questions:

1. In what month do most of the students in this class have their birthday?
2. Which month is second with the most number of birthdays?
3. Which month has only one student's birthday?
4. Which month has no student's birthday?
5. Is it difficult to remember all of this information?
6. How could the information be displayed to better answer those questions?

Activity

Have students select a topic of their choice on which to conduct a survey. Following the survey they organize the information into a graph best-suited to their purpose, selecting from bar, line, or picture graphs.

The creative part comes in the visual attractiveness of the presentation of the information. For example, a survey on the favorite toothpaste may be shown in a bar with the toothpaste shooting from the tube to the appropriate level indicating the number of responses. Students should be encouraged to be as creative and artistic as they can in executing this project.

Follow-Up

Students share the results of their survey and their graphic representations with the class.

Evaluation

Use an analytical evaluation sheet such as that shown in "Graph Evaluation Sheet." Remember to share the criteria for evaluation with the students upon presentation of the project.

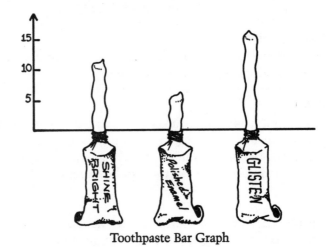

Toothpaste Bar Graph

Graph Evaluation

Criteria	strong 5	4	average 3	2	weak 1	Comments
Accuracy						
Thoroughness						
Appropriate graphics						
Neatness						
Creativity						
Effort						
Total						

Graph Evaluation Sheet

METACOGNITION

Metacognition, an influential trend in developmental cognitive psychology, plays an important part in written and oral communication, memory, and problem solving. Some aspects of metacognition include internal dialogue, the ability to know what we know and what we don't know, the ability to plan a strategy for producing needed information, the evaluation of personal decision-making and problem-solving processes, and the reflection and evaluation of the productivity of one's thinking. Chiefly, metacognition is *awareness of knowing.*

One of the variables of any thinking process is the person, for we cannot separate the process from the person. People are not linear. What we know about ourselves—our attention span, concentration, ability skills, interests, past performance, and expectations—determines our thoughts and actions.

Another variable is the task itself. We can consider the difficulty and complexity of the task, the content and specificity, its representation, our performance, and the criteria for its completion.

Metacognitive strategies can be implemented at three stages of execution—during planning, monitoring, and evaluation. During the planning stage, we can take a linear approach and proceed through a prescribed or self-described sequence to reach the desired goal through outlining, diagrams, time lines, or following directions. On the other hand, we can take a nonlinear approach—starting with the known or the novel, the random or the specific—and proceed in any direction—using conceptual maps, brainstorming, imitating a model, or beginning on a smaller scale.

During the monitoring stage, we can have students summarize, talk internally, engage in means–end analysis where they continually compare where they are to where they are going, self-question, seek outside appraisal for feedback, and set and check subgoals so they are not trying to handle the whole thing at once.

Testing and evaluating strategies can be important aspects of meta-cognition because we can have students make quality judgments when they compare the product to a standard or desired goal. However, we must remember to focus on the process of accomplishing, which is so valuable in learning from doing. Judgments can be made from an outside expert or a peer or be self-generated.

As teachers, we can be effective models by first recognizing the meta-cognitive strategies we use to solve problems and then to take the risk of trying those strategies that we know about but perhaps have not used. Modeling the use of metacognition by describing the thought processes we use to solve problems is critical to the students' understanding of the process. By encouraging self-communication, self-cueing, and self-questioning and by providing challenging problems that are in the "frontier zone" of student knowledge and experiences, we can help students become aware of the metacognitive strategies they already use and expand upon those. Providing feedback and critiquing shared metacognitive strategies in a caring environment is basic to the program. As new information is presented, provide students with organizers they can use to assimilate the new with previously acquired knowledge. At the same time, it is essential that we remember we are all different and that we cannot impose our styles on students. Research also shows that we cannot force strategies when students are not ready to use them.

We can also teach students to recognize options. Many adults assume children are aware of how they think and that a product is the result of this awareness, yet we do not know that. In dealing with metacognition, we should provide experiences that are concerned with the thinking process, not with the amount of material to be covered. Our question should be, "Did I make students aware of their thoughts?" We believe metacognition is a developmental process, but even primary grade students can learn to become aware of thinking processes at their level of development.

Rethinking some current classroom practices is all that it takes to get us started in this program. One way is to model effective self-questioning and self-talk. From our experience, we can predict where students will come upon a stumbling block in a problem. By sharing our thought processes, we can model how we talk to ourselves to work through the problem. We can have the students "double think" their answers by waiting five seconds instead of the usual one and one-half seconds to respond to their answers. By responding immediately, we take away the answering student's and the class' thinking time. When we do respond, we should avoid value responses because that stops everyone from thinking, especially the student who is relieved upon giving an answer. Students should be encouraged to think and rethink and be comfortable to share their thoughts without comparison and without reluctance because a previous answer was noted "good" or "right."

On completion of an assignment or test, have students identify in writing why they missed a question and where the answer could have been found. This makes the testing process more valuable; learning can take place all the time, even after evaluation has been done. Five minutes before homework is to be submitted, have the students place an "understanding level" score on the homework and the reason for that score based on a matrix or a simple scale. This process facilitates reflection and ensures a better understanding of what, how, and why the homework stands as it does. In addition, learning logs help students use writing to understand what they know and don't know. Students can enter comments on specific lessons, validate conclusions on assignments, or comment on questions such as:

- By what means do I learn best?
- Why do I remember some things and not others?
- What methods do I use to reach conclusions?
- If I don't understand, what do I do?
- Why am I better at some things?

We need to give students time to think and also to discuss their thinking. By engaging in metacognition, students begin to understand their thinking and learning processes and thus know better how to help their facilitators to assist them in learning.

SAFE Demonstration Lesson Plan 5.10: Metacognition
Grade Levels: 2–12

OBJECTIVES

Students will

1. be able to reflect on their thinking about their thinking.
2. share their thoughts on this process.

BRIEF DESCRIPTION

Students record their thinking as they do puzzles. They become aware of how and why they behave as they do in completing the work.

PROCEDURES

Metacognition is the process of thinking about one's own thinking. Some aspects include self-talk and the ability to know what we know and do not know. It involves reflection on the person and the task. By allowing students to engage in metacognition, we strengthen their ability to think, reason, and better understand their thinking processes.

Stimulus

Students do a page of problems appropriate to the grade level and record or remember their thoughts on doing the page.

1. Complete all the problems as quickly as you can.

   $5 + 3 =$ $4 \times 8 =$ $10 - 6 =$ $9 \times 7 =$

2. Now try these computations.

   $567 \times 45 =$ $3458 \div 22 =$ $12^3 =$

3. Tom had $10. He treated his friend to the movies. Each ticket cost $3.50. After the movies, Tom treated his friend and himself to 75¢ milkshakes. How much money did he have left?

4. Examine the set of figures. Draw a figure that you think completes the series.

Activity

Students share their responses about how and what they thought about as they completed the sheet of problems. If they need help, you could ask them:

- Did you skip any parts?
- Did you find any problem more intriguing than another?
- How did you feel about the word problem?

Students do appropriate puzzles and activities from a variety of sources and record their thoughts.

Follow-Up

Refer to the section in this chapter on metacognition and use the strategy as described. Be innovative and think of other ways students can strengthen their metacognition.

Evaluation

Observe students, watching for improvement as they become more familiar with the process. Application of the process in activities other than those specified for this purpose would indicate transfer of knowledge and internalization of the skill.

SUMMARY

Confluence of the two brain processes needs to be emphasized for whole-brain education, augmenting the analytical, linear approach with holistic, nonlinear, intuitive strategies. It is comforting to know that we are already using techniques for tapping the right hemisphere. It is important that we first become conscious of these processes and then make an effort to extend these into our lesson plans.

The responsibility for change rests on our shoulders. Studies prove that students produce what is expected by the adult in authority. We can expect that all students will improve in their thinking strategies and that their self-esteem will rise accordingly. Students will enjoy learning in this manner; and when learning is enjoyable, motivation makes learning more effective.

As adults, we can still learn to access our right hemisphere and develop new abilities. We are both learners and role models, open to change and discovery. We must develop the ability to take risks and carry this ability into the classroom. We can balance the highly cognitive verbal teaching with more reflection for independent thinking, encouraging students to become all they can be.

Children come to school as integrated little people with both sides of the brain eager to receive stimulus. We must enter the classroom as integrated adults with childlike enthusiasm to encourage them to develop strategies for processing information with the whole brain.

CHALLENGE

Include color to highlight lesson plans or presentations. One color may denote the important concepts, another the subordinate ideas. A different color may be a specific reminder such as "homework" or "extension idea." Various colors can highlight different levels of thinking in Bloom's taxonomy, thereby making questioning appropriate for the student needing higher-level thinking opportunities.

Create a two-sided lesson plan. Write your lesson plan in the left column and highlight right-brain goals and techniques in the right column.

Generate a metaphor for a unit of study. Start by setting the content goals. Brainstorm a list of metaphors for possible use. After sorting through the list and selecting the ones that best fit the concept as well as highlighting the differences between the subject and the metaphor, plan on how you will bring forth metaphors from students.

Write a unit of study by first mapping your ideas. Allow your ideas to flow and take any form you wish. You might consider colors, geometric shapes, arrows, or codes to connect your ideas. Upon completion, evaluate the process on the basis of enjoyment, thoroughness, and creativity in comparison to your standard approach in developing a unit.

NOTES

1. Tony Buzan, *Use Both Sides of Your Brain* (New York: Dutton, 1974), 17.
2. Robert Ornstein, and Richard F. Thompson, *The Amazing Brain* (Boston: Houghton Mifflin, 1984), 151.
3. Ornstein and Thompson, *The Amazing Brain*, 153.
4. Marilyn Ferguson, *The Aquarian Conspiracy* (Los Angeles: Tarcher, 1980), 177.
5. Karl H. Pribram, *Languages of the Brain, Experimental Paradoxes and Principles in Neuropsychology* (Englewood Cliffs, N.J.: Prentice-Hall, 1971), 145–152.
6. Ferguson, *The Aquarian Conspiracy*, 182.
7. Robert Sylwester, "A Child's Brain, Part I," *Instructor* (Sept. 1982): 90–94.
8. Betty Edwards, *Drawing on the Right Side of the Brain* (Los Angeles: Tarcher, 1979), 78.
9. Gabriele Lusser Rico, *Writing the Natural Way* (Los Angeles: Tarcher, 1983), 18.
10. Buzan, *Use Both Sides of Your Brain*, 102.
11. Georgi Lozanov, *Suggestology and Outlines of Suggestopedy* (New York: Gordon and Breach, 1978), 72.

EXPLORING FURTHER

Buzan, Tony. *Use Both Sides of Your Brain.* New York: Dutton, 1974.
Edwards, Betty. *Drawing on the Artist Within.* New York: Simon & Schuster, 1986.

Ornstein, Robert, and Richard F. Thompson. *The Amazing Brain.* Boston: Houghton Mifflin, 1984.

Williams, Linda Verlee. *Teaching for the Two-Sided Mind.* Englewood Cliffs, N.J.: Prentice-Hall, 1983.

Wonder, Jacquelyn, and Priscilla Donovan. *Whole Brain Thinking, Working from Both Sides of the Brain to Achieve Peak Job Performance.* New York: Ballantine Books, 1984.

The creative process is the emergence in action of a novel relational product, growing out of the uniqueness of the individual. Carl B. Rogers: Toward a Theory of Creativity

CREATIVITY

A first-rate soup is more creative than a second-rate painting. Abraham Maslow: Creativity in Self-Actualizing People

Creativity is the encounter of the intensively conscious human being with his world. Rollo May: The Nature of Creativity

Creativity is the ability to <u>see</u> (to be aware) and to <u>respond</u>. Erich Fromm: The Creative Attitude

CHAPTER 6

Creativity in the Round

Objectives

After reading this chapter, you will be able to

- *Discuss creativity from an informed perspective.*
- *Enhance your classroom environment to promote creative endeavors.*
- *Plan teaching strategies that integrate creative thinking across the curriculum.*

Definitions of creativity focus on the creative acts of talented individuals who relate to their environment through a process that results in products of value. The products may be an invention or discovery, a work of art or a scientific theory, new to the world or new to the individual. An artist may look anew at a subject; a writer may change the style and subject matter; an engineer may design plans for a bridge. In each case, a new product is produced.

As educators, it is important that we be receptive to the creative efforts of students. We must allow students to invent and discover, to see situations from different perspectives, to use prior knowledge and look anew, to create products, and most important, to view the process of creating as vital as the product itself. We must nurture the creative potential in all aspects of learning and thinking to ensure creativity in the real world.

Creativity in the Web

Through the years, certain names are key to the discussion of creativity. Carl Rogers maintains that in education we tend to produce conformists rather than freely creative thinkers. In the sciences, thus, there are many technicians but few to formulate hypotheses. In leisure activities passive entertainment predominates. In industry only a few—the designer, manager, or head researcher—create. Rogers considers the goal of educators to be the stimulation of creativity in students, to give them the enabling skills to think rather than simply to learn.[1]

Joy Guilford, another leading authority in this field, found in the 1960s that creative people have several personality traits in common.[2] Creative people

- have a good sense of humor.
- enjoy doing several things at the same time.
- are enthusiastic about novelty.
- are adaptable to new settings.
- are somewhat sensitive to rebuffs.
- are absorbed in their own goals.
- are nonconformists.
- set a fast, energetic pace.
- have a wide range of interests.

Guilford associates creative thinking with these four abilities:

- *Fluency:* thinking having to do with the fertility of ideas
- *Flexibility:* deserting old ways of thinking and striking out in new directions
- *Originality:* dealing with the unusualness of responses or cleverness
- *Elaboration:* constructing a more complex object

She defines creativity as the ability to overcome a "constraining mental set" and to have the flexibility to diverge from conventional ways of looking at things. This kind of innovative thinking exists in degrees and is involved in everything we do. It is important in art, science, and business, as well as in interior decorating and constructive problem solving in interpersonal relations. With this broad application, we can easily understand the urgency of allowing our students to use their creativity, for in Erich Fromm's words, "Education for creativity is nothing short of education for living."

Edward de Bono, a psychologist and doctor of medicine at Cambridge University, who has researched the behavior of biological systems, discusses extending thinking through lateral thinking—pushing oneself to look further and in different ways. He sees vertical thinking, which is logical and traditional, as proceeding from one state of information to another, like building a structure. Vertical thinking is analytical, a function of the left brain, where the conclusion must come after the evidence. On the other hand, lateral thinking is provocative, a right-brain function, characterized by discontinuity where the conclusion could come before the evidence. This "design" type of creativity, concerned with changing concepts and patterns that everyone can learn, deals with generating new ideas and approaches and with extending capabilities through imagination and intuition. De Bono proposes that whereas creativity usually judges a result, lateral thinking is a process that can be practiced. The processes become thinking tools that can be applied directly to produce a result.[3]

Skill in lateral thinking is a combination of attitudes and techniques. De Bono believes that the purpose of thinking lessons is to enable students to use these devices when they wish. His lateral thinking lessons are based on the premise that if we can move away from the established tracks of our experience and find other tracks, we accomplish a creative result. Divergent thinking is a part of the process of lateral thinking, the latter being concerned more with switching to new and better patterns, not solely the generation of alternatives.

E. Paul Torrance studied many aspects of creativity, providing insight into the characteristics of the creative child at the elementary school level.[4] The tests of creativity he developed generally call for "ideational fluency," rating the person on the quality and number of ideas generated.[5] This concept agrees with de Bono's separation of divergent thinking from the larger process of lateral thinking.

David Perkins, a professor of psychology at Harvard University and author of several books on creativity and thinking, is a more recent researcher in the field. He is highly regarded for his knowledge, especially in his concern with cognitive skills and human development.[6] In contrast with Torrance, Perkins believes that Torrance's tests of creativity do not have much to do with real creativity because people of demonstrated creativity do not necessarily score high, for example, in ideational fluency. This is a critical point because it limits the validity of research. The Torrance Tests of Critical Thinking could be accurately predicting real-world creativity, but Perkins questions their ability to differentiate between more creative and less creative people at the professional level and their ability to determine the effect of instruction. Perkins reports that instructional programs can improve people's performance on the popular instruments for measuring creativity, but there is no hard evidence that instruction improves creativity in the real world.

In his book on creativity, *The Mind's Best Work*, Perkins shows that creativity is not some mysterious gift or process, but something that can be understood in terms of familiar experience.[7] Creative insight often occurs by recognizing a pattern or by remembering something with intention, with the creative person questioning at a different level than do less creative people. Perkins sees creativity as a style of deploying one's abilities. Biographical data show that creativity arises because of the person's intention of seeking the challenge, not necessarily because of a spontaneous reaction.

Problem finding is another area that differentiates the levels of creativity. Creative people tend to be less solution-minded but more concerned with *what* the problem should be. This relates to the more individualistic personality of creative people. It is interesting to note that personality measures point out truly creative individuals with much more reliability than do ideational fluency measures.[8]

Perkins suggests that "creativity by design" is a powerful concept for schools to use in encouraging creativity. Creativity involves creative products, a design with a particular structure adapted to its intended purpose.[9] This broadens our scope in the concept of design from such a concrete thing as a paper clip to such processes as computer programs and to such abstract inventive activities as designing a law or theory. He sees teaching a thinking course as having payoffs across the curriculum; however, integrating thinking allows for depth rather than breadth, making it a preferred process.

The authorities in the field each contribute a different perspective to the study of creativity. Guilford delineates the traits of fluency, flexibility, originality, and elaboration often synonymously referred to as the elements of creativity. De Bono emphasizes the separate teaching of lateral thinking skills to be transferred to all learning. In his creativity tests, Torrance focuses on ideational fluency, which measures creative performance in instructional programs. Perkins deals with problem solving and design, searching for creativity expressed in the "real world," through integrative thinking. Whatever their perspective may be, they all view creativity as breaking away from a "mental set." Despite differing approaches, the educators' goal is developing the enabling skill to think beyond simply learning facts.

SAFE Demonstration Lesson Plan 6.1: Flow to Fluency
Grade Levels: 2–12

OBJECTIVES

Students will

1. use brainstorming to generate a flow of ideas in a group game and individually.
2. learn that the most creative ideas arrive after ridding one's mind of common ideas and by pushing oneself to expand possibilities.

BRIEF DESCRIPTION

Students brainstorm to produce many divergent ideas, first as a class, then as part of a small group, and finally, individually. Students demonstrate their ability to evaluate their ideas. Through the process, students learn the value of brainstorming for fluency development and increase their skills in using this technique.

PROCEDURES

Stimulus

Show the class a common item such as a paper clip, toothpick, or hammer. Ask students to think of as many uses as possible for it. Discuss the process of nonjudgmental brainstorming. Have the students share the results and their reaction to the process, noting the occurrence of piggybacking, where the most unusual answers occur, and the reasons for this. Help students understand that the more creative answers surface after the common ideas have been used.

Activity

Organize the students into teams with a recorder. Give each team the same topic. Use your own topics or choose from these:

- Uses for a brown paper bag
- Things that are both soft and white
- Things that could be used as containers
- Words that describe "mud" (or a color)
- Things you would find in the kitchen

After the students brainstorm for twelve minutes, ask one of the teams to read its list, one item at a time. Any team that has that idea must cross it out. If no other team has that item, the reading team may circle it. Students may challenge an opposing team's idea, and the team may defend its position. The teacher is the arbitrator. All teams will eventually read their lists. The team with the most number of circled items wins.

Evaluate the process:

1. Were there times when someone else's ideas triggered another thought in your mind?
2. Where on the list are most of your circled answers?
3. Did you enjoy the brainstorming process?

Follow-Up

Give students a situation to ponder individually:

- What if all human beings suddenly became blind?
- What if everyone lived to be 200 years old?
- What if gravity did not work today?
- What if you could make yourself invisible at will?

- What if you could talk to animals?
- What if you could fly?
- What if you were the color green?
- What if the Wright Brothers had never invented the airplane?

Have students record their own ideas. Allow about twelve minutes. When time is called, the students will evaluate their own ideas and put a star next to the five ideas they think are most creative. Each student should share a starred item with the group.

Evaluation

Monitor growth in the students' abilities in fluency and in group brainstorming. Allow for differences in divergent thinking levels and accept the highly divergent thinker. Reward all for their efforts.

SAFE Demonstration Lesson Plan 6.2: Flex to Bend
Grade Levels: 4–12

Objectives

Students will

1. engage in activities involving forced changes and adapt to them.
2. be aware of the need for flexibility in everyday living.

BRIEF DESCRIPTION

Upon completion of a puzzle, the solution of which requires breaking the mind set's limited boundaries, students demonstrate their ability to be flexible in changed conditions in the classroom. They keep a log showing the need for flexible thinking in daily living.

PROCEDURES

Stimulus

Give students the following puzzle with these instructions: Draw no more than four straight lines (without lifting the pencil from the paper) that will cross through all nine dots.

This puzzle is difficult to solve if the imaginary boundary enclosing the nine dots is not exceeded; you have to "get out of the box." James Adams explains that this puzzle is a classic because the limit is a block in the mind of the solver, not in the definition of the problem.[10] One possible answer is

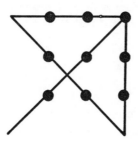

However, Adams received many divergent solutions such as using three lines, not necessarily drawn through the centers of the dots, folding the paper to line up the dots in a straight line, and rolling up the puzzle and drawing a spiral through the dots. Challenge students to pursue other solutions.

Activity

Discuss the need for flexibility in the reality of everyday living. Depending on the grade level, select one of the following activities for the class to try:

- Change the seating arrangement in the class, using a floor plan you have never tried before.
- For a part of the day or all day, do not use books. What kind of learning occurs? What resources are used?
- For a day or part of a day, carry on the regular curriculum without paper and pencil activities. What strategies are used for teaching? For remembering information?
- Keeping to the minimum requirements for basic curriculum, change the schedule for the day.

Follow-Up

Direct students to develop a list of changes that can be reasonably accomplished and carry them out, one a week. Have them keep a flexibility log in which they note their reactions to different situations requiring flexibility.

Evaluation

Allow for unexpected situations to arise. The creative student will see this as an opportunity to impress you with unusual approaches. Look for growth in flexibility in the students' behaviors and in their understanding of the concept in their log notations.

Have students evaluate their progress and write a summary based on their logs.

SAFE Demonstration Lesson Plan 6.3: Preserving Originality
Grade Levels: 4–12

OBJECTIVES

Students will

1. brainstorm ways to preserve or maintain a variety of things.
2. expand their solution into an essay.

BRIEF DESCRIPTION

Given a list of things from blackberries to friendship, students think of ways to preserve or maintain each item. From these possible solutions, they select one item and explain its preservation method in an essay.

PROCEDURES

Stimulus

Ask students to visualize a birthday party they remember especially fondly.

- What is the setting like—place, decorations, surprise?
- Who is at the party—family, friends, special guests?
- What things happen—games, food, activities?
- What gifts do you receive?
- What special feelings do you share on this birthday—love, happiness, joy, excitement?
- Capture the good feelings and setting of this party.
- How can you preserve the feelings and atmosphere of the party?

In a large group, discuss possible solutions. Emphasize the value of divergent thinking that often leads to inventions.

Activity

Have students complete the following worksheet[11] by selecting four of the seven choices. The students are to select one of their four solutions to elaborate in an essay. Direct the students to cluster specific details of their solution before they write.

Preserving Originality Worksheet

We preserve many things in many different ways. To keep fish fresh, we use ice. To keep meat fresh, pioneers used salt. By bronzing baby shoes, many people keep the shoes of their children in the same condition that they were when the shoes were outgrown. Now, we can preserve food by encasing it in plastic. In this exercise, you will think of how a variety of things might be preserved—that is, how they might be kept, maintained, or sustained.

How Would You Preserve

1. Blackberries? _____

   _____

2. The flavor of chocolate? _____

   _____

3. The fragrance of fresh air? _____

   _____

4. The excitement of a holiday? _____

   _____

5. Honesty? _____

   _____

6. A friendship? _____

   _____

7. (Your choice) _____

   _____

Follow-Up

Have students create a product (diagram, collage, construction) to accompany their explanation. Set up a display of the products and their revised essays.

Evaluation

Discuss the criteria for evaluation at the start of the lesson. Cooperatively, list features for student work; thus,

Essay: divergence, clarity, thoroughness, description
Product: accuracy, neatness, appropriateness

In a small-group peer evaluation situation, students evaluate the products and essays based on the criteria.

SAFE Demonstration Lesson Plan 6.4: Elaborate Elaboration
Grade Levels: 2–12

OBJECTIVES

Students will

1. create a new product by elaborating on an existing item.
2. describe its purpose and function in a poster advertisement.

BRIEF DESCRIPTION

Following a brief discussion on the creation of products through elaboration, students use at least one elaborative method to design a new product and establish its marketability in a poster advertisement.

PROCEDURES

Stimulus

Show the class a recent product such as a glass with an attached straw spiraling through it. Discuss how the straw developed through the years from paper to plastic, plain to decorated, straight to bendable. Each improvement was made because of a minor change. Discuss what the next change might be.

Activity

Have students suggest ways of elaborating on an object—for example, changing size, adding something, subtracting something, combining with another item, changing color, substituting an element, or changing the position. Direct them to choose one item to elaborate. They should sketch its new design. Encourage students to create the new product and a poster advertising the product for sale.

Follow-Up

Have students edit the advertisements in peer groups. The posters and any created products should be displayed.

Evaluation

Recognize all students for their new design. Give extra points for exceptional thinking evidenced in

- a combined use of elaboration methods.
- practicality.
- feasibility of production.
- creation of actual product.
- advertising gimmick.
- poster presentation.

Creativity Through the Classroom Environment

Perkins defines creativity as "thinking patterned in a way that tends to lead to creative results."[12] This pattern involves six general principles of creative thinking, an interesting mix of strategies, skills, and attitudinal factors. Creative thinking depends on

- aesthetic as much as practical standards.
- attention to purpose as much as results.
- mobility more than fluency.
- working on the edge more than at the center of one's competence.
- objectivity and subjectivity.
- intrinsic, more than extrinsic, motivation.

Perkins states that education in general works against the creative pattern of thinking because to some extent schools are too "right-answer" oriented and have little tolerance for the maverick. Special-purpose instruction of creative thinking has little impact on creativity because it focuses on strategies for creativity, which are helpful, but creativity needs skill as well. The skills outlined in the six principles require extensive practice applied in a particular field. Also critical to creative thinking are attitudes that cannot be taught directly. Furthermore, the limited time devoted to such special-purpose efforts does not constitute a program.

APPLYING CREATIVITY PRINCIPLES TO INSTRUCTION

In this section we apply the principles recommended by Perkins to various areas of instruction.

1. *Attention to aesthetics:* Besides literature and the arts, we can focus on the aesthetics of the products of human inquiry—scientific theories, mathematical systems, historical syntheses. For example, we can highlight the beauty of Newton's laws and the periodic table or the originality of thinking of history as shaped by geography.

2. *Attention to purpose:* We can provide students with the opportunity to generate and select different purposes. Consider the range of phenomena that spurred Newton to develop his laws and the historical origination of them. How do Newton's laws affect our everyday lives?

3. *Mobility:* We can apply mobility when a task presents major choices—selecting or revising a problem, choosing between empirical and theoretical methods, choosing to write discursively or as a dialogue, or deciding on a thesis to defend.

4. *Working at the edge of one's competence:* We can create a climate that will challenge students to work toward their creative potential.

5. *Objectivity:* We typically do highlight objectivity, but we can improve doing so in the arts.

6. *Intrinsic motivation:* We can provide students with more opportunities to select problems they address and the direction their instruction takes.

To teach for creativity we need to present knowledge as the product of a creative effort to accomplish something and to give students tasks that exercise creative effort. As we contemplate our role as educators and relate it to the encouragement of creative development, we can ask ourselves:

- Am I willing to let students ask questions about whatever puzzles them?
- If a relevant topic arose that was not in my prepared lesson, would I take the time to pursue the discussion if the students were eager to do so?
- Would I encourage a student to be successful even if his or her approach is different from what I had planned?
- Would I withhold criticism or correction long enough to allow a student to discover and correct his or her own errors?
- Would I allow input from a student on possible classroom activities?
- Would I encourage self-initiated learning?

These approaches are inherently tied to both educational excellence and the creative endeavor. Creativity is a vital element to be emphasized along with academic and ethical development.

DESIGNING A CREATIVITY PROGRAM

Synthesizing the research, we can see that a creativity program elicits creative behavior by including the following elements.

Respecting Students' Ideas and Questions

This underlying philosophic element increases not only creativity but also total learning and character development. We can respond with interest and enthusiasm, not necessarily by providing answers, but by turning the situation into an enriching one by leading students to consider, produce, and evaluate a range of possibilities. Providing a safe, positive atmosphere where respect for individuals is upheld lays the groundwork for all learning.

Improving Questioning Skills

We can ask questions that require different kinds of abilities and skills such as those beyond the knowledge level in Bloom and Krathwohl's *Taxonomy of Educational Objectives,*[13] namely, comprehension, application, analysis, synthesis, and evaluation. In this way, we can improve creativity while increasing the students' enthusiasm, problem-solving skills, and depth of understanding.

Recognizing Original Ideas

It is important that we value originality along with information acquisition. The criterion of originality is one of choice, combined with an interpretation of a creative idea. Must it be true, useful, surprising, a step forward, and requiring creative intellectual energy? In our attempt to teach students that the questions we ask do not necessarily have a single correct answer, we must develop our skills in asking questions that call for divergent thinking. In our peer-coaching experiences, it would be valuable to have the coach record a list of all the questions asked and together analyze them, discuss possible alternatives, and chart and note changes.

Elaborating Ideas

The successful creative thinker must be able to elaborate ideas and work out the details, making them practical and attractive, if necessary. One common method of elaborating what is read is having students illustrate what they read or apply other media such as music, songs, rhythmic movement, and dramatics. Writing different story endings or changing a character in some specific way to determine what other changes would occur and expanding on a certain episode are other ways of elaborating what is read. Elaboration can unlock learning difficulties and serve as the key to students learning to read.

Applying Creativity

Encouraging students to think creatively and critically about what they learn makes ideas more useful and exciting. Seeing new relationships and possibilities, synthesizing unrelated elements, redefining the known, and building from it are expectations that should be required of students. Greater depth of learning occurs when students reproduce with imagination, elaborate, transform and rearrange, and extend their learning beyond the classroom walls.

Where better to allow for creative thinking to start than in the classroom? Stretching students to make choices, to "think," and to apply their thinking all rely on our respecting the students and their ideas. We create the classroom environment. Let us allow students to create within it so as to be able later to create without it.

Creativity Across the Curriculum

Is creative teaching equated to teaching that encourages students' creative endeavors? We could debate the issue, but we do know that creativity does not occur in a vacuum so efforts to nurture it must deal with teaching strategies and learning theory. We also realize that no single segment of the curriculum can teach creativity alone; all instruction must contribute to the promotion of creative behavior.

It is said that creativeness begins when individuals pose problems for themselves. The discrepant event creates the problem, raises frustration, and requires the scientist to reexamine the evidence in search of a solution. Ideally, the science student begins to find information in new ways, to process the information through various activities, and to make inferences and predictions and test them.

Valuable social science experiences can be had inside and outside the classroom, providing an opportunity for teacher and student to interact. In mathematics, creative behavior occurs when the student is allowed to play with a problem with almost no direction, instead of being given predetermined stipulations. Freedom to experiment with composition writing and with literature interpretations makes the language arts come alive. This is also true when students approach creativeness through fine-art forms. When they explore reality and can function creatively with the information, they then have the freedom to play with the information.

In all subject areas, a scholarly attitude is typically characterized by much curiosity, which needs careful nurturing teachers. As students seek answers and attack problems, they create their intellect by synthesizing insights and understandings from all areas, becoming a scientist, a historian, a critic, an artist. Creativity is inherent in all subject areas.

SCIENCE

Scientific investigations result in changes in our concepts of the universe at a rapid rate. Many supposedly valid scientific theories will be proved false before students have the opportunity to apply the knowledge in a meaningful way. Clearly, it is not critical that students memorize ideas or processes that are today considered proper scientific technology. What is important is that students develop scholarly attitudes toward learning, an attitude of curiosity and the tendency to question. We can promote this attitude by encouraging investigations rather than simply passing on facts about science. Learning what has been discovered is not learning science and its ways of thinking.

Progress in science comes from original thinking. We should allow students to investigate topics of individual interest as much as possible or at least provide a framework within which the students collect their own data, draw their own inferences, make their own predictions, and test them. This sets the stage for future innovation, experimentation, and creative endeavor because students will become adults with the curiosity required to continue learning.

MATHEMATICS

In mathematics, we often squelch creativity by demanding that students do problems "the right way," not allowing for alternative processes to the solution. For example, in solving for the value of x in the linear equation $4x + 5 = 25$, a student can almost immediately respond that the answer is 5. Many teachers, realizing the student arrived at the answer too quickly, would know the student did not use "the" method of subtracting 5 from each member of the equation and then dividing each member by 4 and would therefore require the student to do so formally. Some teachers may ignore attempts at creativity, hoping they will go away. The rare teacher rewards such creativity with praise.

The beginning algebra student will discover that guessing some number for x in the equation $ax + b = c$ will lead to the thinking process that can determine the answer. Guessing k as the answer, $ak + b = d$. If $d = c$, k is the solution. If d is less than c, the answer is found by adding $(c - d)/a$ to k. If d is greater than c, the solution is found by subtracting $(d - c)/a$ from k. That the procedures will produce the correct answer is easily demonstrated. Students, however, convince themselves that the procedures work by simply thinking about them. EXAMPLE. $4x \times 5 = 25$

1. Guess that $x = 2$. $4(2) + 5 = 13$.
2. Because 13 is 12 less than the desired result (25), 2 is too small.
3. Because the coefficient of x is 4, whenever the value of x is increased by 1, the value of the entire left member will be increased by 4.
4. So the guess must be increased by 12/4, or 3, in order to increase the result by 8.
5. Thus, the answer must be $2 + 3$, or 5.

As teachers, we feel a responsibility to help students know the things we know, to make them fully knowledgeable as rapidly as possible; it is often difficult for us to step back and encourage independence. We need to recognize that we can never hope to pass on all the accumulated wisdom and the vast amount of knowledge that is increasing exponentially. Creators are important in our society. We should not become so wrapped up in passing on information, therefore, to the neglect of encouraging independent thought and creative energy. At the same time, we cannot expect students to create all that came before them. Thus, a compromise between an environment that requires complete creativity and one that allows no creativity is the sensible solution.

LANGUAGE ARTS

"Writing is among the most complex of all human mental activities," state researchers Linda Flower and John Hayes.[14] The writing process covers all the stages in Bloom's taxonomy as writers tap their knowledge, translate it into thought or print, organize ideas, focus within the whole construct, synthesize a framework for communicating the intended message, transform this pattern into written form, and evaluate the product.

Because students must juggle these demands within the constraints of their limited, though growing, abilities, we cannot assign practice tasks in writing and anticipate improvement in enhanced thinking and writing skills. We must structure lessons that increase the intellectual capabilities and provide guided practice in the content and process of composing.

Lessons organized according to the process model of composition—prewriting, writing, sharing, revising, and evaluating—move the student through all levels of thinking from knowledge through evaluation. In working from concrete to abstract levels, writing can be used as a learning tool across the curriculum for expanding and refining thinking. Guided writing practice develops thinking as students internalize the problem-solving process leading to synthesizing, the vital step of the creative effort.

SOCIAL SCIENCE

The content, methodology, and products related to the social sciences also lend themselves to promoting creative processes in students. Human social development in the environment, the solution of social problems, and the study of group interaction offer opportunities for students to pursue creative problem-solving techniques. Opportunities exist in the discovery of a problem, the gathering of pertinent data, the forming and checking of hypotheses, or the evaluation of the process or product.

Guilford's theory of the intellect[15] furnishes the impetus for creative endeavor in the social sciences. Content, process, and product are interwoven in a dynamic cross-transferring process. For example, in the study of an imaginary planet, a problem to solve is the need to make the planet a desirable place to live. The traits of the inhabitants would need definition. From that, decisions on food, climate, communication, transportation, education, recreation, religion, protection, and aesthetics need to be made. Besides the taxonomy of knowledge skills related to these topics, moral and ethical thinking and creative aspects of the topic come into play.

Opportunities to involve students in creative processes are numerous. Audio-visual presentations, construction of maps and dioramas, role playing, sociometric devices, visual artwork, dramatic presentations, music activities, and research, all ongoing presently in the classroom, are the basis from which other creative activities can spring.

PERFORMING ARTS

Create ... re-create ... recreation. These words represent three approaches to the performing arts. The creative artist creates or brings an idea into existence as a playwright in the theater, the choreographer in dance, the composer in music. Actors, dancers, musicians, directors, designers, and conductors re-create or interpret the idea, bringing the creation to life. The audience witnesses this re-creation for their recreation.[16] Creating in the theater is a collaborative effort with each person working at his or her peak of creativity to interpret the artist's conception.

Nurturing creativity in the artist involves encouraging experimentation in the composition with words, sound, movement, and images. In the process, the student becomes aware of the possibility of alternative interpretations of a production. Some methods for stimulating dramatic imagination are creative dramatics, pantomime, eurythmics, and planned improvisation. The creative and interpretive artists develop through experience.

VISUAL ARTS

"What is art?" is a question long-debated. It is not our intention to debate the issue, but a broad concept is needed to address the issue of creativity. Objects become works of art through their inherent artistic qualities, resulting from a person's exploration of his or her ideas and feelings in a medium suited to particular purposes. The object created is a tangible form of an idea.

An important factor in the teaching of art involves establishing conditions in which students can learn the joy and excitement of realizing new forms and be willing to experiment with the unknown. While coloring in numbered pictures is an extreme of the noncreative activity, so is the too-broad latitude of "doing your own thing." The objective is a balance between enough structure for the student to advance with confidence and sufficient freedom of choice to encourage individual expression. The creative art teacher introduces ideas and images and encourages students to synthesize the ideas and images with their own unique ways of thinking. This fosters creative insights.

A rich source of images can be drawn from the work of other artists. Students can become aware of how one artist handled a subject in different ways or compare how several artists handled a particular subject. The trees in a van Gogh landscape can be compared, for example, with the trees in a Constable landscape. Working with an art consultant can make teaching art the creative experience we wish it to be—the development of knowledge and insight about visual symbols and forms and the ability to give form to ideas and feelings.

In working with creative student artists, J. N. Getzels and M. Csikszentmihalyi documented the students' tendency to value stated qualities and their straightforward striving to achieve them.[17] This twenty-year longitudinal study of artists from 1963–1981, when these artists were at midlife, reveals the critical role in the creative thought of finding and formulating problems. To discover the process of creative performance, Getzels and his associate observed how the creative artistic product was achieved. They observed the crucial difference between industrial artists and fine artists: The former work on presented problems, and the latter have to find or create the problem on which to work, thereby working on "discovered problems."

That finding and formulating the problem is an integral phase of the creative process is attested to by these noted researchers:

> The formulation of a problem is often more essential than its solution, which may be merely a matter of mathematical or experimental skill. To raise new questions, new possibilities, to regard old questions from a new angle requires creative imagination and marks real advance in science.   ALBERT EINSTEIN (Scientist)[18]

> The function of thinking then is not just solving a specific problem but discovering, envisaging, going into deeper questions. Often in great discoveries the most important thing is that a certain question is generated. Envisaging, stating the productive question, is often a more important, often a greater achievement than the solution of a set question.   MAX WERTHEIMER (Psychologist)[19]

> I sometimes begin drawing with no preconceived problem to solve, with only a desire to use pencil on paper and only make lines, tones, and styles with no conscious aim. But as my mind takes in what is so produced, a point arrives where some idea becomes conscious and crystallizes, and then control and ordering begin to take place.   HENRY MOORE (Twentieth-Century Artist)[20]

Other than the numerous instruments designed to observe how a person solves a problem, there are no methods or prior studies on the subject of how a person "finds" a problem. From their devised means of thirty-one fine-arts students, Getzels and Csikszentmihalyi arrived at statistically positive and significant correlations that led them to these conclusions:

- The discovery and formulation of problems can be studied empirically.
- Individual differences occur in the finding and formulating of problems just as they do in the solving of problems already created.
- A positive relation exists between the quality of a problem that is found and the quality of the solution that is attained.

SAFE Demonstration Lesson Plan 6.5: I Read, I Write, I Think . . . I Create
Grade Levels: 4–12

OBJECTIVES

Students will

1. read several short selections.
2. respond to the selections they have read in a performing and visual arts medium of their choice.
3. write a response to the unit theme.

BRIEF DESCRIPTION

This thematic lesson ties in literature, oral language, writing, and the performing and visual arts. Depending on the selected theme, social science can be a part of the focus also. Students read at least one short story, discuss what they have read, undertake a project of their choice, and write in response to the theme.

PROCEDURES

Stimulus

Read aloud a short story while students follow in their own copies. A recommended selection is "So Much Unfairness of Things" by C. D. B. Bryan in *Ten Top Stories*. P. S. Wilkinson, the central character, is a student in a private school. He cheats while taking the final Latin examination, and he is observed by another student, reported, and expelled from the school.

After reading, have students cut from magazines any words, phrases, and pictures of objects that they relate in any way with the story. Direct students to create a montage bulletin board using the pictures collected. Use this display to initiate a discussion of the theme.

Guide students to react to these statements, noting their relationship to the story, in small groups:

Man is not the creature of circumstances; circumstances are the creatures of men.
BENJAMIN DISRAELI

It is fortune, not wisdom, that rules man's life.
CICERO

Activity

Have students select other short stories that appeal to them. Possible readings for older students are

- *The Best American Short Stories,* Houghton Mifflin, published every year.
- *Prize Stories, The O. Henry Awards,* Doubleday, published annually.
- *Ten Modern American Short Stories,* edited by David A. Sohn, Bantam.
- *Ten Top Stories,* edited by David A. Sohn, Bantam.

Possible readings for younger students are

- *Great Survival Adventures,* compiled by Robert Gannon, Random House, 1973.
- *Tales Our Settlers Told,* Joseph and Edith Raskin, Lothrop, 1971.
- *Ten Tales of American Immigrants,* Joseph and Edith Raskin.

After reading their stories, students should choose an option from this list of projects. They may decide to work with a small group or individually.

1. *Prepare a Series of Still Photographs:* Students carefully examine the story and select moments that could be dramatized and portrayed on film. They consider costume, setting, camera angles, props, and composition of the photographs and write a caption for each photograph. Students display their project on the bulletin board, with large letters indicating the title of the story.

2. *Prepare a Filmstrip:* Instead of still photographs, students take the shots with the camera focused sideways, as if for height in pictures, and do not cut the film in processing. This will create a filmstrip.

3. *Prepare a Radio Drama:* Students reshape a dramatic moment in the story and communicate it effectively to listeners. They prepare a script, rehearse it, and tape-record it for the class. Students will need some assistance from class members as actors and as voice and sound-effects persons.

4. *Prepare a Brief Drama:* Similar to the radio drama, students prepare a script with notes on the performers' movements, gestures, and facial expressions. They may study a published play to see how the dramatist provides this information.

5. *Prepare a Dramatization for Videotape:* Videotape allows the performers to record dialogue and action. In preparing the script, students consider camera angles and camera movement. They may want to divide the paper into two columns, one for the audio (dialogue, sound effects), the other for video (visual effects, performers' movements, expressions).

6. *Direct an "MTV" Production:* Along the lines of "MTV," students select a song related to the theme or change the lyrics of a song to reflect the theme and videotape a performance highlighting the reading using the song as the audio production.

7. *Prepare an 8-mm Film:* Students need to consider costume, setting, camera angles, and movement. Dialogue will be necessary only if you select to use a camera with sound.

When students are ready to make a personal response to the unit theme, have them choose such formats as:

- a critical essay.
- an anecdote, drawing on personal experience and reflection on the theme.
- a poem, offering emotional and structural freedom to the student.
- a story in fictional narrative form, experimenting with voice, image, and characterization.

Follow-Up

Have groups of students plan a panel presentation of the unit theme, alluding to the different stories read, while class members not on the panel comment and question what is being discussed. This discussion could be videotaped.

Evaluation

Have students evaluate their work on each of the six parts of the unit:

1. Participation in creating the montage
2. Contributions in small-group discussions
3. Understanding of the short story selected
4. Project accomplishment
5. Written response to the unit theme
6. Participation as panel or audience member

SAFE Demonstration Lesson Plan 6.6: Metaphorical Connections
Grade Levels: 4–12

OBJECTIVES

Students will

1. learn about metaphors.
2. generate and discuss metaphors.

BRIEF DESCRIPTION

Following a teacher demonstration on the use of metaphorical connections related to a concept, students select a metaphor to use in reviewing a principle and prepare a review lesson to share with the class.

PROCEDURES

Metaphorical thinking is the ability to see a relationship between two unlike things by recognizing a shared trait or principle between the two things. The connection between one's experience and a new concept makes learning more efficient. Metaphors can be used to introduce a unit, to clarify a concept, or for review.

Stimulus

Ask students, "How is the pumping of blood through our arteries like water running through pipes?" After students share answers such as the involvement of pressure, blockages, restrictions, sizes, and connections, ask them if they are aided in their understanding of the concept of blood flow by the use of an example. They will generally see the advantage of an example, if not in this situation, then in others that you can elicit from them.

Demonstrate this process for students by sharing with them the thinking process that occurs and by eliciting their answers in this example:

1. What do I want to teach about arteriosclerosis? How restriction of arteries causes increased pressure against arteries' inner walls.
2. What is the hazard of the condition? It leads to heart attacks and strokes.
3. What can I think of that would show this pressure? Conduits of sorts (pipes, straws), watering can with holes at the spout, hole in a dam, garden hose.
4. Which of these is most easily demonstrated at school? The garden hose.
5. How is the garden hose different from the arteries? It is not part of the circulatory system, and it does not have a means for the water to return to the source.
6. How do I present this information? I will use a clear straw packed with lard to introduce the condition of arteriosclerosis and pour water through it to show the flow. Then, I will use a garden hose attached to a faucet to show the flow of water when there is no blockage. I will place my finger over the end of the hose and have students notice the pressure of the water shooting forth. This would be similar to the breaking point of the artery.

Activity

Organize students into groups to select a metaphor to use in reviewing a general principle they have been studying. After generating various ideas, they should choose the one that best communicates the concept. Guide them to plan a lesson to present the concept to the class through the use of the metaphor. Students will use your model to generate an appropriate metaphor for the concept they are to demonstrate.

Follow-Up

At the end of the unit, ask students questions based on metaphors to evaluate their comprehension. For example, with the question "Explain how the period leading to the French Revolution was like the building up of a volcanic eruption," students need to know not only the events leading up to the Revolution but also understand them well enough to explain their significance in terms of an analogy, a volcanic eruption. When students are more experienced, they can generate their own metaphors.

Metaphors are also a powerful model in expository writing because students have a tool that promotes understanding and a format for clearly presenting information. Have students write a sentence telling what they wish to communicate, choose a metaphor, and write using metaphor to explain the thesis statement. In creative writing, seeing original connections through metaphor produces powerful pieces. "What color is a dream?" stretches the mind to discover one's creativity.

In a unit that integrates math, science, history, music, and writing, students

1. compare the amoeba with the Massachusetts Bay Colony.
2. fold paper to understand exponential growth and discuss why that is not like the mathematics of amoeba colonies.
3. write to, "If the American colonies were made of cheese, who would be the mice?" and "If amoebas ate light bulbs, what would happen when they reproduced?"
4. become aware of the variations of Beethoven's Fifth Symphony and write about the music likened to amoebas reproducing.[21]

Evaluation

Because the process of learning to make connections is more important than is the content, it is vital that trust be established before evaluation is started on metaphorical thinking. We must remember never to belittle a student's response and also never to ignore it.

When using metaphors to teach substantive content, evaluate the connections on the basis of what you consider an important aspect of the subject. You can make a list of the things that should be included and check the answers against it. An especially creative metaphor will earn extra points.

SAFE Demonstration Lesson Plan 6.7: The I-Search Paper[22]
Grade Levels: 4–12

OBJECTIVES

Students will

1. conduct a search on a topic of interest.
2. write the I-search paper.

BRIEF DESCRIPTION

Students do research on a carefully selected topic and write a report of the search. The I-Search paper is a move away from the traditional research report based on the encyclopedia as the main resource. In an I-Search paper, the searcher and the object are influenced by each other, and this relationship is expressed in the report.

PROCEDURES

Stimulus

Have students create a Möbius strip with strips of paper one-half inch wide and eleven or more inches long, the ends of the paper joined with a full turn and taped together. On one side they write *object* and on the other *searcher* and draw a continuous line from *searcher* along the middle of the strip. It will eventually run into the word *object*. Side one will have become side two. Discuss this model of human searching, the *I* and the *object* flowing into each other. Students should understand that a true report shows the reader how and to what extent the *I* and the *object* have influenced each other.

Activity

After students decide on topics of their choice, topics representing a need to know rather than an assigned task, they find information through people, interviews, library resources, the yellow pages, letter writing.

The format of the paper can be a simple chronological reporting or a division into sections such as

Example 1

1. statement of the problem.
2. procedure.
3. summarization.
4. implications.

Example 2

1. "What I Know."
2. "Why I Am Writing This Paper."
3. "The Search."
4. "What I Learned."

Follow-Up

Have students respond to one another's first draft, using the evaluation sheet as a guide. They should make the necessary revisions and submit the final form to the teacher.

Evaluation

Evaluate the I-Search papers with a holistic scoring rubric. The elements to look for in an I-Search paper are as follows:

- Can the reader see the relationship between the I and the object?
- Are there enough details about the search for the reader to evaluate the most critical judgments made in the paper? Include such other considerations as organization, clarity, and syntax.

SUMMARY

It is important for us as educators to understand that finding and formulating problems should be a major focus of instruction.

A few years ago, some of the world's most distinguished scientists agreed that the most important thing to learn is how to pose the productive problem, how to ask the right question. Sir Hans Krebs, the Nobel Prize–winning biochemist, said of his teacher, Otto Warburg, "He taught me how to go about asking the right kind of questions—a question that is worthwhile and a question that can be tackled with the tools available at the time."[23]

Getzels and Csikszentmihalyi's study shows that to enhance creativity in science, art, and all activities the effective question, the "problem of the problem," is at the heart of the effective solution.

Gertrude Stein says it well: "The whole question of questions and not answers is very interesting. Suppose no one asked a question. What would the answer be?"[24]

CHALLENGE

1. Review the six principles of creative thinking as presented by David Perkins on page 173. Congratulate yourself for any principle you

have mastered and are presently practicing consistently in your class-room. Then select an area with which you would like to work. Set it as a goal and brainstretch ways you can incorporate the principle in your curriculum. Highlight this practice in your lesson plan with a colored pen to heighten your awareness of your effort to promote creativity.

2. Share with your students the five elements for a creativity–nurturing environment described on page 174. Focus on one area for a one-week period. Have students create a poster with the concept clearly explained. You might have a contest of the five most creative posters. Display one of them each day at the front of the classroom and have students keep a log on butcher paper next to the poster of positive experiences that contribute to the accomplishment of that goal for the week—that is, interaction between you and the class, you and an individual, student and student. The other posters may be distributed throughout the school. The next week, transfer the poster and log to a bulletin board and post the next focal area at the front of the classroom. Proceed in the same manner, focusing on the one concept but continuing to build on the previous areas as well. At the end of five weeks, keep the posters on the bulletin board and reinforce the concepts. Encourage students to continue highlighting the creativity–nurturing experiences throughout the year.

3. Select a subject area in which to incorporate the activities of the performing and visual arts. Plan activities such as the following: Allow students to relate a specific element in the topic of study to an art form. In math, a student could produce a videotape on the various ways to creatively attack a math problem. In science, a student could dramatize the process of photosynthesis. In social science, a student could relate the artistic representations to the historical or sociological aspects of a specific period of time.

4. Develop a creativity strand for a unit of study. For example, in a unit on "War: Man in Conflict," some questions might be as follows:

- List all the terms associated with war.
- How many ways can you come up with as solutions to wars?
- How would war look to a pacifist? Survivalist? Mercenary?
- What would a retreat mean from the viewpoint of a commanding officer?
- How would modern weaponry look to Napoleon?
- You are a land mine in a village of Vietnamese children. How do you feel?
- Suppose that you could develop an "antiwar pill." What ingredients would you have in the pill?
- How are peace negotiations like friendship?
- What weapon is most like you? Why?

NOTES

1. Carl R. Rogers, "Toward a Theory of Creativity," *ETC.: A Review of General Semantics* 11, no. 4 (Summer 1954): 249–260.
2. Joy P. Guilford, *Personality* (New York: McGraw-Hill, 1959).
3. Edward de Bono, *CoRT Thinking, CoRT IV* (Direct Education Services Limited, 1975).
4. E. Paul Torrance, *Education and the Creative Potential* (Minneapolis: University of Minnesota Press, 1963).
5. E. Paul Torrance, *The Torrance Tests of Creative Thinking: Norms-Technical Manual* (Scholastic Testing Service, 1974).
6. Ronald S. Brandt, "On Creativity and Thinking Skills: A Conversation with David Perkins," *Educational Leadership* 43, no. 8 (May 1986): 12–18.
7. D. N. Perkins, *The Mind's Best Work* (Cambridge, Mass.: Harvard University, 1981).
8. Brandt, "On Creativity and Thinking Skills," 14.
9. D. N. Perkins, "Creativity by Design," *Educational Leadership*, 42 (Sept. 1984): 18–25.
10. James L. Adams, *Conceptual Blockbusting: A Guide to Better Ideas*, 2d ed. (New York: Norton, 1979), 24–31.
11. Gwenn Doty, *Kids Kan Kreate* (Cupertino, Calif.: Cupertino Union School District, 1977).
12. Perkins, "Creativity by Design," 19.
13. Benjamin S. Bloom, and D. R. Krathwohl, *Taxonomy of Educational Objectives: The Classification of Educational Goals* (New York: David McKay, 1956).
14. Linda Flower, and John R. Hayes, "The Dynamics of Composing," in *Cognitive Processes in Writing*, eds. Lee W. Gregg, and Erwin R. Steinberg (Erlbaum, 1980), 33.
15. J. P. Guilford, "The Structure of Intellect," *Psychological Bulletin* 53 (1956): 267–293.
16. John Edward Blankenchip, "Performing Arts," in *Teaching for Creative Endeavor*, ed. William B. Michael (Bloomington: Indiana University, 1968), 230–236.
17. J. W. Getzels, "Problem Finding and the Enhancement of Creativity," *NASSP Bulletin* 69, no. 482 (Sept. 1985): 55–61.
18. Albert Einstein, and L. Infeld, *The Evolution of Physics* (New York: Simon & Schuster, 1938), 92.
19. M. Wertheimer, *Productive Thinking* (New York: Harper, 1945), 123.
20. H. Moore, "Notes on Sculpture," in *The Creative Process*, ed. B. Ghiselin (New York: Mentor, 1955), 77.
21. William Gordon, and Tony Poze, *Strange and Familiar, Book VI* (Cambridge, Mass.: Porpoise, 1972), 67–76.
22. Ken Macrorie, *Searching Writing* (Hayden, Inc., 1980).
23. J. H. Maugh, "Creativity: Can It Be Dissected? Can It Be Taught?" *Science* 184 (1974): 184.
24. Getzels, "Problem Finding and the Enhancement of Creativity," 61.

EXPLORING FURTHER

Getzels, J. W., and M. Csikszentmihalyi. *The Creative Vision: A Longitudinal Study of Problem Finding in Art.* New York: Wiley, 1976.
Perkins, D. N. *The Mind's Best Work.* Cambridge, Mass.: Harvard University Press, 1981.

CHAPTER 7

Extending Comprehension Skills

Objectives

After reading this chapter, you will be able to

- *Understand the meaning of comprehension as a learning skill.*
- *Discern the levels of comprehension found in instructional materials.*
- *Recognize the research implications for comprehension skills instruction.*
- *Identify the connection between the comprehension skills tested by standardized reading tests and instruction for thinking.*
- *Describe the importance of linking activities for both auditory and reading comprehension.*
- *Create activities for helping students increase their comprehension skills.*

Every learner, even the very brightest, has experienced that period of confusion when learning stops. For many learners, this lapse occurs in studying mathematics or sciences; for others, in learning a foreign language or analyzing a piece of literature. If the learner doesn't overcome this block, this inability to understand a concept, idea, or theory, the result is frustration or sometimes even failure. Comprehension does not always happen automatically.

For teachers, such learning disruptions pose two major problems: recognizing student misunderstanding and providing effective instructional intervention, which allows students to continue the learning task. Our success in solving these two problems determines the degree of our students' accomplishment of the goals we establish in our classrooms. Therefore, if we want our students to improve as learners and thinkers, we need to help them develop more powerful comprehension skills. This chapter examines various aspects of comprehension.

Exploring Comprehension

DEFINING COMPREHENSION

Comprehension is the foundation upon which higher-level thinking skills programs are built. Unless students possess genuine proficiency in comprehension, they cannot be expected to perform capably such critical thinking skills as application, analysis, synthesis, and evaluation.

Webster's New World Dictionary defines *comprehension* as "the act of grasping with the mind," and the "knowledge that results from this." But, in actual practice, the meaning of comprehension and its applications are not so straightforward. Roger Shuy identifies how the problem of definition relates to reading tests:

> ... The really useful area of measurement in reading, comprehension, is so ill-defined that current measurement is not helpful. Standard procedure seems to be to give a short passage for silent reading followed by four or five short responses for selection. The right answer is one of these short responses.[1]

In effect, current practice reduces comprehension instruction to either searching for main ideas or remembering important details.

Obviously, comprehension is more than identifying main ideas or recalling facts. R. David Pearson summarizes research efforts on reading comprehension by observing that such comprehension is "a complex interactive process in which a reader varies his focus along a continuum from primarily text-based processing (concentration on getting the author's message straight) to primarily reader-based processing (concentration on predicting what the author's message ought to be)."[2]

Benjamin Bloom defines comprehension as "grasping the meaning of material." He identifies the cue words involved in the process of comprehension as *recognize, locate, report, express, identify, explain, restate, review, paraphrase, cite, tell, summarize, describe, support, document, precis,* and *abstract*. This list of behavioral indices represents a wide range of cognitive skills.

Gaining meaning, comprehension, in its fullest sense, thus requires a variety of mental processes. For our purposes, we define comprehension as understanding the meaning of oral or written material that allows students to perform higher-level cognitive skills.

LEVELS OF COMPREHENSION

Thomas Barrett identifies five levels of comprehension:

1. Literal comprehension
2. Reorganization
3. Inferential comprehension

4. Evaluation

5. Appreciation[3]

It is interesting to compare this listing with the comprehension skills typically presented in reading tests and basal readers: main idea, sequence, cause–effect, and fact–opinion. Although Barrett's listing more clearly identifies levels of skills, all these skills are necessary aspects of comprehension. Our task as teachers is to help students expand their abilities with all components that comprise comprehension.

IMPLICATIONS OF RESEARCH ON COMPREHENSION

One clear implication of research on comprehension instruction is that we need to spend more time teaching for comprehension. In two broad studies of the teaching of reading comprehension, Durkin found that during periods of time set aside specifically for reading instruction only 1 percent of the time focused on comprehension.[4]

Another important implication is that both content and process factors are involved in reading comprehension. This means that the more we know about a subject or topic under investigation, the more we will understand and be able to integrate new information,[5] and that we recall and recognize information better when it is presented in familiar forms.[6] These research findings emphasize the importance of sequencing instruction so that students move along a continuum of familiar content and structures into less familiar ones.

Research also indicates that *direct* instruction of comprehension skills produces greater gains on standardized measures than does *incidental* instruction.[7] Collectively, the research studies cited here reveal that not enough time is devoted to comprehension instruction in most classrooms, but in cases where there is systematic direct instruction with carefully selected content organized in familiar literary forms, students do increase their comprehension skills. Comprehension can be taught!

Researchers unanimously acknowledge that there are levels of comprehension ranging from low to high, simple to complex, or concrete to abstract. Many studies show that the after-reading questions from basal readers and other classroom reading assignments are mainly of the literal comprehension type requiring only recall or recognition of details and facts from the stories. The common recommendation therefore is that more attention be given to working with higher levels of comprehension through questions requiring the use of inference, evaluation, and application.

CONNECTING READING AND THINKING SKILLS

Books present a visual record of an author's thinking. Besides asking our students to think about what they are reading, we should also remember to emphasize that most of their reading, whether required or for pleasure, represents thinking. Whether our students are reading fiction or nonfiction, they are reading "thinking." As readers, students enter into a transaction with the author, working with the author to construct meaning.[8] Students apply their prior knowledge to this task of "making meaning." Through reading, students encounter expressions of values and attitudes, universal human needs, stances on issues and events. They need opportunities to discuss these ideas, to question the author's beliefs, and to draw their own conclusions.

Another motivation for reading is the opportunity to share vicariously in the experiencing of a new place, a different adventure. This probably helps explain an individual's preference in reading matter. Very often we prefer to read about people who are confronting and solving problems similar to our own. Again, this relates to sharing in the author's thinking about a subject. We need to proceed with caution in "teaching" a book to our students. We probably perform a greater service by first stepping aside and letting them find their own meanings, connections, and learnings in the books. Then, we can share our instructional agenda, the things we wish them to gain from the books. Later in this chapter, you will find specific suggestions for allowing students to interact with their reading materials out of their own needs and interests.

Another important task we face as teachers of comprehension skills is determining an appropriate allotment of instructional time. To decide what might constitute a reasonable amount of time, we first must identify the expected outcomes. Our task can be overwhelming if we select too long a list of objectives. An alternative is to begin with concepts or skills commonly tested on standardized reading tests, thus reducing the size of our responsibility, for example:

1. Details
2. Inferences
3. Sequence
4. Main idea
5. Cause/Effect
6. Comparison
7. Predicting outcomes
8. Drawing conclusions[9]

Examining this list reveals that most of these skills are generally considered comprehension skills. This list implies that our responsibility in teaching reading skills, insofar as standardized tests go, is not so overwhelming at all. Each of these eight topics and skills can be addressed in a relatively short period of formal instruction, then regularly reinforced through thinking in broader contexts. This allows additional time for other instructional activities related to thinking and comprehension.

In designing lessons to teach comprehension, remember to select activities that provide for both auditory and reading comprehension. Help your students make the important link between oral and written communication and reinforce the need for purposive listening as well as reading. Beginning with oral discussion and talking through ideas is a good pre-reading introduction to thinking activities.

To assist students in refining their comprehension skills, you may try an incremental approach to both content and form. Because the sentence is the basic unit of communication, for a varied approach, begin with single sentences of different lengths, types, and subject matters. Take these sentences from the literature used in your classrooms.

After students have gained acceptable proficiency with the sentence, move on to paragraphs. You might follow this simple model of three sequential steps for developing skill in paragraph comprehension:

First, find the key words in each sentence.
Second, find the key sentences in the paragraph.
Third, find the main thought in the paragraph.[10]

Do not, however, remain overly long with instruction based on isolated sentences or paragraphs, but move to multiparagraph selections. Remember to let your students find their own meanings as they analyze literature selections. Take your students beyond mere factual comprehension into critical thinking. Have them paraphrase an essay or write an analysis of a poem. Activities such as these help students make connections between beginning comprehension skills and higher-level thinking abilities.

Moving into more advanced thinking skills, we might focus on inference, a complex skill that includes many outcomes. Students will be able to

1. infer details not given, draw conclusions and evaluate.
2. perceive relationships: part-whole; cause–effect; general-specific; place, sequence, size, and time.
3. make generalizations.
4. interpret figurative expressions.
5. identify character traits, reactions, and motives.
6. anticipate what will happen next in a story.
7. make hypotheses.
8. forecast and predict story outcomes.
9. predict how a change introduced by the author affects events in a story.
10. forecast the effects or acts of nature in a story.

11. make inferences.
12. apply ideas and integrate them with past experience.[11]

Obviously, this list includes far more complex thinking ability than the skills usually assessed on reading tests. To provide extensive involvement with higher-level thinking by students, we must plan integrated literature-based learning activities. This implies that we teach our students to be careful, thoughtful listeners and readers. We should realize, however, that their mastery of these skills is part of an ongoing process of becoming effective learners. They may grow at different rates in different aspects of comprehension. These abilities will be supported by learning experiences in all subject areas as well as experiences outside the school.

Working with other teachers, you can develop objectives for various comprehension skills groupings, thus:

Comprehension Skills Involving Categorizing:
1. Classifying ideas
2. Distinguishing fact and fantasy
3. Distinguishing real and unreal
4. Distinguishing fact and opinion
5. Distinguishing relevant and irrelevant information
6. Integrating new information with old
7. Choosing correct and applicable meanings

Comprehension Skills Involving Deductive Reasoning:
1. Identifying supportive information and details
2. Inferring details
3. Analyzing conclusions
4. Giving examples
5. Applying information gained to new situations
6. Providing visualizations

Comprehension Skills Involving Inductive Reasoning:
1. Making generalizations
2. Identifying character traits and motives
3. Interpreting the author's style, bias, attitude, and purpose
4. Getting the main idea
5. Interpreting figurative and idiomatic language

Comprehension Skills Involving Predicting Events:
1. Anticipating future actions
2. Making hypotheses
3. Forecasting and predicting outcomes
4. Understanding the use of foreshadowing/foreboding
5. Making educated guesses

Comprehension Skills Involving Predicting Consequences:
1. Predicting causal relationships
2. Anticipating the effect of character's actions
3. Predicting affects of change of events
4. Forecasting effects of natural events[12]

Such lists are applicable across the curriculum. The discrete skills listed are usually not taught alone. They are part of instruction in many academic areas, furthermore, reminding us that every teacher has a responsibility to help students gain meaning through listening or reading. All too often, the reading teacher or the English teacher is seen as the sole agent for helping students become better readers. Because developing and using thinking permeates all learning, a responsibility this great must be shared by all teachers.

General Suggestions for Improving Comprehension

AUDITORY COMPREHENSION

Even though many of our students spend hours watching television or listening to the radio, auditory comprehension is still a problem, something to be learned. One important reason is that students have learned to listen selectively, quickly tuning out what they do not wish to hear. Another reason is that "individuals vary greatly in their relative ability to comprehend by listening and by reading."[13] This being the case, if our classroom activities are out of balance, favoring one learning modality or instructional methodology over another, some students will inevitably suffer. We need to include oral language as part of our planning for student learning.

We can assist our students in improving their auditory comprehension by providing activities that require frequent use of listening skills. One such activity is dictation. A short passage of fiction or nonfiction dictated to students once or twice a week offers them the opportunity to sharpen their listening skills and auditory comprehension. By judicious selection of literature passages for dictation, you can give your students extensive practice with varied sentence patterns and usage fundamentals. You might select sentences from literature to dictate that

1. illustrate different sentence patterns.
2. contain prepositional phrases.
3. contain comparative adjectives.
4. contain correctly used pronoun cases.
5. illustrate standard English usage.
6. illustrate the correct placement of adverbs.

7. contain possessive nouns and pronouns.
8. illustrate the rules of capitalization.
9. illustrate punctuation marks.
10. use vocabulary words in context.
11. are compound.
12. are complex.
13. illustrate subject–verb agreement.
14. illustrate pronoun–antecedent agreement.
15. illustrate various verb tenses.
16. contain homophones.
17. contain indefinite pronouns.
18. contain sensory details.
19. contain synonyms for words such as "say" and "walk."
20. contain similes and metaphors.[14]

After you have finished dictating the sentences, give students time to process what they have heard. They can analyze the dictation passage for the rules of grammar and usage implied and for the logic of structure and organization. They can also practice writing their own sentences, using the dictated sentences as models. Through such activities, students are directly engaged in improving comprehension and thinking as well as writing abilities.

Dictate literature selections to your students that represent varied types of writing, both fiction and nonfiction. Through careful attention to your choices, you can also introduce your students to interesting and rewarding books, short stories, poems, and essays. To fit with your course objectives, you might choose dictation selections that

1. contain descriptive material.
2. show how suspense is created.
3. demonstrate point of view.
4. illustrate tone.
5. show the use of slang.
6. provide meanings of words and phrases from context.
7. can be rewritten in modern English.
8. give a fresh or unusual view of something ordinary.
9. contain examples of dialogue.
10. illustrate denotation and connotation.[15]

After dictating these selections, have your students analyze them for content and style. They might also try to infer what led to your choice of each selection. Give them time to write short analyses or reactions for each selection. You might read the full literature selection together after student interest has been piqued.

Another useful strategy for auditory comprehension is the game Twenty Questions. Divide the class into two teams. Each side has twenty questions to ask in trying to identify a person, place, or thing selected by the other side. All questions must be framed so that they can be answered simply either "Yes" or "No." Through the process of narrowing and defining their questions to get the correct answer, students learn the value of listening carefully and focusing their questions based on each new bit of information. Thus, listening links clearly with thinking. After your students become more adept at questioning, you will probably find you need to reduce the number of questions to twelve.

To offer still another type of auditory experience to your students, read a descriptive poem that has strong imagery of mood and place, for example, "The Highway Man." Then have students draw pictures of the scenes or settings suggested by the poem. As they compare their creations, students will gain an understanding of how their fellow students imagined the scenes from the poem.

You can also read a story to the class, omitting the opening and closing passages. Have students suggest beginnings and endings based on what they heard. Then read the author's version as students compare their ideas with the original. More comprehension occurs as they study their ideas, hear those suggested by other students, and listen to the author's writing. Such listening comprehension activities support reading comprehension.

READING COMPREHENSION

Learning researchers have found both a high and positive correlation between listening comprehension and reading comprehension. Generally, the good listener tends to be a good reader. The learning activities we have already looked at for improving our students' auditory comprehension lead naturally into suggestions for enhancing reading comprehension.

Comprehension Corner

One idea for helping students who encounter difficulties with reading comprehension is creating a comprehension corner in your classroom. This is a place where special exercises and materials for comprehension development are available for students to use on an individual basis. For example, you could have crossword puzzles based on vocabulary from books currently being read in the class. Include cloze exercises, where students fill in blanks in a selected passage from literature. Audiotapes of short passages can be followed by various levels of comprehension questions for students to answer. Students can be assigned to this area or go voluntarily when they have time for extra study. Take special pains to provide high-interest materials for this area and change them frequently.

Comprehension Development Day

Another way to highlight the importance of comprehension is observing a special comprehension development day on a regular basis. This is a day devoted to exploring a wide variety of activities for increasing reading comprehension. Here is a chance to apply some of the comprehension skills from Bloom's taxonomy. You might try such activities as these:

- Have students paraphrase short passages from literature.
- Have students write a character sketch of an important character from a story or book.
- Select a difficult passage of poetry or prose and discuss its meaning in depth with students.
- Pair students and have them explain and discuss confusing passages from books or stories.
- Bring in guest speakers to provide additional information about scientific, mathematical, and historical concepts.

You can choose some of these activities, but let your students suggest others that they think would be useful as you conduct classroom research on comprehension together. You might team with another teacher so both of your classes participate. This expands the area for involvement throughout two classrooms. Try it!

Skill Attack

Still another idea for stressing comprehension growth is to declare occasional skill attacks. These occur during the silent-reading period. Select a specific comprehension skill and present a quick, short instructional exercise. Skills such as finding the key words, getting the meaning of words from the context, deriving root words and word families, and identifying syntactical relationships lend themselves to these brief, intense lessons. As soon as the "attack" is over, students resume their assigned reading.

Listing

Listing is also a useful activity for your students to perform as they are reading. Many different topics lend themselves to listing, but don't assign more than one list at a time. Students might list

- things learned about a particular place or period of time.
- good and bad influences on a character.
- good and bad experiences of a character.
- ways a character is like you.

- problems encountered by a character.
- strange or unusual happenings.

Have your students generate other ideas that they might like to try. After your students have finished reading a book and compiling their lists, give them time to process these lists. What did they learn from making the lists? What inferences can they draw about a character or the book itself? Listing is a simple device for turning passive readers into more active ones.

Selecting

Another valuable way of involving students actively is selecting. After they have finished reading a story or book, you can ask them to select certain things, defending their choices orally or in writing. Assure your students that they are not in a guessing game with you over the "right" choices. You simply expect them to make selections and defend their reasons for their choices. The following is a list of a dozen possible elements to select from a story or book:

- Three most important incidents
- Three most interesting incidents
- Three most important sentences (in a story)
- Three most interesting sentences (in a story)
- Three most unbelievable incidents
- Three funniest incidents
- Three saddest incidents
- Three most surprising incidents
- Three most frustrating incidents
- Three most boring incidents
- Three most frightening incidents
- Three well-written passages

As the class grows familiar with this activity, your list could be expanded considerably. Remember, you want your students first to summarize the incidents selected and then to give reasons for their choices. Your own familiarity with specific stories and books will assist you in knowing appropriate elements to assign.

The Reading Log

This final activity for improving reading comprehension is actually one that many students have already experienced: note taking. Keeping a reading log, however, gives note taking a new slant. The log is an excellent device for student interaction with literature before you present your instructional agenda for the material. What you want students to record in their logs should not be a summary of the book's plot. Instead, the log entries should be made up of the students' questions, comments, and opinions about their reading matter. This sample page is from a student's reading log on *The Catcher in the Rye*:

p. 9 I love how he casually says his parents will be irritated about him being expelled.

p. 9 It's funny how people make things more obvious and notice-able by trying to hide them.

p. 11 It's funny how you feel like you can't get any lower, then your teacher starts saying he doesn't want to fail you or you aren't the type of guy that should fail and then you feel lower. Does Holden really think all teachers are phonies?

p. 12 Holden is really a screwed up guy if he doesn't mind that he's failing.

p. 13 I hate when people ask me how I feel when I've really screwed up. How do they think I should feel? I feel like the pimple on the butt of humanity!

p. 14 I think Holden creates phonies. Does he wonder if he's one himself?

p. 15 Holden sounds like he's in more of a rut than a phase.

p. 16 Holden is your average liar. You can tell he is lying and he thinks he's great and that makes him average.

p. 16 I don't think being a mortician would be a very interesting ca-reer. They make a killing on a good funeral, but I like jobs where I can be with people, but only live people.

p. 17 I don't like it when people spell out exactly what you should do just because it happens to work for them.

p. 17 It's strange how it's always easier to remember something that is rude or crude rather than something that is good. Did the writer of this book have a bad childhood?

p. 18 I think it would be nice to live in a dorm and go to a boarding school.[16]

As you can see, what this student has written is more interesting to read than the usual summarizing notes. The thinking involved in writing the notes is also more valuable for the student's skill development. You can assign a specific number of pages of notes for each story or book. The reading log serves as a way to involve your students with stories and books and as a basis for discussion of reading assignments during individual conferences between your students and you. It can also be useful in small-group discussions of the same book by students.

Be patient, your students will get better with their reading logs as they practice note taking and as they share ideas with other students. Besides the sorts of notes included in the example, you can encourage them to write questions about unfamiliar words or phrases, character behaviors, plot developments, and aspects of style.

If your students protest that keeping the reading log slows them down and lessens their enjoyment of reading, tell them just to note on a sheet of paper the page numbers they want to take notes from and go on with their reading. They can also put check marks in the book in pencil and then erase these as they write their notes upon finishing their reading.

Tell your students that they don't have to write a note for every single page of the book. They may take two or three notes from some pages and then read several without taking any notes at all. After all, it is your intent to get a sampling of their thinking processes as they read, and the reading log provides a visual representation of that process for them and you. Discuss the value of the log for developing student thinking and comprehension, and both they and you will find the reading log a worthwhile learning activity.

SAFE DEMONSTRATION LESSON PLANS

On the following pages, you will find several SAFE Demonstration Lesson Plans, which demonstrate strategies for extending both auditory and reading comprehension skills.

SAFE Demonstration Lesson Plan 7.1: Quiet Argument
Grade Levels: 4–12

OBJECTIVES

Students will

1. express their views on an important or controversial issue.
2. recognize an opposing view's points of argumentation.

BRIEF DESCRIPTION

Students analyze current issues, examining both pro and con arguments. Then, they work in pairs to argue in writing about a selected issue. After reading the full argument, students summarize the points made by their opponents.

PROCEDURES

Stimulus

Brainstorm with your class current issues or problems about which people have strong feelings. List these on the board. Have two or three students role play a typical argument that might occur based on one of these issues. Stop after three minutes and then discuss the elements of the mock argument. After you have elicited a number of these, tell students they are going to argue in pairs, but they are going to do it without speaking a word aloud.

Activity

Pair the students and have them take two sheets of paper for their arguments. Have each pair select one of the issues from the board. Tell them to decide which side each will take for the sake of arguing the issue. After each has chosen a position on the issue, give students time to think of several arguments for their point of view. Then tell them to move their desks together and start the argument. Arguments will be written on the paper they are using with each student reading and responding to the others' arguments as they swap the papers back and forth. The argument ends when both sheets are full. Students should write only two or three sentences during each swap of the papers. They are to do this silently with no oral comment. Stress the importance of their presenting the best reasons they know in support of their position and of reading carefully so they fully comprehend the opponent's position.

Follow-Up

After all students have completed their arguments, tell them each to take a clean sheet of paper and, in summary form, restate their opponent's argumentation from memory. When they have finished, have students reread the original arguments they wrote to see if they included most of the arguments.

Evaluation

Collect their papers, both the original two sheets of argumentation and the two sheets of summary of the opponent's argumentation. Assign two grades: one for the thoroughness of their argumentation in the first part of the activity and a second for the quality of their summaries. Read some of the more interesting arguments to the entire class before returning the papers.

SAFE Demonstration Lesson Plan 7.2: Talk Back to an Author*
Grade Levels: 4–12

OBJECTIVES

Students will

1. locate the important point in each sentence of an author's essay on a timely subject.
2. express an opinion of their own about each sentence.
3. explain what they learned from talking back to an author.

BRIEF DESCRIPTION

Students respond sentence by sentence to an essay written about a timely topic. They share the expanded essays in small groups. Then, they evaluate the work of their peers based on an established rubric on which all have agreed.

PROCEDURES

Stimulus

Select a paragraph from a newspaper or magazine column written by a featured columnist on a subject of general interest. Put the paragraph on an overhead transparency, leaving room after each sentence to write in a response. Go through the paragraph sentence by sentence with the class, first reading each sentence carefully for its meaning and then writing in a response to each sentence. The responses may express agreement, disagreement, or additional information on the same idea. Tell the class that this is a way of talking back to an author.

Activity

Let each student select a short essay to read and respond to in the manner demonstrated to the class. Have a number of magazines, newspapers, and books on hand to give students a variety of choices. After all have chosen, tell them they are to copy each sentence from the essay, think about its meaning or implication, and then write a response for it. Tell students that their responses must be in complete sentences and should indicate that they have understood each sentence. Give students time to complete

---

*This lesson is adapted from an idea by Toby Lurie, a San Francisco poet and educator, which he calls conversation poems.

the assignment completely. Move about the room and assist with clarification of vocabulary or ideas as needed.

Follow-Up

Group students by fours and have them share their efforts by passing their papers around their groups. Have them select one paper from each group to be shared with the rest of the class. After this sharing, ask students to turn their papers over and write an explanation of what they learned through this process of reading and responding. Collect their papers.

Evaluation

Evaluate the papers for both the quality of their responses to the author and the thoroughness of their explanations. Use a five-point scoring rubric and give each paper a numeric score. Share the rubric with students when you return their papers. Remind the students of these evaluation criteria immediately preceding a second assignment using this method.

SAFE Demonstration Lesson Plan 7.3: Do I Look Like a Toad?
Grade Levels: 8–12

OBJECTIVES

Students will

1. locate a piece of writing that has special significance for each of them.
2. paraphrase the ideas in the piece of writing they have each selected.
3. express in writing or orally why they selected the piece of writing.

BRIEF DESCRIPTION

Students select a short piece of writing that has special significance to them. They write a paraphrase of this writing, thus restating the thinking of another person. Speaking for themselves, students explain their reasons for enjoying the writing they selected.

PROCEDURES

Stimulus

Write this poem by Stephen Crane on the board or on an overhead transparency:

Think As I Think

"Think as I think," said a man,
"Or you are abominably wicked;
You are a toad."
And after I had thought of it,
I said, "I will, then, be a toad."

Discuss the poem with the class. Arrive at a general consensus about its meaning. Discuss why being a toad was preferable to the speaker. Ask the class for examples of times they had to refuse to think the way someone else did, of times when they willingly chose to be "toads."

Activity

Let each student look through a number of books to find a short piece of writing—poem, paragraph, or short essay—that for some reason has special significance for him or her. After each student has chosen, ask students to write a paraphrase of their selected piece of writing. You might need to conduct a brief lesson on paraphrasing at this point or review this skill. Explain that paraphrasing is, in a sense, a way of thinking as someone else thinks but in your own words. Give them time to write their paraphrases. Ask some students to share their writing with the class.

Follow-Up

Now that they have become "toads," ask students to make a choice about how they wish to explain why they chose the piece of writing they did. They may explain orally or in writing. The point is to make it clear precisely what struck them or appealed to them in the piece they chose. Let students have time to prepare their explanations. Have those who wish to give theirs orally present theirs first, then have those who wrote read to the class. Take a class vote on the three that were most convincing.

Evaluation

Assign points for both the paraphrases and the explanations. Take into consideration the difficulty of the paraphrased material. Because this is a comprehension activity, check the quality of comprehension reflected in the paraphrase.

SAFE Demonstration Lesson Plan 7.4: That's Not the Way I Saw It!
Grade Levels: 4–12

OBJECTIVES

Students will

1. observe a scene from a television show or movie.
2. describe what they saw when they watched the scene.
3. cite reasons or details to show why their descriptions are accurate.

BRIEF DESCRIPTION

Students observe a scene selected from a television show or movie. After viewing the scene, they attempt to describe the scene as accurately as possible. Students compare their descriptions, filling in details. Then, they view the scene again to check on accuracy.

PROCEDURES

Stimulus

Select a seven- to ten-minute scene from a television show or movie to tape-record for student viewing. Select a scene that has a fairly high level of complexity in terms of character revelation and/or plot development. Have the tape ready to play. Ask your students about memorable scenes they have watched on television or in movies. List the characteristics that made these scenes especially vivid to students. Then tell them you want them to watch a scene you have selected so they can describe it accurately after it is over.

Activity

Play the videotape. After it is over, remind them of the list of characteristics on the board. Have them describe the scene they watched, giving as many specific details as they can remember. They should each do this in writing. After students have finished, ask the first one done to read her or his account. Then ask the last one to read hers or his. Tell the rest of the class to compare their accounts with the two that were read. Fill in any important details omitted from these accounts. Divide the class into three groups. Give each group a different reason for your selection of the scene; keep these reasons secret from the other groups. One of the three reasons you give should be authentic and the other two should be false. Let each group have time to argue for the validity of its reason to the other two groups.

Follow-Up

After each of the three groups has made its presentation, replay the video-tape, stopping it briefly from time to time to focus on details brought out by each of the groups. After it is completed, have the class vote for which of the three reasons is the authentic one. Then tell them which one actually was correct. If students guessed the wrong one, discuss why this happened.

Evaluation

Award a prize or privilege to the group that made the most convincing presentation. Collect the individual descriptions and assign grades based on the level of comprehension reflected in each paper.

SAFE Demonstration Lesson Plan 7.5: Comprehension Circle
Grade Levels: 6–12

OBJECTIVES

Students will

1. locate the most important ideas in a series of stories from the front page of a newspaper.
2. restate these ideas into a condensed version of the paper's front page.
3. create a found poem by combining their selected ideas into a poetic unity.

BRIEF DESCRIPTION

Students analyze the ideas in stories that appear on the front page of a newspaper. Selecting key words from the stories, they rewrite the page in condensed form. Afterward, students create found poems based on the key information presented.

PROCEDURES

Stimulus

Collect front pages of a number of different newspapers. Go over the headlines of the different stories from one of these front pages with your class. Have students speculate about the content of the stories based on what the headlines say. Then pick one of the stories and read it aloud. Have students write down key words and phrases from the story as you read. Write their selected words and phrases on the board. Read these aloud and discuss whether they convey the sense of the original story.

Activity

Group students by fives and have a representative from each group select one of the front pages to work with on this activity. Tell the groups to divide up the stories from the front page they are using among the members of the group. They are to read their assigned stories and select key words and phrases as in the stimulus activity. Then, students are to use these selections to write a condensed version of each of the stories on their front pages. When they have finished, tell students to compare their new version of the front page with the original. Were they able to create an impressionistic version of the original? Ask one member from each group to tell the other groups about their "new" front page.

Follow-Up

Next, have each group take their condensed front page and randomly extract whichever words or phrases suit their fancies. Then, they should create a found poem by combining these selections into a pleasing poetic form. (You may need to explain *found poem* and give some examples.) Share these aloud when all students have finished.

Evaluation

Evaluate each group's efforts separately. The emphasis with the activity is on comprehension. Create a comprehension scale of one to eight and judge the condensed versions of the front pages against the original in terms of the level of understanding and thoroughness represented in each. Discuss each group's strengths and weaknesses with them. Decide on an attractive way of displaying the found poems and display them for all the class to view.

SUMMARY

To quote an old proverb, "He who would climb the ladder must begin at the bottom." You can help your students climb the ladder toward higher-level thinking by getting them started confidently on the comprehension rungs. This chapter explored the meaning of comprehension and its levels. We have seen that research indicates an urgent need for more intensive instruction in comprehension skills. We have looked at the necessary link between reading and thinking skills. Also, we have examined the connection between listening comprehension and reading comprehension. One truth emerges above all others: Comprehension is synonymous with thinking. We can assist students by providing scaffolding as they ascend the rungs of this ladder.

CHALLENGE

1. The following is a guideline for improving reading comprehension instruction:

> Teachers should encourage all children to utilize their higher level cognitive abilities by systematically planning instructional experiences which introduce and invite children to try a variety of reading comprehension strategies such as storying, visualizing, inferencing, summarizing, generalizing, and drawing conclusions based on intuition, the information in the text, and logic.[17]

Evaluate your own efforts at reading comprehension instruction based on this guideline and assign yourself a grade. Explain your "grade" to a friend or fellow teacher.

2. Select a novel you plan to teach. Read this novel while keeping a dialectical journal with pages lined in columns, thus:

Page	Author's ideas	My ideas

After every page or two, jot down comments and questions in each column. These ideas will be useful in creating learning activities for your students as they read the same novel.

Your students can also keep a dialectical journal as they read a novel. For younger students, ask them to copy a quotation from the novel after every other page and to respond to that quotation. This enjoyable way of checking on comprehension gives students specific things to discuss in small groups.

NOTES

1. Roger W. Shuy, "What the Teacher Knows Is More Important Than Text or Test," *Language Arts* 58, no. 8 (Nov./Dec. 1981): 928.
2. R. David Pearson, "A Context for Instructional Research on Reading Comprehension," in *Promoting Reading Comprehension*, ed. James Flood (Newark, Del.: International Reading Association, 1984).
3. Thomas C. Barrett, "Goals of the Reading Program: The Basis for Evaluation," cited in "Developing Questions That Promote Comprehension: The Story Map," by Isabel Beck and Margaret McKeown. *Language Arts* 58, no. 8 (Nov./Dec. 1981): 914.
4. Nancy L. Roser, "Teaching and Testing Reading Comprehension: An Historical Perspective on Instructional Research and Practices," in *Promoting Reading Comprehension*, ed. James Flood (Newark, Del.: International Reading Association, 1984).
5. Pearson, "A Context for Instructional Research on Reading Comprehension," 3; citing studies by Neilsen, 1977; Omason, 1978; Stein and Glenn, 1977; Thorndyke, 1977.
6. Pearson, "A Context for Instructional Research on Reading Comprehension," 5; citing studies by Mandler, 1977; Stein and Glenn, 1977; Thorndyke, 1977.
7. Pearson, "A Context for Instructional Research on Reading Comprehension," 7; citing studies by Day, 1980; Gordon and Pearson, in press; Hansen and Pearson, 1980; Raphael and Pearson; Tharp, 1980.
8. Louise Rosenblatt, *The Reader, the Text, the Poem: The Transactional Theory of the Literary Work* (Urbana, Ill.: NCTE, 1978).
9. Jo Stanchfield, in a speech to members of the Central California Council of Teachers of English at Asilomar, Calif., 1984.
10. H. Alan Robinson, "A Cluster of Skills: Especially for Junior High School," in *The Improvement of Reading*, ed. Ruth Strang, Constance McCullough, and Arthur Traxler (New York: McGraw-Hill, 1967).
11. "Desired Outcomes in Developing Inferential Skills," a handout at a South Bay Writing Project summer workshop, not attributed as to authorship, California State University, San Jose.
12. "Comprehension Skills and Thinking Instruction," a handout at a South Bay Writing Project summer workshop, not attributed as to authorship, California State University, San Jose.
13. Ruth Strang, Constance McCullough, and Arthur Traxler, *The Improvement of Reading* (New York: McGraw-Hill, 1967), 29.
14. "Dictation," a handout at a South Bay Writing Project summer workshop, not attributed as to authorship, California State University, San Jose.
15. "Dictation," California State University, San Jose.
16. From a student's reading log for *The Catcher in the Rye*, Gilroy High School, Gilroy, Calif., 1985. Used with permission.
17. "Guidelines for Improving Reading Comprehension Instruction," a handout at a conference on critical thinking, source not attributed, authorship by committee for California State Department of Education, 1986.

EXPLORING FURTHER

Flood, James, ed. *Promoting Reading Comprehension*. Newark, Del.: International Reading Association, 1984.

Jensen, Julie, ed. *Composing and Comprehending*. Urbana, Ill.: National Council of Teachers of English, 1985.

Mallick, David, Peter Moss, and Ian Hansen, eds. *New Essays in the Teaching of Literature*. Australian Association for the Teaching of English Inc., 1982.

Page, William D., and Gay Su Pinnell. *Teaching Reading Comprehension*. Bloomington, Ind.: ERIC Clearinghouse on Reading and Communication Skills; and Urbana, Ill.: National Council of Teachers of English, 1979.

Russell, David H., and Etta E. Karp. *Reading Aids Through the Grades*. New York: Bureau of Publications, Teachers College, Columbia University, 1961.

Strang, Ruth, Constance C. McCullough, and Arthur Traxler. *The Improvement of Reading*. New York: McGraw-Hill, 1967.

Ungerleider, Dorothy Fink. *Reading, Writing, and Rage: The Terrible Price Paid by Victims of School Failure*. Jalmar Press, 1985.

A series of writing assignments is a
series of thinking assignments and
therefore a sequence of internal
operations.
James Moffett

Clear thinking becomes clear
writing: One can't exist
without the other.
William Zinsser

Writing is the basic stuff of
education. It has been sorely
neglected in our schools.
Donald H. Graves

. . . Writing can be a powerful process for
discovering meaning rather than just
transcribing an idea that is in some sense
waiting fully developed in the writer's
mind.
Arthur N. Applebee

I don't know
what I think
until I see what
I've said.
E. M. Forster

CHAPTER 8

Composing Thinking

Objectives

After reading this chapter, you will be able to

- *Design lessons that use the writing process at each stage.*
- *Organize a writing continuum, which includes the basic modes of discourse, for your class.*

Thinking and writing are synonymous. Effective school writing programs incorporate this truism into the very core of their structure. They ensure that writing is a means of learning in all curriculum areas and provide a wide range of writing experiences in all subject matter areas. They build on students' interests and on their reading and oral language experiences. Such programs help students discover that writing is a way of learning about themselves and about the world, of developing thinking skills, of generating new ideas, and of helping them to survive in an increasingly complicated society.[1]

With the advent of such efforts as the National Writing Project, the National Center for Research in Writing, and other writing centers across the country, research about writing processes has generated a large body of common knowledge:

- Teachers already know much about which practices in teaching the writing process are effective.
- The act of writing, in and of itself, does not necessarily improve the quality of a student's writing.
- Praising what students do well improves their writing more than correction of what they do badly.
- The language arts are interrelated and are more difficult to learn when they are taught in isolation from each other.

The latest work by researchers focuses on the process of writing itself and less on teacher behavior and writing as a finished product. While the

writing process is of central concern to any writing program, so is awareness of the various modes of discourse in which one writes. This chapter
is concerned with both the writing process and modes of discourse.

The Writing Process

The writing process includes several complex stages, or phases, including
prewriting, drafting, responding, revising, evaluating, and postwriting.
All stages are not included in every lesson nor must stages always be
followed in any particular order. Students and teachers need awareness
of the recursive nature of the writing process. For example, during the
writing stage, some students might edit for the conventions of writing
(spelling, punctuation, grammar, usage) as they proceed with composing
their ideas. Still others and many of the former will revise again later
after they participate in response groups or receive feedback from the
teacher to what they have written.

DEFINING THE STAGES OF WRITING

The first stage of the writing process is, of course, prewriting. This stage
includes any experience, activity, or exercise that stimulates a person to
write. It can generate material and ideas as well as focus a writer's attention on a particular subject. Prewriting moves writers from thinking
about a writing task to the act of writing. The "Stimulus" part of this
book's SAFE demonstration lessons, particularly in this chapter, illustrate prewriting.

Composing a first draft, the second stage of the writing process, involves the writer in narrowing his or her thinking to include only the
subject at hand. It is therefore necessarily a synthesis of the writer's experiences. Writing entails identifying a purpose and an audience for whom
the written piece is intended; however, only after students have developed fluency as writers will they be able to consider fully the needs of
their audience and the purpose for which they are writing.

Response or reaction from a reader or listener represents the third
stage of the writing process. Responses are usually expressed through
questions, suggestions, and statements to the writer about the content or
form of what was written. The responder can be a teacher, a peer, a group,
a holistic scoring team, or anyone who responds to a piece of writing. At
this stage, writers often can clarify their ideas and purposes and eliminate
many mechanical errors that block reader comprehension.

Revision or editing, the fourth stage of the writing process, allows writers to "resee" and "rethink" their writing. Such matters as unity, development, order, clarity, emphasis, word choice, and organization are the major issues. As stated earlier, this stage is recursive in that it takes place during writing, rewriting, reading, and rereading. It is through editing that students learn how to improve their writing.

Editing continues in the refinement stage of the writing process. Errors in grammar, usage, capitalization, punctuation, spelling, paragraphing, and syllabication are corrected. Taking editing a step further leads to concerns such as diction, syntax, accuracy of text, and proper manuscript form. Peers, teachers, tutors, aides, and parents may assist in the editing process.

Developing skill with the conventions of writing can occur at any time during the writing process. For example, vocabulary is often expanded during prewriting activities such as brainstorming and clustering. Concerns about usage and grammar are key factors during the revision stage. Spelling and punctuation usually are taught as part of editing. Learning grammatical analysis, usage, and other conventions makes little sense to students until they are engaged in the act of writing.

Evaluation, the final stage of the writing process, is only one aspect of the activities following actual writing. As such it needs to be kept in perspective. Evaluation must be used to support, not thwart, growth in writing. Analytical scoring, holistic scoring, and primary trait scoring are three methods that are used to evaluate writing for different purposes. Analytical scoring entails evaluation of the strengths and weaknesses of specific areas such as punctuation, syntax, grammar, paragraph development, and organization. Holistic scoring is used to judge writing as an entity. It focuses on the overall effectiveness of the piece, rather than on the strength or weakness of one part. Primary trait scoring looks for characteristics of a particular genre. This might include such features as tone or vocabulary appropriate for a given audience.

Postwriting, a final and important stage of the writing process, includes all the activities that can be done with a finished piece of writing. For example, it can be charted, illustrated, posted, published, mailed, discarded, or even saved. Making students aware of the postwriting activities planned or possible during the prewriting stage motivates students and gives them a sense of audience.

There are, of course, several types of writing assignments that purposely do not include certain parts of the writing process. Journal writing or other brief fluency writing assignments may not require as much attention to each of the stages as does essay writing or narrative writing. Nevertheless, conscious efforts should be made to provide students with experiences in each of the stages of the writing process.

SAFE DEMONSTRATION LESSON PLANS

The three SAFE Demonstration Lesson Plans that follow demonstrate all stages of the writing process and show how to apply the information in this section directly to your classroom.

SAFE Demonstration Lesson Plan 8.1: The Signs of Spring
Grade Levels: 4–10

OBJECTIVES

Students will

1. recall experiences.
2. categorize pictures taken of family and friends, of places of interest, and of natural objects and scenes.
3. discuss why some pictures are the most memorable.
4. identify the features of authentic Japanese haiku.
5. record signs of spring by taking notes on a walk around the school grounds and selecting items from their lists of signs that would make good subject matter for haikus.
6. emulate the characteristics of traditional haikus.
7. create pen names for themselves.

BRIEF DESCRIPTION

The traditional haiku form of three lines, five-seven-five syllables, has been so simplistically taught that the intended content of a good haiku has all but been forgotten in many instances in the classroom. Thus, as in this lesson, a return to the examples by the masters of this art is essential. This lesson combines sensory notation of nature (the ingredients of haiku) with a thorough grounding in the basics of rich traditional haiku. Students take notes based on the signs of spring, fall, or winter, depending on the season, that will later be used to write haiku.

PROCEDURES

Stimulus

Ask students if they have ever taken pictures while on a vacation. What were some of the sights and scenes snapped, aside from people? Elicit several responses, listing them on the board. What pictures are usually the most memorable ones? (Establish the idea that glimpses of nature, often in a very simple state, furnish the ingredients of many prized photos.)

Read the following haikus aloud at least twice. In addition, display them on the board or a transparency.

This fall of new snow
that sags my hat is my own
and it's light as down.
KIKAKU

Wake up, old sleepy
Butterfly! Come, come with me
On my pilgrimage!
BASHO

Out of the sky, geese
Come honking in the spring's cold
Early-morning light.
SOIN

Ask students the following questions about these haikus:

1. What is the season of the year in these haikus?
2. How do you know?
3. Is there optimism in any of these poems?
4. What verb tense are these poems written in?
5. How many syllables are there in each line?
6. Is the poet a participant in any of these poems?

Depending on the particular haiku examples used, various other characteristics can be elicited, such as a sense of wonder, surprise, and humor and the frequent use of a mixed sensory image (for example, "flowers chimed a peal of fragrance").

Some Possible Characteristics of Haiku

- Seasonal references
- Optimistic outlook
- Present tense
- Five-seven-five syllables
- Poet is a participant
- A sense of wonder
- A sense of surprise
- Humor
- Mixed sensory images

Activity

When all the major characteristics of a good haiku have been established, take the class for a brief walk around the school yard (fifteen to twenty minutes). Each student should carry paper and pencil and should observe and list the signs of the current season. Upon returning to the classroom, go around the room and have each student recite a sign aloud. Some may be willing to share their entire list.

Review the characteristics of haiku poetry. Display the list students compiled. Have students write haiku using their observation notes and modeled after traditional haikus.

Follow-Up

Have students select their best haikus for "publishing" on a bulletin board. Provide plain 5 × 8-inch index cards for each student. Obtain calligraphy pens and ink and provide a few lessons in calligraphy so students can write their best haiku on the cards in calligraphy.

Have students make up a Japanese pen name for themselves using the first two letters of their first and last names: for example, Ralph Samuels would be RASA or Margaret Tupper, MATU. Sometimes the last letters work better, or more than the first two are needed to make a phoneme. A Deborah Schlinkledorf could simply be DEBBA.

Because a major characteristic of haiku is that it is seasonal, have the class prepare haiku calendars for the whole year or a portion of it. These make good Mother's Day presents. Duplicated calendar graphs can be distributed to each student. Artistic embellishments or pictures cut from magazines can be added to each calendar page to complement the haiku.

Evaluation

Grade haikus on a point system:

- Proper form (five-seven-five syllables) = ten points
- Seasonal content = ten points
- Optimistic tone = ten points
- Present tense = ten points
- Poet participates = ten points
- Sense of wonder = ten points
- Sense of surprise = ten points
- Humor = ten points
- Mixed image = ten points
- Pen name = ten points

Some students will create much better haikus than others, no matter how thorough the instruction is. Therefore, being objective about grading removes you from judging this very personal kind of writing.

SAFE Demonstration Lesson Plan 8.2: At One with Nature
Grade Levels: 4–12

OBJECTIVES

Students will

1. listen to a poem read by the teacher.
2. observe an object of nature.
3. imagine themselves to be on a fantasy trip, which involves the object, led by the teacher.
4. compare meditative experiences with others in the class.
5. create a poem, essay, story, sketch, or other short piece based on the natural object and/or their experience of it.

BRIEF DESCRIPTION

The teacher brings a natural object such as a piece of driftwood to class to use as the focal point for a meditation exercise. The main purpose of the lesson is to help students learn to focus as entirely as possible on one thing and to thereby bring their own creative energies to a peak. A segment of Walt Whitman's poetry sets the mood followed by a teacher-led fantasy exploration of the object. After a short discussion, students write a short piece that relates to the object imaginatively.

PROCEDURES

Stimulus

Bring in a small branch, an interesting large rock, a shell (a chambered nautilus would be perfect), a piece of driftwood with an unusual shape, or some other natural object.

After placing the object in front of the room where everyone can view it easily, tell the class that you are going to conduct them through a simple meditation exercise. To set the mood, ask students to close their eyes as you slowly read such quotations as the following, selected to stimulate their imaginations:

This moment yearning and thoughtful sitting alone;
It seems to me there are other men in other lands yearning and thoughtful,
It seems to me I can look over and behold them in Germany, Italy, France, Spain,
Or far, far away, in China, or in Russia or Japan, talking other dialects,

And it seems to me if I could know those other men I should become
    attached to them as I do to men in my own lands,
O I know we should be brethren and lovers,
I know I should be happy with them.

WALT WHITMAN

Poems don't just happen. They are luckily or stealthily related
to a readiness within ourselves. When we read or hear them,
we react. We aren't just supposed to react—any poem that asks
for a dutiful response is masquerading as a poem, not being
one. A good rule is—don't respond unless you have to. But
when you find you do have a response—trust it. It has a
meaning.

WILLIAM STAFFORD[2]

Instruct everyone to center their focus on the object. Ask them to
gaze steadily at the object with the idea in mind that they are making a
time-lapse photograph of it. Every detail of the object will be recorded in
their picture. Do this for at least two minutes.

Have students close their eyes and look at their time-lapsed photo,
which is now recorded clearly in their "mind's eye." Suggest that they
allow their "eye" to travel freely around the perimeters of the object, up
and down each line in the driftwood or into each crevice of the rock.
Speaking softly, conduct them on a journey around and into the object.

Ask students to open their eyes for a few moments to compare their
time-lapse image one last time with the actual object. Tell them to close
their eyes when they feel satisfied and to continue meditating on the
object. Allow about one or two more minutes, depending on the level of
the class.

Activity

Ask students to share the various experiences that they had when meditating. Ask them whether they focused on the entire object or on only a
part, whether it was difficult to picture the object, and so forth.

Write on the board as the class brainstorms possible forms a piece of
writing might take: poems, essays, stories, sketches, and so on. Ask the
class to write about the object that they now know so well. Avoid stifling
this assignment by harnessing it with a particular form.

Follow-Up

Have students meet in response groups of three to five to read aloud and
exchange comments about the rough drafts they have written. Because a
variety of kinds of writing should come from this assignment, encourage

responses to focus on originality, singleness of purpose in each case, and individual style.

Have students revise and write their final drafts for "publication." Prepare a bulletin board display that contrasts the varied responses to this assignment.

Evaluation

Before posting the finished papers, have students evaluate them for originality, singleness of purpose, and style.

Note the degree of enthusiasm for this assignment. If students are willing to polish and revise their rough drafts for "publication," it might be worth repeating the assignment again with a different object.

The following creative responses were inspired by a piece of driftwood presented to an eighth-grade class.

The Driftwood

MIKE GEIMER

There's a piece of driftwood in the front of the room, the kind that has the look of an old Indian pueblo filled with activity. Indian women are carving buffalo into clothes and meat for the tired hunters returning from their day of following the herd of mustangs.

Some of the younger braves try to tie up the strong ponies the men have brought in. A baby cries and is instantly comforted by a soft blanket and warm fire.

The sun sets majestically as everyone gathers around the bonfire for a meal and many stories which will last long into the night.

Slowly, one by one, the group diminishes until only the aged chief is alone, left with only his own thoughts to listen to . . .

The image fades until only a lonely piece of driftwood is left.

The Giraffe

KIM HELBING

It's a giraffe.
It's a giraffe in the jungle
Eating from a tree.
It's a giraffe in the jungle
Looking at me.

I can see the look of fear in its eyes.
I can see its nose quivering in the air.

It seems to be saying,
"There is danger here.
Run for your life,
And run real fast,
For I, at least
Can see the danger."

It's a fire!
A fire, I say,
Hurry up and run for the bay!"

I too see the fire,
A wild blaze of smoke and heat
Racing across the mountain
And through the jungle.

Eating up everything with the heat of itself
Spreading itself all around
Trying desperately to gain more ground.

Now the elephants,
Beasts with water,
Are spraying the wild blaze
And extinguishing its life.

And the giraffe,
The one eating leaves,
Leaves no trace behind except its shape,
Its shadow against the last standing tree,
A tree made of wood.

SAFE Demonstration Lesson Plan 8.3: Talking to Time
Grade Levels: 8–12

OBJECTIVES

Students will

1. imagine what a conversation with an abstract noun would be like.
2. interpret the purpose and meanings in a poem.
3. identify other abstract nouns.
4. invent an exterior monologue with an abstract noun.

BRIEF DESCRIPTION

Poetry is used to introduce a new writing concept. Students have the choice of composing poetry or prose once they understand exterior monologue. The teacher first leads students in a close analysis of a poem and then brainstorms with them other variations of abstract nouns for possible topics in their own exterior monologues. Thus, students have an excellent model for writing their first exterior monologues.

PROCEDURES

Stimulus

Prepare copies of the following poem for each student.

Time, You Old Gipsy Man

RALPH HODGSON

Time, you old gipsy man,
  Will you not stay,
Put up your caravan
  Just for one day?

All things I'll give you
Will you be my guest,
Bells for your jennet
Of silver the best,
Goldsmiths shall beat you
A great golden ring,
Peacocks shall bow to you,
Little boys sing.
Oh, and sweet girls will
Festoon you with may,
Time, you old gipsy,
Why hasten away?
Last week in Babylon,
Last night in Rome,
Morning, and in the crush
Under Paul's dome;
Under Paul's dial
You tighten your rein—
Only a moment,
And off once again;
Off to some city
Now blind in the womb,
Off to another
Ere that's in the tomb.

Time, you old gipsy man,
  Will you not stay,
Put up your caravan
  Just for one day?

Ask the class to imagine what it would be like to have a conversation with Time. (Some will probably say that Time can't talk.) Explain that such a conversation then would actually be a monologue because the intended listener would not respond.

Tell the class that the poem you are going to read is a one-way conversation with Time. Ask students to listen to the poem as you read it to discover the speaker's purpose in talking to Time. Then read the poem.

Activity

Pass out copies of the poem to the class and reread it or have a student read it as the rest follow along. Discuss the following questions:

1. What was the speaker's purpose? (To get Time to stand still; to stop Time)
2. Why does the speaker want to stop Time? (Because Time makes life pass and end eventually)
3. Beginning with "Last week in Babylon," ask the class to explain what this verse means, which ends with the line, "Ere that's in the tomb." (Time passes by so quickly that one day is dead in one part of the world even before a new day is born in other places.)
4. Is the title "Old Gipsy Man" appropriate for Time? (Yes, because gipsies move on all the time too.)

Have members of the class brainstorm associations with other abstract nouns like Time. Love, Hate, War, Death, and Jealousy are a few examples you might use.

Follow-Up

Have members of the class create a one-way conversation or monologue with an abstract noun other than Time. Suggest that they use the following guide:

1. Decide what it is they want from the subject.
2. Invite the subject to behave in some way contrary to its usual pattern.
3. Think up some enticements to try and convince the subject to accept their invitation or suggestion.
4. Write a poem or monologue fulfilling these tasks.

"Publish" a class book of the completed monologues.

Evaluation

Include several comment pages in the front of the class book where readers may feel free to write their reactions to the poems and monologues. Ask other faculty members to read and comment on the monologues.

Display the booklet at an open house and encourage parents to write responses.

Use the first three steps of the guide above as grading criteria.

Modes of Discourse

Whereas the writing process provides the composition teacher with a format to follow, an understanding of the essential modes of discourse might be said to provide content. In *Active Voice*, James Moffett distills the relationship between writing and thinking through a progression of assignments that "externalize thinking processes—how people conceptualize and synthesize their accumulating experience. That's why the concept of abstraction is central. Abstracting is distilling."[3] As writers, we are constantly in the process of observing, selecting from our many perceptions, and "recapitulating in writing what goes on all the time anyway in our mental processes."[4]

Moffett believes that all writing teaches exposition and expresses ideas regardless of mode. He sees as a model for a composition course a single circle that gradually splits into three separate circles of first, second, and third persons and that eventually merely touch. If we think of these circles as representing a person talking to someone about any topic, the three basic segments of the writing curriculum—inner speech, dialogues/monologues, and narrative into essay—then the overlapping of one form of discourse into another makes sense. Moffett believes that all modes of writing must be taught, and he is critical of teachers who create an atmosphere of panic about teaching exposition. If students are not taught first to write monologues, dialogues, letters, diaries, and narratives, they will never learn how to write exposition.[5]

SAFE DEMONSTRATION LESSON PLANS

This section includes four SAFE Demonstration Lesson Plans inspired by the basic modes of discourse delineated by Moffett. Lesson Plan 8.4 begins with spontaneous inner speech, or first-person voice. Lesson Plan 8.5 deals with dialogue, or second-person voice, in a dramatic format. Lesson Plan 8.6 explores narrative writing and the relationship between narration and exposition. Lesson Plan 8.7 provides an opportunity for synthesis of several modes.

From Spontaneity to Composition

Students must become aware of their inner sensations, memories, thoughts, and feelings. They need to witness something first and then to compose meaning out of it. The lesson in this section begins with what

Moffett calls "noting down." Thus, students are engaged in a spontaneous activity during which they take notes that later become the material for a composed piece of writing.

SAFE Demonstration Lesson Plan 8.4: In Someone Else's Shoes
Grade Levels: 6–12

OBJECTIVES

Students will

1. observe a place from a selected point of view.
2. imagine sensory impressions from a selected point of view and record only those sensations.
3. select items for a composed piece of writing.
4. characterize the imagined person in his or her role as an observer.
5. invent a short piece in which the voice and tone of the speaker emulates the imagined role portrayed.

BRIEF DESCRIPTION

Students assume the role of a specific person observing their school. While walking around the school, students take notes using the senses of the person they select. During the walk, the teacher also takes a role and makes notations along with the students. The following day the class writes their point-of-view stories.

PROCEDURES

Stimulus

Tell the class that they are going to go for a walk around the school but that they are going to be "wearing someone else's shoes." Compile a list of the types of people who might have a reason for observing the school—parent, teacher, principal, vice principal, counselor, new student, foreign exchange student, superintendent, state official, board member, neighbor walking a dog, and so on.

Take the class on a fifteen-minute walk during which each takes notes from a selected point of view. For example, a parent might notice excess trash and loud classroom noise whereas a vice principal might be concerned about students who are out of class.

Upon returning to class, ask students to read aloud at least one of their notes.

Activity

Read aloud one or more of the short pieces that follow, examples of what an observer wrote:

The State Evaluator

Here I am at Stevenson Junior High. My job is to evaluate the school and note any changes needed. It's up to me to make sure the children of America learn all they can. There it is, surrounded by fences and gates, a prison-type atmosphere. So far, so good. The halls are empty, so I reason it is class time. Wait, I hear laughter coming from one of the rooms. That must be stopped. Kids are here to learn, not fool around. Now, around this corner here I hear the vice-principal yelling at two of the beasty kiddies. Ah! Music to my ears.

Now the bell is ringing. Hordes of the little runts are pouring into the halls. They shouldn't be acting like this. They should be neat and orderly. They seem to be all heading out to this large area full of basketball courts and crowding onto the benches. Now what is the vice-principal doing on the roof? It sure would be a shame if he fell off, wouldn't it? I'll have to see about building a guardtower in the middle.

JOHN

A Former Student

I sure feel funny walkin' up this hill again—well, there she is—my old alma mater—dear old Stevenson Junior High School. Never thought I'd say "dear" or consider this place with any kind of term of endearment. Same old cracks in the pathway leading up to the back playground—I remember how I used to imagine that my initials and those of the blond babe in my math class were together, "T.B. and J.S." Yeh, here it is, just like I remember it, but with lots more weeds in the cracks. Wonder what ever happened to old J.S. I thought she was the most perfect girl in the world—her hair was perfect, her clothes were just right, and her smile with her braces was so sweet. Oh well, that was just a fantasy. She's probably married and has four kids by now.

This fence is new around the school. So many vandals these days, I guess—not angels like we all were.

I wonder if any of my old teachers are still here. Ha! I spoke too soon. I hear Johnson booming forth in room 10. And here comes old man Barstow toward me. I'd better not remind him of who I am—just walk on by—whew!

Miss Pringle, Mrs. Dubury—they're still here too. Nothing's really changed.

TERRY

After reading each example, ask students to comment on the tone of each.

Tell students that they are to select from their list of notes those that sound appropriate for their chosen point-of-view role. Then have them write rough drafts of short point-of-view pieces.

Follow-Up

Form response groups of three to five students and have each "author" in turn read aloud to the others in the small group. Tell students to restrict their comments to appropriateness of observations and tone for a particular role.

Have students make revisions, additions, and deletions to their rough drafts; then have students write final drafts of their revised papers. Before accepting final drafts, require each student to have his or her paper read by two other persons (students, parents, siblings) and signed by each. (The purpose here is twofold: to create an expanded audience and to perhaps incidentally, cut down on some of the mechanical errors.)

Evaluation

Grade the finished papers for selection of content and tone appropriate to the chosen point-of-view role.

"Publish" these writings by posting them on the bulletin board for other classes to read and enjoy. Finally, encourage students to submit well-written, clever point-of-view pieces to the school newspaper as features.

From Duologue to Monologue

There are many kinds of prewriting activities that can facilitate these types of writing. In general, these involve transcribing taped conversations, simple interviews, impromptu drama activities, and surveys, which collect oral information such as jokes, riddles, and so forth, that can be either recorded and transcribed or simply written down in an interview fashion.

The lesson in this section samples one of Moffett's ideas, that of the duologue. Moffett's further progression into exterior and interior monologues and one-act plays would be a natural extension of this beginning. (See SAFE Demonstration Lesson Plan 8.3 for a lesson using exterior monologue.)

SAFE Demonstration Lesson Plan 8.5: Budding Playwrights
Grade Levels: 4–9

OBJECTIVES

Students will

1. imagine a conversation between two unrelated people whose pictures have been clipped out of magazines.
2. imitate the style of script writing by recording that conversation.
3. dramatize with a partner simple written dialogue.
4. examine published plays to see how scripts are written complete with settings, stage directions, and other information.
5. compose a lengthy dialogue between two people.
6. direct other students in a dramatization of his or her script.

BRIEF DESCRIPTION

This lesson is actually two lessons in one. The stimulus, used here as a prewriting exercise, can actually stand alone, but it also provides a nice warm-up and nonthreatening exercise for the duologue part of the assignment because it involves students working with partners.

Creating conversations of people from magazine pictures prepares students to do the major task of the lesson, which is to write an original script for two people. The follow-up activity of directing two classmates to act out the duologue is usually taken in stride by students once they have become comfortable with the dialogue form.

PROCEDURES

While watching television or sitting in the faculty room, prepare the stimulus for this "never-fail" lesson. Simply tear out pages of old magazines that contain pictures of people who could be talking to someone. Trim the pictures and pair up enough sets for the whole class and put each pair in a separate envelope. Now you have the stimulus for this lesson that pairs up students to write the conversation between the two people in the envelope.

The following is an extended duologue produced by an eighth-grade student:

A Sample Duologue

Cast: Narrator
      Marlene
      "Borrower"
      Karen

Setting: Marlene, a new student, goes to homeroom at her new school. It's morning and kids are everywhere, rushing one place and another. Marlene sits at her seat and looks around.

NARRATOR: Marlene is very excited about being at a new school. She'll have many more classes than she did last year.

BORROWER: Hi! What's your name? (Friendly)

MARLENE: Marlene. What's yours? (Interested)

BORROWER: Elizabeth. Can I borrow a pen?

MARLENE: Sure, but give it to me tomorrow. O.K.?

(Next day at school in Marlene's homeroom)

MARLENE: (To borrower) Can I have my pen now?

BORROWER: Oh! I forgot it in my locker! Can I keep it?

NARRATOR: Marlene figures that if she gives the pen to Elizabeth, she won't need to ask her or anyone else for a long time.

MARLENE: I guess. (Reluctantly)

BORROWER: Thanks. (The bell rings.) Bye! (She leaves the room.)

NARRATOR: During the day, Marlene goes to a couple of classes. Marlene goes to her third-period math class. She sits at her usual desk and takes a pencil out of her notebook. A person sits at a desk beside her and opens her book.

BORROWER: Can I have a pencil?

MARLENE: Here. (Handing her a pencil from her notebook.)

NARRATOR: Marlene suddenly feels like pounding her head as soon as she realizes that the girl intends to keep the pencil and that that was her last pencil. Marlene has to use a pen for math.

(After class, just as the bell rings)

BORROWER: Thanks for the pencil! (She leaves.)

MARLENE: Sure. (Disappointedly)

(Next day at sixth-period social studies)

NARRATOR: Marlene sits at her seat in a corner.

MARLENE: Hi, Karen. (Her new friend)

NARRATOR: As soon as Karen and Marlene begin a conversation, the bell rings and class is in session.

KAREN: Can I borrow a pencil for the day? I'll return it tomorrow. Okay? (Whispered because the teacher is talking)

MARLENE: All right. (Taking a pencil from her pencil case) Here.

KAREN: Thanks.

(Marlene nods her head.)

(Next day; at the same class)

MARLENE: Can I have my pencil back please?

KAREN: What pencil?

MARLENE: The pencil you have in your hand! (Frustrated)

KAREN: Oh, I'm sorry! Can I borrow it for the rest of the period? I don't have anything with me to write with.

MARLENE: Yes. (Angrily)

(After class)

NARRATOR: As Marlene asks for her pencil back, Karen leaves the classroom. Marlene leaves the room frustrated to catch the bus.

(Next day; during lunch)

NARRATOR: Marlene is eating lunch, and a girl comes over.

BORROWER: Can I borrow a pen just for a minute?

MARLENE: Yeah, here. (Handing her a pen)

(Just as soon as she hands over the pen, the gates to the lockers open.)

MARLENE: Wait! Give me back my pen! (Excitedly)

(The girl runs in through the opening gates quickly, forgetting about returning the pen.)

(At Marlene's fifth-period language class)

NARRATOR: Marlene leaves her desk to get a drink of water and comes
back to her desk to find her pencil gone.

MARLENE: Have you seen my pencil?

BORROWER: Yeah. (Taking her pencil out of his desk) Right here.

MARLENE: Give it back!

BORROWER: Can I just borrow it today? . . . Thanks . . .

MARLENE: No. Give it back!

BORROWER: Please! (Pleadingly)

MARLENE: Okay.

(Next day at her sixth-period social studies class)

NARRATOR: Marlene is noticing that her pens and pencils are disappearing
one by one, so finally she decides that if she carries around only one
pencil or pen, she won't have to buy a packet of pens and pencils
every week. Today, she has only one pencil with her.

MARLENE: Hi, Karen! (Enthusiastically)

KAREN: Hi, Marlene. Oh, by the way, can I borrow that pencil?

MARLENE: No, it's the only one I have with me. Sorry.

KIM

Stimulus

Distribute an envelope containing two pictures of people cut from magazines to every two students. If the class contains an uneven number, the
teacher can be the partner of one student. Explain to students that in turn
they are to write exactly what these people are saying to each other in
script form. They must make up names for their characters, use colons
after each name, and then write a response passing one sheet of paper
back and forth between them. There is to be no talking during this exercise!

At the end of the period, collect each script and set of pictures. Before
the next class meeting, make two copies of each script, one for each partner. The teacher retains the original for possible posting on the bulletin
board later along with the pictures.

The following day in class, return the photocopied scripts to each pair of students along with their pictures. Allow five minutes for practice before having each pair come up in front of the class to read alternately their script while showing their pictures.

Activity

Locate a play script that contains a brief description of a setting, stage directions, and so forth. Make enough copies of one page for each member of the class. Conduct a discussion with the class based on conventions of writing the play form.

Ask each student to create two characters that are having a conversation and to write their miniplay in the proper play form. Designate the length according to the level of pupils, but insist on enough length to cover an entire conversation. Suggestions might be a conversation between a parent and child, a teacher and student, two friends, a boyfriend and girlfriend, and so forth. The circumstances surrounding the conversation should be clear—for example, an argument between a parent and son or daughter about going to a rock concert or a discussion with a salesclerk about which tropical fish to buy. This assignment can be done at home and in class, depending on the students' abilities. A portion of the writing time should be spent in class for answering questions and helping the less able.

Follow-Up

At the appointed time, collect the manuscripts from all students. Reproduce three copies of each script, retaining the original for grading. (Prior to returning the scripts to students for the next stage, "production," peruse the scripts to ensure propriety.)

Return the three copies to each student "playwright/director." Each "playwright/director" must now select his or her cast to perform the script in front of the class. A good rule of thumb is not to allow a student to be both a performer and director. The preparation and presentation of these duologues take several days if all students in the class are to have a turn directing.

Evaluation

An informal ranking of the class scripts can take place prior to "production" if there is a shortage of time and/or if you feel that only a select number of the scripts should be performed.

Grade each completed script based on how well it communicates its issue or subject. Stage directions, setting, and traits developed for each character are the essential characteristics to be judged.

Have the class make nominations and vote on the three best productions. Perhaps these could be polished and presented to another guest class.

From Narrative Forms to Essays

The various forms of discourse present a complex tapestry of interwoven threads. The fact that narration embeds dialogue is a case in point. In other words, as Moffett has pointed out over and over again, there is no clear-cut separation between one mode and another; they all blend into one another. According to Moffett, "narration becomes exposition by gradual shifts, and this continuous bridging between abstraction levels needs to be followed in some way, sometimes as an order of writing, sometimes merely as a focus of awareness for teacher and students."[6]

Lesson Plans 8.6 and 8.7 show how one form of discourse often carries over into another. Lesson Plan 8.6 begins with a model from literature and engages students in writing an imaginative narrative but eventually has them analyzing the narrative for its possible effects. Lesson Plan 8.7 begins with a combination of noting down information during a field trip as well as interviewing subjects but gradually shifts to writing a distilled, impressionistic report of information.

SAFE Demonstration Lesson Plan 8.6: Is That Really What I Want to Be? Grade Levels: 6–12

OBJECTIVES

Students will

1. compose a story about themselves.
2. speculate, in a follow-up essay, about the positive and negative effects if fantasies were to come true.

BRIEF DESCRIPTION

This lesson offers students a chance to be imaginative, idealistic, or just plain funny about their own uncertain futures through writing a short narrative following that modeled in "The Secret Life of Walter Mitty" by James Thurber.

Students listen as the teacher reads the story aloud. Rather than analyzing Thurber's story, students write about their own secret lives by imitating the Walter Mitty model. In a follow-up assignment, students take another look at their fantasies in order to write speculative predictions.

This two-part lesson involves narrative writing and expository writing on the same subject.

PROCEDURES

Stimulus

Read aloud "The Secret Life of Walter Mitty" by James Thurber.[7] Discuss with the class how transitions are made from fantasy to reality and vice versa. (Walter Mitty is driving a car while commanding a Navy hydroplane; Walter Mitty drives by a hospital and begins fantasizing about being a world-famous surgeon; a newsboy's announcement of a trial instantly casts Mitty as a "crack shot with any sort of firearms" on trial for murder; an article in the newspaper entitled "Can Germany Conquer the World Through the Air?" thrusts him immediately into the role of Captain Mitty, fearless World War II bomber pilot; and, while smoking a cigarette and waiting for his wife, Mitty imagines himself before a firing squad having his last cigarette.)

Activity

Brainstorm with the class all the different daydream fantasies a teenager might have. (Students might imagine themselves as rock stars, television stars, sports heroes, Olympic greats, and so forth.)

Tell the class to imagine themselves in the Walter Mitty mode of daydreaming to escape the reality of their own lives. Have students write a short narrative piece in which they indulge in at least one daydream that contrasts sharply with their actual life.

Follow-Up

Form response groups of three to five students and have each member read his or her daydream fantasy in turn. Ask each group to select one to be read to the entire class.

In a class discussion, speculate about both the negative and positive effects being a rock star, for example, might entail. (Or use an example from one of the students' own papers.) Ask each student to analyze one of his or her own daydream fantasies by speculating about both the negative and the positive effects.

Have students write an analysis of one of their daydreams in which a logical hypothesis concerning their speculation about the negative and positive effects of the daydream coming true is presented. Insist that they describe in detail what they think would happen if their daydreams came true.

Evaluation

Hold a class discussion in which, possibly through a Venn diagram, the two types of writing in this lesson are compared for their similarities and differences.

Have students write a comparison between the two types of writing that stem from the same subject matter in this lesson. Evaluate the narrative piece for its imaginative qualities and the expository piece for its logic.

NOTE

Adapt this lesson for younger students by using such books as *Sam, Bangs, and Moonshine* by Evaline Ness (Holt, 1966) or *Lizzie Lies a Lot* by Elizabeth Levy (Delacorte, 1976). Both present characters that fantasize more than usual which gets them into trouble.

SAFE Demonstration Lesson Plan 8.7: Photography with Words
Grade Levels: 5–12 (Adapt for grades 1–4)

OBJECTIVES

Students will

1. observe details on a field trip to any place of interest.
2. record selected aspects of the place being visited.
3. conduct an interview, if appropriate, of key people at the place visited.
4. examine information collected in order to characterize the experience.

BRIEF DESCRIPTION

This lesson suggests a combination of noting down data and interviewing to accumulate enough information to write a reporter-at-large essay. In the same way that a photographer moves around to get just the right angle on a subject, an information report needs its special angle or slant. Merely stating the findings won't do; young writers need to be made acquainted with stance. Once they have collected all their information, they must arrange it in such a manner as to attract a reader. This kind of synthesis of the subject may begin even before the class goes on a field trip as a prewriting set, but the process of arranging and rearranging material in the best light doesn't end until the final period is placed.

Any field trip or experience offers the opportunity to use this lesson. It doesn't matter whether the class is taking the trip as a stimulus to a new unit, as the grand finale to a subject, or for no special reason at all.

The important thing is not to miss the opportunity to have students become reporters-at-large where their minds must assimilate information and then distill it in an appropriate manner for others to understand.

PROCEDURES

Stimulus

Go on a field trip with the class. (Visit a museum, an exhibit, a live performance, a rest home, a senior citizens' center, a college campus, a newspaper publisher, a television studio.) Tell the class that they are expected to take many notes about what they see, hear, sense, read, smell, taste, and so forth and that these notes will be used later to write a special composition. Each should bring a notebook and pen or pencil.

If interviews are in order on the field trip, be sure to have students plan five to ten interview questions *before* leaving. (For example, a trip to a senior citizens' center could entail interviews with people over age sixty who remember the Depression—a great opportunity for a social studies class to get oral histories!) If brochures are available, be sure to have students pick them up or get at least one to duplicate for everyone upon returning to school.

Activity

Armed with observation notes from the field trip, interview answers, and brochure facts, conduct a class discussion that focuses on the distinctions among the three types of information collected. Point out that the observation notes might provide the raw material for narration, the interview the raw material for drama, and the brochure facts the raw material for exposition; all three are important modes of composition, which will be interwoven in the writing assignment that is to follow.

Read the opening paragraphs to two or three reporter-at-large articles to acquaint students with possible ways to start writing. Discuss at length the idea of angle or slant before students begin to write. Have them pretend they are photographers, showing the field trip or event attended through a series of photos.

Brainstorm with the class several possible ways to characterize the place visited. (For example, a television studio might be characterized as being unglamorous.) Finally, have students write the rough drafts of their reports.

Follow-Up

Form response groups of three to five students and have each author read his or her rough draft to the others. In response groups, insist that students focus their discussion on the following:

- A balance of facts, narration/description, and dialogue (if interviews were included)
- An unusual angle or slant
- A clear *idea* of the character of the place that pervades the essay

Have students revise and edit their compositions for a class collection.

Evaluation

Send copies of the completed reports to the place visited, if appropriate, and request feedback for your students. Have students score each composition for its inclusion of the three criteria listed above.

SUMMARY

The following ideas concerning improving student writing were developed by the South Bay Writing Project in San Jose, California.[8]

This We Believe ...
1. Writing is a process that involves thinking; it should not be defined as assignments or products.
2. Students need a prewriting warm-up, a stimulus that is often oral, before they begin to write. Oral language provides the foundation for both writing and reading.
3. Our first emphasis in a writing program should be on developing fluency. Students need to write daily, and they need to experience a variety of forms and types of writing to write effectively.
4. Writers need to be aware of the audience for whom they are writing: this audience should not always be just the teacher.
5. Teachers should draw from a variety of theories and strategies for teaching writing.
6. An effective writing lesson includes (a) prewriting (talking, gathering ideas), (b) writing (organizing thinking, sharing, responding, editing, rewriting), and (c) postwriting (making the writing public).
7. Not every piece of writing goes through the full editing process; many will be short "finger exercises" designed to develop fluency and to break down writing apprehension.
8. A teacher should not expect to read or to grade every piece of writing that students do.
9. Teachers should write frequently with their students to model the writing process and to show value for writing as well as to share themselves.

10. Writing develops critical thinking skills and facilitates learning across the curriculum.
11. Evaluation of writing should be ongoing and should emphasize more than just the correct use of conventions. Students should engage in self-evaluation, peer evaluation, and conferences with the teacher.
12. Writing is the most difficult of the language skills, so we should appreciate what students are able to achieve.

CHALLENGE

1. Devise a note-taking activity as a prewriting exercise for a later composition. The activity can be based on a walk around the campus, or on an object as a meditation subject.
2. Collect enough pictures from magazines to make up a class set and pair them off into envelopes for a partner predialogue assignment.
3. Find poems that represent both exterior and interior monologues. Design composition lessons based on poems that you especially enjoy.
4. Select a short story that could be used as the stimulus and/or the model for a lesson in narrative writing.
5. Consider the subject matter and the forms of several short stories for analytical content for lessons on expository writing.
6. Plan a field trip that includes the collection of interviews, brochures, and sensory notes, all of which will be synthesized into expository writing.

NOTES

1. *Handbook for Planning an Effective Writing Program* (Sacramento: California State Department of Education, 1983).
2. William Stafford, "Introduction" to *Since Feeling Is First* by James Mecklenburger and Gary Simmons (Glenview, Ill.: Scott, Foresman, 1971), 7.
3. James Moffett, *Active Voices* (Upper Montclair, N.J.: Boynton/Cook, 1981), 14.
4. Moffett, *Active Voices*, 14.
5. Moffett, *Active Voices*, 146.
6. Moffett, *Active Voices*, 72.
7. James Thurber, "The Secret Life of Walter Mitty," *21 Great Stories* (New York: New American Library, 1969).
8. South Bay Writing Project (San Jose, Calif.: San Jose State University English Department).

EXPLORING FURTHER

Caplan, Rebekah, and Catharine Keech. *Showing Writing: A Training Program to Help Students Be Specific.* Berkeley: Bay Area Writing Project, University of California, 1980.

Cooper, Charles R., and Lee Odell, eds. *Research on Composing: Points of Departure.* Urbana, Ill.: National Council of Teachers of English, 1978.

Garrison, Roger. *How a Writer Works: Through the Composing Process.* San Francisco: Harper & Row, 1981.

Gere, Anne Ruggles. *Roots in the Sawdust: Writing to Learn Across the Disciplines.* Urbana, Ill.: National Council of Teachers of English, 1986.

Grubb, Mel. *Using Holistic Evaluation.* Encino, Calif.: Glencoe, 1981.

Healy, Mary K. *Using Student Writing Response Groups in the Classroom.* Berkeley: Bay Area Writing Project, University of California, Berkeley, 1980.

Kirby, Dan and Tom Liner. *Inside Out, Developmental Strategies for Teaching Writing.* Upper Montclair, N.J.: Boynton/Cook, 1981.

Koch, Carl, and James M. Brazil. *Strategies for Teaching the Composition Process.* Urbana, Ill.: National Council of Teachers of English, 1978.

Martin, Nancy et al. *Writing and Learning Across the Curriculum, 11–16.* Upper Montclair, N.J.: Boynton/Cook, 1986.

Moffett, James. *Active Voices* (4 volumes). Upper Montclair, N.J.: Boynton/Cook, 1981.

Moffett, James, and Betty Jane Wagner. *Student-Centered Language Arts and Reading, K–13: A Handbook for Teachers,* 3d ed. Boston: Houghton Mifflin, 1983.

Moffett, James. *Teaching the Universe of Discourse.* Boston: Houghton Mifflin, 1983.

Olson, Carol Booth, ed. *Practical Ideas for Teaching Writing as a Process.* Sacramento: California State Department of Education, 1986.

Squire, James, ed. *Dynamics of Language Learning.* Urbana, Ill.: National Commission on Research in English, 1987.

Tiedt, Iris. *Writing: From Topic to Evaluation.* Needham Heights, Mass.: Allyn and Bacon, 1989.

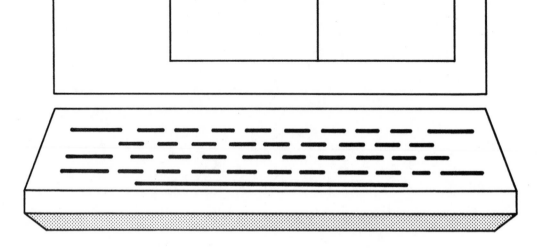

Creativity is the disposition to make and recognize valuable innovations.   *H. D. Lasswell*

Mathematical invention is but a case of invention in general, a process which can take place in several domains, whether it be in science, literature, in art, or technology.   *Jacques Hadamard*

The ability to relate and to connect, sometimes in odd and yet in striking fashion, lies at the very heart of any creative use of the mind, no matter in what field or discipline.   *George J. Seidel*

It is obvious that invention or discovery, be it in mathematics or anywhere else, takes place by combining ideas.
                                                                                      Jacques Hadamard

The reciprocal relationship between culture and creativity is such that a creative product is not really an invention unless it is socially accepted. The creative product has to operate within the culture; it has to work. If it does not work, it is a failure as an invention.   *Morton I. Teicher*

CHAPTER **9**

Thinking with Computer Power

Objectives

After reading this chapter, you will be able to

- *Discuss the educational uses of the computer and the value of computers in enhancing thinking skills.*
- *Plan lessons that use the computer in word processing.*
- *Incorporate cooperative learning with computer time.*
- *Adapt any current, creative activity for use with the computer.*
- *Devise ways to engage students in using the computer to promote thinking.*
- *Research available resources.*

We all have been affected in some way by the use of computers in education. Although they represent a relatively new technological tool in education, computers are familiar to students. We must use this medium to its fullest, taking advantage of new knowledge.

However, no new computer instructional package will completely revitalize education. Educational reform relies on principals and teachers who will take the initiative in instructional design. Whether we are speaking of computer instruction or teacher direction, the basic questions of student interest, learning style, skill development and application, and inquiry methods prevail. It is the combination of educational theory, teaching strategies, technology, and materials that enables educators to provide a modern, well-rounded education for their students. The need goes beyond selecting, coordinating, and using existing resources to designing new materials and applications that meet the levels of thinking and learning we seek.

Computer Uses in Education

ROLES OF THE COMPUTER

In the educational process, computers play different roles in the students' interaction with them, all of which promote thinking and learning. The computer is all of the following:

- Assistant to the teacher
- Handy tool
- Simulator of events
- Programmable machine
- Technological advancement

Assistant to the Teacher

The computerized instruction components of presentation, questioning, judging, feedback, review, and routing comprise the computer-assisted instruction (CAI) program. A tutorial program presents a complete learning episode, simulating the dialogue between student and tutor. The drill and practice strategy focuses on question, response, and feedback, providing the repetition some students require. Effective programs that offer instruction and drill not only on grammar, usage, and punctuation but also on style, sentence variety, and analogies are available as well. Problem-solving programs can guide students through the writing process, taking the students' response, and moving them on to the next step of development.

Handy Tool

As a tool, the computer allows users to devote time to the larger aspects of their work. For both the master science teacher and the beginning science student, the computer observes, records, and compares data. For the writer, it is a word processor. For the manager of the classroom, the computer is an electronic filing system. Instructional management involves keeping records of student work, diagnosing needs and prescribing remediation, testing, maintaining statistics, and generating correspondence. For the administrator, software that provides executive reports without the help of additional people to record or organize makes administrative management more efficient.

Simulator of Events

The computer has captured the imagination of problem solvers in complex "adventure games," "guess-and-rule" programs, and historic journeys, offering the potential for addressing thinking skills. Scientific experiments are simulated for students' analysis and evaluation.

Programmable Machine

Students learn computer languages such as BASIC, LOGO, and Pascal and apply logic and proper format to write their own programs, debugging as necessary to achieve desired results. Programmers can write programs on how to solve a problem or how to prepare a presentation with sound and graphics. This requires critical and analytical thinking skills, the level at which we endeavor to have students think.

Technological Advancement

Computer science classes focus on the computer literacy topics of history, uses, computer architecture, and operating systems. On a higher level, discussion centers on issues such as human values and the computer revolution, robotics and job displacement, computer crime, copyright piracy, and computers and the disabled.

Computers provide individual instruction and instructional management, reinforce concepts, simulate events and experiences, evaluate student performance, and develop critical thinking skills through open-ended questions and generation of student ideas. In addition, computers present a relevant learning mode that is motivating to students. Any intimidation caused by the unfamiliar technological tool is dispelled when we realize the power we have with the computer, which can only do what it is programmed to do. We need to be aware of how computers can free us to use instructional time more efficiently. It enables us to do what we do best, that is, to interact with students, discussing, sharing, and questioning.

TEACHER EDUCATION

Without doubt, we are living in the computer age, and technological advancements are being made every day. It is therefore imperative that all teachers acquire the competencies necessary to develop a computer literacy curriculum for students. These are the abilities to

- integrate the computer across the curriculum.
- read, write, and execute simple programs.
- use educational application software.
- locate and use sources of up-to-date information on computing in education.

For educators, a present and future concern is how best to prepare students for the microelectronics world while teaching curriculum. We should expect technological advancements to make administration and teaching easier. Computers are tools that can free teachers to work individually with students and build the personal relationships that a "high-tech," "high-touch" society needs.

Teachers are the instructional decision makers who design ways to integrate the computer into their classrooms. The computer can be used as a tool for teachers in many ways, for example:

- Grade book programs, which will print missing assignments for a student or class, a list of grade points, students' grades with your remarks, class averages, and statistical information about each test
- "Personalized" letters to parents and students
- Time-efficient interim reports
- Game creator, which generates word searches, crosswords, and word scrambles for use with vocabulary and spelling
- Test creator, which prints out tests of all kinds with different tests for each student and stores tests that can be easily revised
- Awards and notepads created by "Print Shop"
- Easily revised reading lists
- Curriculum design tool as a desktop publishing alternative to a textbook

For a comprehensive explanation on creating your own CAI program in composition, a recommended source is Cynthia L. Selfe's *Computer-Assisted Instruction in Composition: Create Your Own!* (see "Exploring Further").

The following is a list of ways teachers with amateur computer status can begin to use the computer with students:

1. Allow the student computer experts to help inexperienced students.
2. Introduce a new program to three students who become the experts on that program. Eventually, all students can become experts on at least one program.
3. Utilize cross-grade tutoring, having upper-grade students assist younger students. Training in giving instructions and solving problems are the by-products gained by the experience.
4. Request the aid of a media specialist or a parent volunteer to take students in small groups to teach word processing or other programs on the computer.
5. Hook up an adapter that splits the signal coming from the class computer to display on a large monitor for large-group investigations.
6. Know the software you select, being careful to consider not only how each one relates to your instructional goals but also how each fits into your classroom management plans. Some programs, such as simulations, are too long for the twenty-minute blocks of time often set for use by individuals or pairs of students.

7. Upon previewing software that meet your standards and needs, allow students to select programs that interest them. Shared ownership of decisions at the early stages allow all to learn together.

Incorporate appropriate software into everything you teach. In reading, thinking skills are enhanced when the reading group can discuss the strategies they use to work through programs such as "Gertrude's Puzzle" (The Learning Company). In math, problem-solving skills are used, for example, in seeing number patterns in "The King's Rule" (Sunburst). Integrate spelling while teaching keyboarding, by practicing language arts lessons on the computer. For example, students can type adjectives that begin with *a*, thus reinforcing the location of the *a* key in relation to the other keys.

EDUCATIONAL COMPUTER CONCERNS

Four concerns about the role of the computer in the classroom should be examined. A major concern is that we *promote quality thinking by upholding the concept of integration,* by directing the students' minds to the synthesis of curricular elements. Much as a course on American history examines the social, political, and economic aspects of life in its relatedness, computer technology should be integrated into the classroom curriculum. Rather than add computer activities, we should design or adapt present activities to include the computer.

Another concern is the *proper use of the computer.* Rather than allocating time at the computer for games as rewards, time should be scheduled for curriculum-related work by individuals or small groups. Furthermore, the curriculum-related work should require thinking strategies and not be simple fill-in-the-blanks, replacing the "purple peril" ditto or workbook pages. Increasing computer use in education will no doubt improve their use as instructional tools per se in subject matter courses across the curriculum. As schools provide computer training and assistance in integrating computers into the curriculum and as teachers demand quality programs, educators will see this technological advancement as a faithful tool, enhancing education and the thinking of their students.

Some argue against the need to teach "computer literacy" issues and programming because familiarity with current computer languages will not help a student succeed professionally. A third concern therefore is the *demotivating factor of starting students on the computer with a literacy and programming base,* a valid concern. However, keeping all elements in perspective, programming, while not necessary for all, does have its place in the computer science classroom where logic, physics, engineering, and other sciences relate to the development and operation of computers. Higher-order thinking skills are drawn upon in discussion on the ethical and moral consequences of computer power.

Recently, computer technology and thinking skills advocacy have fused into a synthetic diamond that needs careful cutting and polishing if the facets are to shine brilliantly as an educational advancement. This is a concern, for in understanding the dynamics of the issue, *guidelines should be developed* by individual school systems regarding educational goals: the definition of "thinking"; the technological vision of computers in education; hardware and software supply, use, criteria, and evaluation; and training for educators.

The value of the computer is that it provides yet another instructional tool that adds to our choices. Teachers ultimately make all instructional decisions. If we are computer literate, we can decide to use word processing, CAI, management systems, data bases, and desktop publication as additional ways to teach for thinking and learning.

The Computer as Word Processor

Word processing—the use of computer-controlled writing systems—facilitates creating and revising written material. This system provides ways to correct errors, insert or delete words, search for a given sequence of letters and replace it with another sequence, move sections of text, format the printout margin and line spacing, save the writing, and print the material. Advanced word processors include a dictionary and thesaurus and can check surface features such as spelling and syntax. Because physical aspects of producing and editing text become easier, students can pay more attention to the thinking process. Ease of making changes makes editing and revising fun rather than a chore. Therefore, many classroom teachers report that students enjoy writing more, are more willing to revise, and therefore produce better compositions.

With its capabilities, the word processor facilitates the writing process. We are aware of the value of brainstorming, the generation of creative thoughts that blossom into intriguing concepts. Because of the temporary nature of words on the screen, students can type every idea with the option of deletion later, thereby being less inclined to edit ideas in their heads. Prewriting strategies such as clustering, brainstorming, free writing, and invisible writing (explained below) are ideal on a word processor. These steps are important because research on writing competence shows that students who think before writing are better writers.

With thematic development and organizational concerns, the text-movement abilities of the word processor enable ready expansion and change. Students learn to view writing as an ongoing process, which is open to real change with addition of new insights and major reorganization. Revision, no longer laborious, is almost magical to the delight of the students.

During the revising stage, mechanics and style checkers lead students to review these elements as well as the logic and organization of their writing. Questioning is best done at the revision stage because the prewriting phase involves the free-flowing production of ideas. Good writers tend to express their ideas freely as they compose, revising only after their thoughts are in writing. It has been noted that poor writers tend to revise too much too soon, losing their train of thought in their concern for immediate editing, error avoidance.

An interesting technique that increases this flow of ideas, uninhibited by premature revision, is "invisible writing." The process involves students in writing with inkless ballpoint pens on paper over carbon paper, making immediate revision impossible. This strategy has been adapted using the word processor with the monitor turned off. This is a good example of the application of computer technology to adapt or facilitate a recognized instructional strategy. When carefully directed, increased concentration and improved flow of ideas result.

The psychological sense of empowerment the students receive in having control over the process makes the word processor a valuable tool. Control is also strengthened through the production of clean legible copies to share with a proud sense of ownership. The physical separation between the writer and the temporary text on the screen and the psychological distance thereby created also facilitate freer critiquing as opposed to the pen extensions of the fingers and keys of the typewriter.

Studies on the effect of word processing on student revision vary widely in their results. There is no consistency among those comparing revision using a word processor and revision with pen. Some researchers report improved products from the use of word processing, some find no difference, and some conclude that students revise less with the computer. Research does suggest that the word processor's value to the students' writing process depends more on adjunct guidance than on the computer's facility to revise.

Colette Daiute studied three groups of students: those composing with pen, those composing on the computer, and those using the word processor with guiding questions.[1] Her word-processing program called "Catch" offers fourteen types of text analysis and comments to help students pose questions to themselves in revising their writing beyond the simple correcting of errors. Her study evidenced a marked difference between revisions made by students using the computer alone and those using the computer with guidance. The crucial variable appears to be the guidance through questioning provided.

The results of Daiute's study suggest that empowering the student with self-revising through questioning techniques result in more effective communication through meaningful revision. Yet, the best guide may be the personal, verbal questioning of the teacher. Simultaneously, good computer-based instruction frees the teacher to direct student use of technological tools effectively to achieve instructional goals. It is important to remember that the computer is a tool; the teacher must assess the ways new technology can enhance student learning and thinking.

The word processor not only facilitates the writing process and allows writers to concentrate on the thoughts and the semantics behind the words but also improves the teaching of writing. Teachers begin to see writing as a process and therefore emphasize the process to students, rather than focus on the final product alone. Clearly, it is teaching, not just the computer, that makes the difference.

WORD-PROCESSOR ACTIVITIES

The exciting thing to remember about using the word processor is that any creative activity you are presently doing in your classroom can be adapted for use with the computer. The following is a beginning list intended to suggest ideas for integration of the computer into your ongoing classroom activities:

- *Intraschool Computer-Based Message System:* Students can use the system to exchange or ask for information, take surveys, and other such uses.
- *Poetry:* Because poems are short, all students can produce a finished product for publication. An illustrated anthology of student poems from a class would require less than ten pages. Each student can enter his or her poem on a page where it fits. Art can be added on the computer or later on the printed copy before the anthology is duplicated.
- *Graphics:* Use a graphics-designing program like "Print Shop" to create greeting cards and stationery. Students develop an artistic ability to recognize quality and effectiveness in the presentation of material.
- *Issues:* Students can think and write about the impact of technological societies. Older students may take on any of the issues related to human values and the computer revolution: "Will computers change the meaning of being human?" "How am I affected by the Computer Revolution?" Other topics may range from robotics and job displacement to computer crime, copyright and software piracy, an individual's privacy, and computers and the disabled.
- *Book Reviews:* For a change of format, each student can evaluate a book. A class compilation serves as a "Book Review Digest" that can be shared as a way of motivating reading.
- *Newspaper:* Students can write articles, set headlines, select graphics to accompany the stories, lay out the pages, and print the newspaper.
- *Group Journal Writing:* Primary students would especially enjoy seeing their thoughts changing into words. Students can describe experiences

throughout the day, starting with the weather, breakfast, clothing, getting to school, recess, and ending with a summary of learnings and plans for the next day.

- *Plays:* Creating a play on the word processor gives students an open, creative relationship with the script. Students can revise the play as they become more familiar with it. If writers want to change a character's lines, it is easily done.

- *Study Journals:* Through metacognition, students focus on their ideas and feelings, becoming the center of their own learning process and more responsible for their own learning. After students read a chapter, see a film, do an experiment, solve a problem, they can write their reactions: thoughts and feelings about what they have done, read, seen or heard; agreements and disagreements; plans for further inquiry.

SAFE Demonstration Lesson Plan 9.1: Class Profiles
Grade Levels: 1–12

OBJECTIVES

Students will

1. interview classmates.
2. write student profiles.

BRIEF DESCRIPTION

This is an example of an activity that is usually done in a regular classroom without a word processor. It serves to show how any activity can be adapted for use with the computer.

PROCEDURES

Stimulus

Read a short article about a celebrity, one admired by many in the class. Discuss how we are all interested in knowing about other people and how we can learn from knowing about their lives.

Activity

Create a list of the students in your class, numbering each person. (Use your grade book list.) Write the numbers on slips of paper. After each student has picked a number, reveal the person they are to interview.

Generate a list of questions to be asked: interests, hobbies, memories, concerns, ideas, wishes, and dreams. Students may add other appropriate questions as they see fit. Tell students they may opt not to answer any question they feel uncomfortable answering. Students can use a worksheet, filling in the interviewee's answers.

Arrange a schedule for student times at the word processor. Each student is responsible for creating a student profile for a class magazine. Using "Print Shop," students design a border that highlights each interviewee's profile.

Follow-Up

Combine the results into a class magazine with a page devoted to each student. Students may enter a cover design contest if they wish. Distribute copies to everyone in the class and contribute copies to the library.

Evaluation

As a class, evaluate the interview process, the questions, the word-processing application, and the final product. Discuss the side benefits of the project (developed friendships, improved self-concept, computer skills, fun) in addition to those of the writing experience.

Computer Cooperative Learning

Cooperative learning is a proven classroom strategy that is readily incorporated throughout the curriculum and adapted to the computer. The following elements are essential for a successful cooperative learning experience:

- *Team Formation:* A heterogeneous mix of students is the goal. Take into account sex, cultural and language differences, behaviors, and past performance. At other times, form teams randomly, expecting students to work together no matter where they are assigned.
- *Positive Interdependence:* The idea that no one is successful unless everyone is successful must be communicated clearly in advance. Before the work starts, establish what the payoff is, the evaluation criteria.
- *Direct Teaching of Group Skills:* The direct teaching of group skills is like the teaching of any lesson. The skill is specified, its importance emphasized, practice role played, and follow-through monitored. This enables learning to be cooperative.
- *Student Accountability:* Each student must know ahead of time that he or she will be accountable for individual knowledge whether it be an oral explanation or a printout.
- *Evaluation:* Taking time to discuss the process, student learnings, and their goals for improvement is vital for the teamwork philosophy to remain strong.

COLLABORATIVE WRITING

Collaborative writing on a word processor is an effective technique for encouraging writers to think and talk about language. The following advantages enable groups of students to work as a unit:

1. The fluid nature of the text on the screen allows for easy word changes and manipulation of passages.
2. A record of the text provides for easy analysis and modification.
3. The screen focuses attention on the same text.
4. Sharing of cognitive tasks (editor, graphics, designer, proofreader, co-writer) is facilitated.
5. Each student's awareness of the ways language can be used is enhanced.
6. An explicit overall plan and intermediate goals can be formed.
7. The thinking/writing process is facilitated, enhancing communication of ideas.
8. There is increased awareness of language choices and a willingness to make critical judgments about them.
9. There is an immediate presence of audience.
10. There is group security in the result of a shared effort.
11. An appreciation of writing results.
12. Confidence and skills acquired from group writing transfers to individual writing.

The benefits of cooperative learning on the computer are many. People predicted that the computer would further isolate students from their teachers and from each other and that programmed instruction would reduce learning to drill and practice. What is happening contradicts that notion. Rather, it is around the computer that students are interacting and learning from each other. New strategies for formal and informal cooperative learning are emerging as teachers experiment with various arrangements and activities.

SAFE Demonstration Lesson Plan 9.2: Poet Co-op
Grade Levels: 4–12

OBJECTIVES

Students will

1. create a metaphor.
2. write a poem collaboratively.

BRIEF DESCRIPTION

This lesson extends the students' knowledge on metaphors. It follows the lesson called "Metaphorical Feathers" on page 144. Following a discussion on metaphors and Emily Dickinson's poem, students create a class poem using a metaphor. This is followed by a metaphorical poem written collaboratively on the computer.

PROCEDURES

Stimulus

Read a poem to the class such as Emily Dickinson's extended metaphor of a train likened to a horse.

> I like to see it lap the miles,
> And lick the valleys up,
> And stop to feed itself at tanks;
> And then, prodigious, step
>
> Around a pile of mountains,
> And, supercilious, peer
> In shanties by the sides of roads;
> And then a quarry pare
>
> To fit its sides, and crawl between,
> Complaining all the while
> In horrid, hooting stanza;
> Then chase itself down hill
>
> And neigh like Boanerges;
> Then, punctual as a star,
> Stop—docile and omnipotent—
> At its own stable door.[2]

Explain what a metaphor is—a figure of speech in which one thing is likened to another in an implied comparison. Discuss how Emily Dickinson brings out the characteristics of a train and a horse in her poem without naming either.

Activity

Ask students what animal they would have selected to compare to a train. With varying answers, point out how everyone has different ideas and the value of that in making the world interesting. Select an animal by majority vote and create a class poem likening the train to that animal.

Discuss how the cooperative effort created a satisfactory group poem. It is important that students understand that the poem is not their own individual product. They should not be frustrated or upset if the poem moves in a direction different from the original intent. Each student could probably write just as admirable a poem individually; this experience provides a different dimension to expressing ideas.

Have students compose a poem collaboratively on the computer. They should select a subject and a metaphor by which to describe that subject. Each student takes a turn writing a line after reading the preceding lines until the first writer adds the final line to complete the circle and the poem.

Follow-Up

Students may, as a group, revise the poem. They may use a program like "Print Shop" to add appropriate graphics and publish their work by posting it on the bulletin board.

Evaluation

Students evaluate their group effort with an evaluation sheet:

As a group, we	Yes	No
1. accomplished our goal.	____	____
2. arrived at decisions well.	____	____
3. helped each other with ideas.	____	____
Each member		
1. contributed ideas.	____	____
2. contributed a line to the poem.	____	____

Something I did to make the group more successful in doing its work: _____

_____

What I like about our product: _____

_____

SAFE Demonstration Lesson Plan 9.3: The Writing Co-op
Grade Levels: 4–12

OBJECTIVES

Students will

1. write a piece cooperatively using the word processor.
2. write a piece similar in nature individually.

BRIEF DESCRIPTION

Following a demonstration and discussion on popping corn, groups of students use the word processor to write a collaborative description of popping and eating popcorn. They then write a piece individually describing eating an orange. The writing process continues with peer editing and an evaluation.

PROCEDURES

Stimulus

Bring popcorn and a corn popper to class. Students contribute to the prewriting activity of describing eating popcorn from popping it to licking the salt from their fingers. Elicit from students the attributes of good descriptive writing and the elements that "show" the corn popping and the kernels squeaking as they are chewed.

Activity

Direct students to use the word processor to write cooperatively about popping and eating popcorn, borrowing from the prewriting ideas generated as a class. In sharing these group pieces, have students identify the attributes that make each piece powerful.

Students should then write a similar piece individually, describing eating an orange from peeling it to swallowing the last segment. Students must include the features described in the class discussion that "show" rather than "tell" the description.

Follow-Up

Students then respond to their peers' writings. Sitting in two large circles, each person in one circle faces a member of the other circle. Each student reads his or her piece to the person he or she faces and receives feedback from that partner, taking turns in this one sitting. Then have one of the circles rotate by one seat and repeat the process. Students read their pieces at least three times, receiving feedback each time, and hearing other pieces of writing that may influence them.

Evaluation

Create an evaluation checksheet including the points discussed after the cooperative writing part of the activity. You may evaluate each paper using this checksheet. Also have students use the checksheet to evaluate two pieces of writing, giving the writer three evaluations upon which to reflect.

NOTE

Other possible writing assignments are

- a different ending to a short story.
- an interpretation of a popular song.
- a summary of a historical event.
- an explanation of a math concept.
- a comparison of two scientific elements of study.

Keyboarding

When typing became popular, educators noticed that the keyboard offered special help to the language disabled who had trouble seeing, hearing, and sensing the interconnections basic to using written language. People who could not easily sense the pattern of the spelling of a word when writing by hand found they became touch spellers as they became touch typists. Some students need to experience a word kinesthetically in order to see it and to write the word in order to read it through the media of paint, clay, macaroni, or sandpaper. Students can see the result of every keystroke lit on the monitor when they use the computer.

The value of typing itself is clear, but the basic question related to keyboarding is, What instruction do students need to enjoy writing? Teachers generally agree that

- students must use the word processor efficiently if they are to benefit from using word processing.
- there is no need to worry about full keyboarding instruction if students use the computer for an hour or less a week; devoting an hour of instruction to the home row and vital keys is all that is necessary.
- third, fourth, and fifth graders need twenty to thirty hours of instruction if they are to type as quickly as they write with a pencil.
- keyboard instruction should be given just prior to writing on the computer.
- students should keyboard as efficiently as they write with a pencil before they begin to use the computer for their daily writing.

Without instruction, upper elementary students write half the rate they write with pencil (five words per minute instead of ten). This is a problem because transcription should be an automatic skill so the students' mental energy can be used to think creatively and to express ideas easily. The keyboarding task added to the already complex writing process makes writing very difficult.

Components of a good school district keyboarding instructional program include the following:

- Collaboration between business education teachers and other teachers
- Elementary teachers skilled in keyboarding who can deliver the skill to students
- A scripted teacher's guide for direct instruction
- A good keyboarding software program that includes a recordkeeping component and a variety of teacher-dictation and disk-based practice.

The computer literacy class is an ideal place for keyboard instruction. Twenty minutes of the fifty-minute class can be devoted to keyboard instruction. This leaves the language arts teacher time to teach writing with the computer as a tool. Creative primary grade teachers incorporate keyboard learning in physical activity using a keyboard painted on the playground blacktop or floor mats. Students can make up hopping games.

Good keyboarding programs that you are considering should have the following:

- *A Language-Based Approach:* Spelling and composing skills are reinforced through typing logical letter combinations. The word-processing approach not only increases accuracy and speed in typing but also allows for development of basic spelling and writing skills whether they are average fourth graders, bilingual, special education students, or language disadvantaged.
- *Separation of Speed and Accuracy Skills:* Current research on the teaching of typing shows the importance of skills in a hierarchy of correct technique, stroking speed, and accuracy. Students should be able to concentrate on their accuracy without being overly concerned about speed and proceed to the opposite situation until both can be achieved simultaneously.
- *Introduction to Word-Processing Editing Features:* We are learning to use a new technology. After sufficient fluency on stroking patterns is achieved, the use of the DELETE key on an edit screen is a handy tool.

The issue of keyboarding is when it is best for instruction to be given and who provides it. This is another decision teachers must make in using the computer as an instructional tool in the classroom.

Software

As software develops beyond short-answer workbook-type responses into more critical, thoughtful analysis, computers will be even more powerful instructional tools that help students think, learn, and discover. Rather than name software that focus only on skills, we will briefly discuss some of the features of software available that promote thinking.

PROGRAMS THAT PROMOTE THINKING

Writing Activity Disks with Word-Processing Functions

These programs develop composing, revising, and editing skills for students in kindergarten through grade twelve. They address all major areas of written language: story, poetry, letter, journal, report, and essay writing.

Integrated Software Programs

Some programs include spreadsheet, data base, and word processing. These can be used with sample files, which students can modify and on which they can base inferences and predictions. These programs also can be used as templates into which students insert information or as a tool for thinking where students generate formats and solutions for their own problems, analyze similarities, and create graphs. A data base also can be used as a class-management tool. The class secretary can enter the day's activities and homework for easy reference when students return from absence.

Software That Integrates the Curriculum

Stories and poems are created to demonstrate particular writing techniques that students can imitate. Examples include math problems based on classical fairy tales, myths, fables, or stories that require the scientific method for problem solving. Stories may also integrate science, history, literature, and creative writing. Thus, the computer promotes the integration of learning across the curriculum.

Play-Writing for the Middle Grades

This program encourages the student's own language in monologue and dialogue to translate the intended ideas so that the student's imagination controls the images instead of the images controlling the student's mind. Writers can integrate the activities of picking the cast, building a set, creating music, and writing a script to produce a play.

A SAMPLING OF PUBLISHED PROGRAMS

A few specific programs that appear to be especially valuable in developing thinking skills are "The Oregon Trail," "CompuTHINK," and "HOTS: Higher-Order Thinking Skills."

"The Oregon Trail"

Simulations are valuable strategies to use in having students learn specific curricular skills while integrating content through computer use. As an example, "The Oregon Trail" (Minnesota Educational Computing Corporation, 1985) is a reality based model that can be the focal point of an interdisciplinary unit, especially integrated with American history. You might try these related student activities:

1. From your reading of a diary, historical fiction, or textbook and your experiences in the simulated journey, summarize the history of a particular group who participated or was affected by the movement (Donner Party, Mormons, Native Americans).

2. Record your journey as you participate in the simulation. Note data in your journal: accompanying travelers, sites, activities, provisions, and any other details you find interesting or important.
3. From reading an account of an emigrant to Oregon in the 1840s, explain ways the computer simulation supports the experiences of your emigrant.
4. "Travel" the Oregon Trail twice, the first time as a farmer and the second time as a banker. Take notes on each trip about such things as your preparations, stopping places, and health. Compare the two trips.
5. From the simulation, your readings, and your study of the westward expansion, explain five reasons why people left the East to travel over 2000 miles in a covered wagon.
6. Prepare a full-screen graphics of a landmark. Pretend you are standing, for example, near the summit of Chimney Rock. Draw the landscape you see.

"CompuTHINK"[3]

Funded for dissemination to schools throughout California, "CompuTHINK" has been certified as an exemplary project by the Educational Technology Unit of the California State Department of Education. It provides educators with a conceptual framework classifying thirty-three specific thinking skills from recall to complex problem solving, a tested strategy for identifying the cognitive skills emphasized by any educational software program, and a resource guide that matches the cognitive skills framework to existing computer programs and extensive reviews of thirty programs evaluated by "CompuTHINK" criteria. A "CompuTHINK Resource Diskette" for Apple IIe and IIc provides a quick reference to the skills framework definitions and quick retrieval of programs reviewed by grade level and specific cognitive skills.

"HOTS: Higher-Order Thinking Skills"[4]

Drawing from cognitive psychology theories of the organization of information in the brain, Stanley Pogrow developed the "HOTS" program. The goal is to use higher-order thinking activities to improve basic skills and social confidence while improving problem-solving ability. The assumption is that the key to improving thinking ability is to increase the students' repertoire of strategies and to develop sophisticated networks of concept associations. "HOTS" is different from other computer curricula in that it uses a wide variety of commercially available software in accordance with learning theory. Students (grades three to six) work in a computer lab on problem-solving and linkage activities. A thinking discussion in which students articulate the consequences of their strategies and in which the teacher poses challenge questions precedes work on the computer.

SOFTWARE RESOURCES

The following is a list of selected companies that produce thinking skills software:

- Apple Computer
  20225 Mariani Avenue
  Cupertino, CA 95104
- CBS Software
  One Fawcett Place
  Greenwich, CT 06836
- Chalk Board, Inc.
  3772 Pleasantdale Road
  Atlanta, GA 30300
- Educational Materials
  P.O. Box 17
  Pelham, NY 10803
- The Learning Company
  4370 Alpine Road
  Portola Valley, CA 94025

- Minnesota Educational
  Computing Corporation
  3490 Lexington Avenue, N.
  St. Paul, MN 55112
- Midwest Publications Company
  P.O. Box 448
  Pacific Grove, CA 93950
- Spinnaker Software Corporation
  1 Kendall Square
  Cambridge, MA 02139
- Sunburst Communications
  39 Washington Avenue
  Pleasantville, NY 10570

Additional resources for teachers include periodicals that review computer equipment and software. The most readily available resource of software reviews is a subscription to such publications as the following:

- *Computers, Reading and Language Arts*, Modern Learning Publishers, Inc., 1308 East 38th Street, Oakland, CA 94602.
- *Courseware Report Card*, Educational Insights, 150 West Carob Street, Compton, CA 90220.
- *Digest of Software Reviews: Education*, 1341 Bulldog Lane, Suite C, Fresno, CA 93710.
- *Electronic Education*, Electronic Communications, Inc., Suite 220, 1311 Executive Center Drive, Tallahassee, FL 32301.
- *Electronic Learning*, Scholastic Inc., 730 Broadway, New York, NY 10003–9538.
- *Teaching and Computers*, Scholastic Inc., 730 Broadway, New York, NY 10003–9538.
- *The Computing Teacher*, The International Council for Computers in Education (ICCE), University of Oregon, 1787 Agate Street, Eugene, OR 97403–1923.

SUMMARY

The far-reaching limits of the educational uses of computers to enhance student learning are yet to be known. Computer use in schools may always lag behind technology's instructional vision, but only through experimentation, creative efforts, and critical evaluation will educators meet the challenge of high technology's influence in the schools. If we can act on the experts' promise for technology's impact on thinking and learning and prepare students for their future by polishing this diamond faceted with technology and thinking, we will rise to the challenge in brilliant form. As educators, we have the ability to be the "high-touch" teacher capable of molding a "high-tech" curriculum.

Whether we look at the computer as thinking for the student with its complicated processing or as stimulating the student to think through problem solving or writing, it does create time for the teacher and student to engage in more complicated thinking tasks. Learning environments that include the computer enable students to think, learn, and explore in a complex fashion.

CHALLENGE

1. Select one of your favorite writing lessons and adapt it for use with the word processor.
2. Select an appropriate cooperative learning activity and adapt it for use with a computer.
3. Check into obtaining the "CompuTHINK" program. Use it to acquire a solid background for integrating thinking skills and technology.
4. Select an appropriate simulation for your students and integrate curricular content through computer use.

NOTES

1. Colette Daiute, "Can the Computer Stimulate Writers' Inner Dialogue?" in *The Computer in Composition Instruction: A Writer's Tool*, ed. William Wresch (Urbana, Ill.: National Council of Teachers of English, 1984, ED247602).
2. Emily Dickinson, *Poems for Youth*, ed. Alfred L. Hampson (Boston: Little, Brown, 1934).
3. John Cradler (Project Director), South San Francisco Unified School District, 398 "B" Street, South San Francisco, CA 94080.
4. Stanley Pogrow, College of Education, University of Arizona, Tucson, AZ 85721.

EXPLORING FURTHER

California State Department of Education. *Computer Applications Planning; Computers in Education: Goals and Content; Educational Software Preview Guide.* Sacramento: Author, 1985.

Costa, Arthur. "Computers and Thinking" in *Developing Minds: A Resource Book for Teaching Thinking.* Alexandria, Va.: ASCD, 1985.

ERIC Clearinghouse on Reading and Communication Skills. National Council of Teachers of English. 1111 Kenyon Road, Urbana, IL 61801. (Request publication list.)

Hunt, James B., Jr., "Action for Excellence, Excerpts from the Task Force Report." *Educational Leadership* 18 (Sept. 1983): 15–16.

Nickerson, Raymond. "Computer Programming as a Vehicle for Teaching Thinking Skills." *Thinking, The Journal of Philosophy for Children* 4 (1983): 42–47.

Papert, Seymour. *Mindstorms: Children, Computers, and Powerful Ideas.* New York: Basic Books, 1980.

Selfe, Cynthia L. *Computer-Assisted Instruction in Composition: Create Your Own!* Urbana, Ill.: National Council of Teachers of English, 1986.

Turkle, S. *The Second Self: Computers and the Human Spirit.* New York: Simon & Schuster, 1984.

Walker, Decker. "Reflections on the Educational Potential and Limitations of Microcomputers." *Phi Delta Kappan* (Oct. 1983): 103–107.

Winston, P. *Artificial Intelligence,* 2d ed. Reading, Mass.: Addison-Wesley, 1984.

Let me exhort everyone
to do their utmost to
think outside and beyond
our present circle of
ideas. For every idea
gained is a hundred years
of slavery remitted.
Richard Jefferies

The vitality of thought is in
adventure. Ideas won't keep.
Something must be done about
them. When the idea is new, its
custodians have fervour, live for it,
and if need be, die for it.
Alfred North Whitehead

If Erasmus saw the classroom as the new stage for the
printing press, we can see today that the new situation
for young and old alike is the classroom without
walls. . . .
Marshall McLuhan

CHAPTER 10

Integrating Thinking Across the Curriculum

Objectives

After reading this chapter, you will be able to

- *Discuss the positive aspects of an integrated curriculum.*
- *Design a unit of study based on a theme that crosses curriculum boundaries.*
- *Develop unit activities that challenge student thinking while allowing students to stretch their minds across the disciplines.*

Thinking operates naturally in interdisciplinary learning situations. James Moffett summarized this position in 1968 in *The Universe of Discourse:*

> ... The division of learning into English, Mathematics, Science, Social Studies is a huge mistake. ...
>
> So I would like to propose that educators work toward a future reorganization of the total curriculum that would eliminate conventional subject divisions and would base learning on the central process of human symbolization. The distinctions between modes and levels of abstraction are far more important than distinctions in subject content. The most important things children of today will need to know when they are adults are how experience is abstracted, communicated, and utilized, whether the data are recurring phenomena of nature and society or the private truths of the heart.[1]

Imagine a humanities block, a core program combining social studies and English, or a self-contained elementary school classroom in which learners continuously make connections between form and content. Barriers of subject matter don't get in the way to cloud thinking and prevent students' minds from distinguishing between "modes and levels of abstraction." Higher-order thinking skills—applying, analyzing, synthesizing, and evaluating—are the most natural thought processes to employ,

265

once the traditional lines of the curriculum have been erased. We explore the possibilities for integrating thinking across the curriculum in this chapter.

Integrative Approaches to Teaching

Interdisciplinary studies are supported by the trend in education today to emphasize thinking in the curriculum. A high school offers humanities as a course that fulfills credit for English or social studies. Junior highs combine social studies and language arts classes with the intent that teachers will relate the two subject areas together in unified lessons. The self-contained elementary classroom has one teacher handling the entire curriculum for a single group of students. These interdisciplinary arrangements facilitate the use of integrative methods that challenge students to become independent thinkers.

WHY CHOOSE AN INTEGRATED APPROACH?

Students are much more likely to take ownership of their own learning when teachers use an integrative approach. When the historical, economical, and architectural aspects of Gothic cathedrals are meshed with a study of illuminated manuscripts and literature of the Middle Ages, the learner's mind can make great leaps rather than just be a receiver of portions of knowledge that seldom come together in the separated disciplines of the curriculum.

A special bonus offered by this integrated approach to learning is that it eases the teaching load. Instead of having two separate classes of language arts and social studies, the core teacher has one class of students for two periods. High school humanities classes often are coordinated with art and music lectures, again with the same students ideally meeting together or at least having the same exposure. Rather than sending students to "specialists" for "skill" work, the elementary teacher should consider having the "specialists" come to the regular classroom to facilitate the needs of deficient learners, thus allowing students to remain in the mainstream of learning. Such arrangements can make the classroom teacher's job easier.

ORGANIZATIONAL ARRANGEMENTS

Humanities

Many high schools, junior highs, and even elementary schools have recently added humanities studies to their curriculum. The National Endowment for the Humanities has boosted this trend in recent years by offering secondary teachers and administrators stipends to attend summer seminars at colleges and universities throughout the country. Traditionally, humanities is an interdisciplinary study of literature, history, philosophy, art, and music.

In humanities we stress an attitude of study in which the student constantly asks, What is the artist (author, composer, historian, philosopher) trying to say in this particular work? Objectivity and the quest for truth make the pursuit of humanistic studies similar to scientific inquiry. The word *humanities* connotes the crucial difference, however. Human interests and values color the field of humanities allowing great human achievements to live again and again through interpretation and appreciation. A true humanities course serves to integrate the fields of literature, history, philosophy, art, and music by helping students discover connections, perhaps through historical periods. Ideally, a humanities course pivots around and parallels other great works in different disciplines. The students have many opportunities to apply varied thinking skills as they explore these integrative studies.

Sample schedule for a high school humanities student

Sophomore: American Literature/ American History (humanities), two periods:

- French
- Biology
- Geometry
- Athletics

Senior: World Literature/ World History (humanities), two periods:

- German
- Physics
- Calculus
- Residential Planning/Design

Core Curriculum

Core curriculum, commonly used in middle school or junior high school to combine two or more class periods into a block of time, is not a new idea. Usually, the block combines language arts and social studies; occasionally, a reading class is combined with language arts. Ideally, three blocks of time or half of a student's day is integrated into one class with one or a team of teachers who interrelate the subject matter.

The social studies curriculum may dictate the course content; however, particularly if reading is included, so can a work of literature. Writing and speaking activities are generated through the interrelated studies of historical, geographical, social, and literary events, which become the focal points of such courses. Thus, through natural learning experiences, students explore new dimensions, gathering data at the knowledge level of thinking, then analyzing, evaluating, and creating.

Sample schedule for a junior high (core) student
Language Arts/Social Studies (Core), two periods:

- Science
- Algebra or Math
- Physical Education
- Spanish, Band, or Elective
- Reading or Great Books

The Self-Contained Classroom

Most conducive of all to interdisciplinary studies, it would seem, is the self-contained elementary classroom where one teacher and one class of twenty to thirty students have the luxury of an entire school year together. Unfortunately, far too many elementary teachers are systematized into lock-step programs, which dictate learning solely on the basis of basic skills achievement. Breaking free from such a regime takes courage on the part of the teacher, but the horizons that are possible become limitless.

Units of study focusing on such diverse topics as "Mexico and Its People," "Change in Our Lives," "The Need for Love," and "How Language Affects Us" offer opportunities for individual students to choose specific investigations. Studies have purpose and function as students integrate thinking, listening, speaking, reading, and writing. Studies range across the curriculum as students explore and share their findings through small-group discussions, written reports, or presentations to parents and other students. Multicultural education falls naturally into place within such comprehensive studies.

HOW TO DEVELOP A UNIT STUDY AROUND A THEME

Development of a theme across the curriculum at any grade level is essentially the same. The basic steps in planning are as follows:

1. Select a theme.
2. Establish goals and objectives.

3. Identify resources.
4. Develop a knowledge base.
5. Create learning activities.
6. Plan evaluation procedures.

The first step, that of selecting a theme, can be done one of two ways. A theme can relate to curriculum units already prescribed by a social studies text or it can be based on a work of literature. Some examples of social studies units that suggest themes are "The First Americans and Their Land," "The Middle Ages," "Turning Points to the Present," and "Asia and Oceania Today."

Two lesson plans in this chapter, from a unit that received its impetus from a seventh-grade social studies book, illustrate this idea. The text unit was entitled "Asia and Oceania Today," but the core teachers wanted to find a work of literature that could serve to focus learning on one country. By "postholing," or narrowing, the focus to China, the team was able to develop goals and objectives that would relate to their primary source, *The Good Earth*. Activities related to science, art, and even music promoted writing and thinking skills as projects developed that entailed analyzing, applying, synthesizing, and evaluating.

Another lesson plan in this chapter on Gothic cathedrals could easily be part of a fourth-, fifth-, or sixth-grade unit, "Wonders of the World"; a junior high school unit on "The Middle Ages"; or a high school unit on "Medieval Human Achievements." Infinite parts of the curriculum unfold to suggest the study of illuminated manuscripts and perhaps to include calligraphy as an activity, the study of architecture as it relates to cathedral designs of the Middle Ages, a study of secular and sacred history as reflected in stained-glass windows of the period, or a study of feudalism and its place in the social structure.

Using a simple mapping procedure, the various directions a unit theme might point become graphically clear. (See "Mapping for a Gothic Cathedral.")

Mapping for a Gothic Cathedral

Mapping for *Alice in Wonderland*

Alice in Wonderland at sixth-, eighth-, or tenth-grade levels provides a foray into a classroom "wonderland." One lesson plan in this chapter shows how an activity can integrate literature with math. Other activities in the unit might include such projects as constructing lighted peek boxes, which illustrate perspective—an art concept—while showing the hallway where Alice first followed the White Rabbit. Students masquerading as Alice and the White Rabbit, who run into classrooms to invite others to their classroom "wonderland," provide still another dimension to the unit—drama in the form of unforgettable dramatic vignettes. (See "Mapping for *Alice in Wonderland*.")

An openness on the part of the teacher is helpful once a unit based on a theme begins to unfold: One idea leads to another, and students will want to contribute suggestions for activities and directions to follow. Responsibility for developing a knowledge base are shared by teacher and students jointly as are planning for evaluation. Many lesson plans in this chapter illustrate research techniques and simple evaluation procedures that involve the students as much as the teacher.

SUMMARY

The humanities teacher, the core instructor, and the teacher of a self-contained classroom all share the unique opportunity to focus on the great works of the world without concern for artificial subject boundaries. Indeed, we owe it to our students to disclose great humanistic achievements whenever the opportunity arises. The vast treasury of human expression is the birthright of all young minds at all stages of development and at all levels of intellect. No one group has a corner on the rich marketplace, and no one should have to wait until college to discover impressionist art or the treasures of King Tut. Likewise, we should not leave it to films to acquaint our children with *The Odyssey* or to Broadway musicals to give them their first experience with a Shakespearean theme.

Planning Instruction

Dozens of different connections are possible for developing a sound inter-disciplinary study in high school, junior high, and elementary school. The lesson plans that follow could be used in a humanities class, a core curriculum, or in a self-contained classroom. These lessons suggest only a few of the possible cross-disciplinary connections, the myriad directions and designs that can be woven when thinking across the curriculum occurs. Although the depth of penetration into these studies will vary according to the maturity and abilities of students, the organizing principles are essentially the same. We explore lessons that begin with a work of literature, lessons that begin with a topic from social studies, and lessons that begin with art.

BEGIN WITH LITERATURE: SAFE DEMONSTRATION LESSON PLANS

All journeys across the curriculum must begin somewhere. Frequently, a class reads a work of literature and quite naturally finds itself delving into other disciplines in order, perhaps, to understand the work better. Ties with social studies, history, art, and even science and math can evolve easily from a rich classic. This section presents lessons that begin with a good book and diverge to other disciplines of the curriculum.

Novels with universal qualities serve to posthole, or focus, units of study at all levels. A junior high core's study of Asia can be launched with an oral reading of *The Good Earth. Cry, The Beloved Country,* which focuses on South Africa, magnetizes appropriately for our times the problems of apartheid and thus launches the study of present-day Africa. *Animal Farm* could serve as a good choice of literature to focus a social studies unit on Russia.

In Lesson Plan 10.1, the first of two lessons from a unit on Asia, *The Good Earth* is used to develop a science project in which students plant beans, the food that saves the lives of Wang Lung's family during the drought. Lesson Plan 10.2, also based on *The Good Earth* and its use as a postholing factor for a study of Asia in a junior high core class, serves as a culminating project.

The Hobbit by J. R. R. Tolkien, basis for Lesson Plan 10.3, transforms into a wonderful puppet show complete with apple-head dolls for the puppets. The dried apple-head dolls that are usually "grannies" make perfect dwarves, a wizard, and a hobbit.

There are several classics that lend themselves to Lesson Plan 10.4 where students become journalists. An all-time favorite to use with sixth or seventh graders is *The Wind in the Willows* by Kenneth Grahame.

Even the skills of mathematics have their place occasionally when classes are allowed to operate naturally without regard for "disciplines." In Lesson Plan 10.5, excerpted from a unit on *Alice in Wonderland*, a junior high core class really got excited about graph making.

A seventh-grade core class that had just finished reading Paul Zindel's *The Pigman* felt the urge to celebrate and share their excitement over the book. Hospitality, a characteristic we generally associate with the home economics department, became the guiding principle for what was called "Pigmania" (Lesson Plan 10.6).

SAFE Demonstration Lesson Plan 10.1: Bean Products, Inc.
Grade Levels: 7–9

OBJECTIVES

Students will

1. select earth in which to plant beans.
2. plant beans and cultivate their growth.
3. analyze the progress of the plants by keeping a daily log.
4. create a poster, an advertisement, a poem, a story, a cartoon, or other written product.

BRIEF DESCRIPTION

A natural activity for the Asian study stimulated by studying Pearl Buck's *The Good Earth* is to have each member of the class plant beans in a foam cup. Students must obtain their own soil as part of the learning process; however, the teacher supplies a foam cup and three beans. Watering, fertilizing, and complete cultivation of the plants are the responsibility of each student. A contest for the best three plants adds incentive; when the story is finished, the "Wang Lung," the "O-lan," and the "Ching" awards are presented to the top three "farmers." Because a daily log has been written throughout the growing of the beans, a natural off-shoot of this lesson is to have students create something original to show for all their labors. Notice that this activity could be used with younger students reading different literature.

PROCEDURES

Stimulus

Call attention to the time in *The Good Earth* when Ching gave Wang·Lung a handful of beans so his family could survive the drought. Give each student a foam cup and instruct them to bring soil the following day for planting beans.

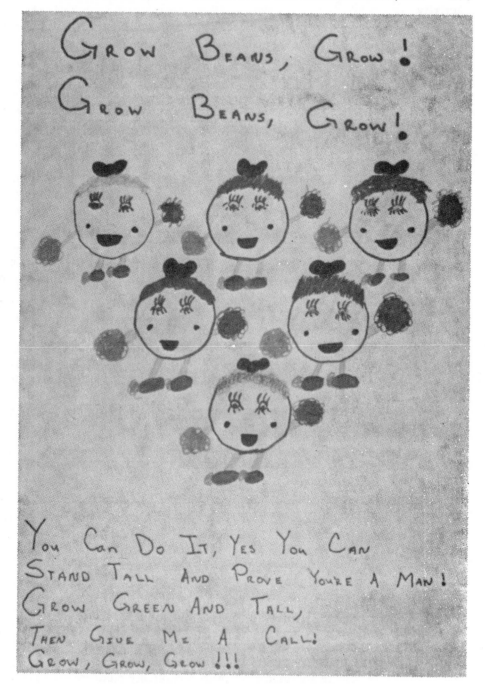

Activity

Give each student three beans to plant in the cups. Allow five minutes each day for "farming" to take place. (At this time, students may water, transplant, stake, or set their plants out in the sun.)

Each class period, have students write a log entry on the progress or lack of progress of their bean plants. Then invite volunteers to share their daily entries from logs. Finally, inform students that the top three plants will receive special awards at the end of the growing season.

Follow-Up

When *The Good Earth* has been completed by the class, it is time to give out the awards for the best three bean plants. Use a computer graphics program if possible to make the "Wang Lung," the "O-lan," and the "Ching" awards.

Using their logs, have students create cartoons, posters, advertisements, stories, poems, or any other appropriate mode that comes to mind and which can be included as a part of Bean Products, Inc. (See poem, "Grow Beans, Grow!")

Evaluation

Evaluate the bean plants themselves because a bean-growing contest is used to motivate this lesson. Evaluate each student individually. Those who are successful "farmers" will win prizes, those who are conscientious log keepers will be pleased with their entries, and those who like to go a step further with a cartoon or wanted poster will experience a special joy as well.

SAFE Demonstration Lesson Plan 10.2: Universalizing *The Good Earth* Using Pictures from *National Geographic* Grade Levels: 7–12

OBJECTIVES

Students will

1. select pictures to illustrate *The Good Earth.*
2. arrange pictures in a sequence.
3. construct transparencies of the pictures.
4. create and tape a script to accompany pictures.
5. introduce a literature selection to another class.

BRIEF DESCRIPTION

In this lesson, students use their knowledge of *The Good Earth* as a basis for comprehension, application, and synthesizing exercises by tying *National Geographic* magazine pictures to the text of the story in the form of a taped slide show.

PROCEDURES

Have students purchase a copy of *The Good Earth* voluntarily. Read one chapter aloud each day at the beginning of the period as the class "tracks." (More mature students can be assigned the reading on their own.)

Stimulus

After reading *The Good Earth*, divide the class into groups of five or six. Give each group several copies of *National Geographic*. Direct each group to search the magazines to locate pictures that could serve as illustrations of *The Good Earth*. Pin the pictures in front of the classroom for a class session on sequencing the pictures to match the story. Divide the pictures among groups in the class. Groups will make final selections and place the pictures in an appropriate order.

Activity

Form the class into "expert" groups (for example, slide makers, background-music arrangers, script writers). Each expert group researches its specialty. Include one person from each working group.

The slide makers make experimental "slides" using the clay-transfer technique. (Cut each picture to an appropriate size, place it face down on clear contact paper and rub it with a hard object such as a scissors handle, place it in warm soapy water for two minutes, rinse it gently with a clean, damp sponge to remove the paper, and allow it to dry. Later, the transferred transparent pictures will be mounted in construction paper or manila tagboard "frames.") The background-music group investigates the school library record collection as well as music available from students in the class. Possible theme music is brought to class for listening. The script writers work on an introduction, transitions, and a conclusion, which will later be taped.

All class members return to their original home groups to make the "slides" for which they are responsible. (If the teacher has used the expert groups correctly, each home group should now have one or two slide makers, background-music arrangers, and script writers.)

Each home group makes its slides and writes any dialogue needed to accompany each picture. Narrators and a cast are selected by the teacher

Posters to Advertise a Slide Show

or through tryouts, and the entire "show" is taped, complete with background music and sound effects.

Follow-Up

Make advertising posters and show the prepared "slide" show of *The Good Earth* to selected audiences for feedback. Invite other core classes to see it. Schedule it to be shown to parents at Open House.

Evaluation

Observe the degree of involvement by students in this project as well as the accuracy of the universal ties made. Form evaluation teams among each of the expert groups. Each group fills out a simple checklist concerning the success of the two other counterparts.

SAFE Demonstration Lesson Plan 10.3: Hobbitry
Grade Levels: 4–10

OBJECTIVES

Students will

1. write a script. (See "Sample Script for *The Hobbit*.")
2. construct scenery.
3. create apple-head hand puppets.
4. cast and rehearse a puppet show.
5. invite other classes to attend a puppet show.

THE HOBBIT (Script for a Puppet Show)
(Based on Chapters I, V, VIII, and XII)

NARRATOR: (from beginning on p. 11 to Now you know enough to go on with, on p. 12)

NARRATOR: By some curious chance one morning long ago in the quiet of the world there was less nose and more green, and the hobbits were still numerous and prosperous, and Bilbo Baggins was standing at his door after breakfast smoking an enormous long wooden pipe that reached nearly down to his wooly toes (neatly brushed)—Gandalf came by

BILBO: Good Morning.

GANDALF: What do you mean? Do you wish me a good morning, or mean that it is a good morning whether I want it or not; or that you feel good this morning; or that it is a morning to be good on?

BILBO: All of them at once, and a very fine morning for a pipe of tobacco out of doors, into the bargain. If you have a pipe about you, sit down and have a fill of mine. There's no hurry, we have all the day before us.
(BLOWS A SMOKE RING)

GANDALF: Very pretty. But I have no time to blow smoke-rings this morning. I am looking for someone to share in an adventure that I am arranging, and it's very difficult to find anyone.

BILBO: I should think so- in these parts. We are plain quiet folk and have no use for adventures. Nasty disturbing uncomfortable things. Make you late for dinner. I can't think what anybody sees in them, (BLOWS ANOTHER SMOKE RING AND READS HIS MORNING LETTERS)
(Gandalf continues to lean on his stick and to stare at him)
Good morning. We don't want any adventures here, thank you. You might try over The Hill or across The Water.

GANDALF: What a lot of things you do use *Good morning* for. Now you mean that you want to get rid of me, and that it won't be good till I move off.

BILBO: Not at all, not at all, my dear sit. Let me see, I don't think I know your name.

GANDALF: Yes, yes, my dear sir. And you do know my name, though you don't remember that I belong to it. I am Gandalf, and Gandalf means me. To think that I should have lived to be good-morninged by Belladonna Took's son, as if I was selling buttons at the door.

BILBO: Gandalf, Gandalf. Good gracious me. Not the wandering wizard that gave Old Took a pair of magic diamond studs that fastened themselves and never came undone till ordered. Not the fellow who used to tell such wonderful tales at parties, about dragons and goblins and giants and the rescue of princesses and the unexpected luck of widows' sons. Not the man that used to make such particularly excellent fireworks I remember thoe. Old Took used to have them on Midsummer's Eve. Splendid. They used to go up like great lilies and snapdragons and laburnums of fire and hang in the twilight all evening. Dear Me. Not the Gandalf who was responsible for so many quiet lads and lasses going off into the Blue for mad adventures, anything from climbing trees to stowing away aboard the ships that sail to the Other Side. Bless me, lide used to be quite inter - I mean, you used to upset things badly in these parts once upon a time. I beg your pardon, but I had no idea you were still in business.

Sample Script for *The Hobbit*

BRIEF DESCRIPTION

Once favorite chapters from *The Hobbit* have been selected, the class is divided into groups to write dialogue, paint scenery, make the puppets, record a sound track, and develop lighting. If a regular puppet stage is available, it saves a lot of time; however, a simple one could be constructed by the students. The process of drying the apple "heads" does take time, so allow at least a week or two. (We used diluted vinegar on ours to prevent rot.)

PROCEDURES

Stimulus

The class reads *The Hobbit*.[2] In a lower-grade level, this should be done orally by the teacher with the class "tracking." In upper grades, the reading can be assigned independently. Play a tape or show a film of the book, if it is available, to augment the reading and to give the class a feeling for its dramatic possibilities.

Activity

As a whole-class activity, reach a consensus of favorite chapters to be converted to a puppet show. Divide the class into the following groups: script writers, puppet makers, scenery designers and painters, sound track, and lighting. Allow at least two weeks for the stage-craft tasks to be completed.

Follow-Up

Hold tryouts and cast the puppet show; spend at least one week rehearsing the show. Invite other classes one period at a time to come and be the audience.

Evaluation

Evaluate the success of the puppet show on the basis of scene choices that can be successfully dramatized. Measure the success of this lesson by the enthusiasm of the audience.

SAFE Demonstration Lesson Plan 10.4: Hot Off the Press
Grade Levels: 4–7

OBJECTIVES

Students will

1. select several events in a novel to rewrite as news.
2. create newspapers featuring several aspects of the book.
3. imitate headlines and front-page stories to cover the events.

BRIEF DESCRIPTION

Students read a classic literature selection. They then create a newspaper based on events and characters in the book.

PROCEDURES

Stimulus

Read *The Wind in the Willows*[3] aloud to the class as they "track." A taped recording could be played as an alternative.

Activity

Brainstorm with the class the favorite chapters to be covered by the newspapers each small group will create. Divide the class into newspaper groups, being careful to place one or two leaders in each group. (Groups of four work well for this activity.) Brainstorm with the class names that newspapers are called such as *Herald, Star, Gazette,* and *Times,* for example.

Assign each group its chapter to cover in their bogus newspaper. Have each newspaper group choose an editor, illustrators, and reporters. It is a good idea to have a strong student serving as editor.

Follow-Up

Allow one week for newspapers to be named, headlines and stories to be written, and illustrations to be added. (Such newspaper names as *Animal Gazette*—see "Student Newspaper"—and *The Riverbanker* can be quite amusing as can such headlines as "War at Toad Hall!" or "Gypsy Wagon Smashed to Pieces at Roadside.")

Show students how to fold large plain white pieces of construction paper together like a real newspaper. Share the completed newspapers with other classes or put them on display in the school library.

Evaluation

Judge the newspaper done by each group as a whole and give each member a group grade. Grade each individual's contribution also.

1.

ANIMAL GAZETTE

Wednesday, May 12, 1978

GYPSY WAGON SMASHED TO PIECES AT ROADSIDE

Yesterday afternoon a terrible accident happened along the highroad, at about 2 o'clock pm.

A motorcar discribed as a "... glorious stirring sight. The poetry of motion ..." by Mr. Toad, residence of Toad Hall, was coming along the highroad at top speed. Taking no heed of the canary-coloured gypsy wagon, driven by the famous Mr. Toad and his two compan-

ions, Mr. Mole and Mr. Rat, raced right past it, forcing it to the side of the road. The horse reared from sheer fright of the "... rival mariners..." as called by Mr. Rat, broke loose from

—turn to page 2., col. 1.

Student Newspaper

SAFE Demonstration Lesson Plan 10.5: A Chart for All Sizes
Grade Levels: 5–10

OBJECTIVES

Students will

1. keep track of the shrinking and growing Alice while reading *Alice in Wonderland*.
2. design and make a growth chart.

BRIEF DESCRIPTION

This project is only one of many exciting ones that relate to the classic, *Alice in Wonderland*.[4] It can be done as the story unfolds in a daily oral reading of each chapter; it can be assigned to be done independently by students; or it can be done after the entire story has been read.

PROCEDURES

Stimulus

Bring several types of graphs to class, such as bar graphs and line graphs from the newspaper or other sources. Duplicate or show each type on an overhead projector. Have students bring their math books to class and turn to the sections on graphs.

Ask the class how the principles of graphs could be applied to *Alice in Wonderland*. (Most students will catch on fast to the idea of graphing Alice's shrinking and growing.)

Activity

Tell students to make a list of all the times in the story when Alice's size changes. (This can be done at the beginning of the reading or after the entire story has been read.) Have students design their own graphs depicting Alice's many sizes. (See "A Graph on Alice's Shrinking and Growing.")

Follow-Up

Have available tagboard for students to make enlarged and colorful graph charts, which can be displayed on the bulletin board or included with other projects based on *Alice in Wonderland*.

Evaluation

Evaluate each graph for its originality of design and accuracy. Have students evaluate each others' graphs and rank them as to how well they successfully illustrate the story.

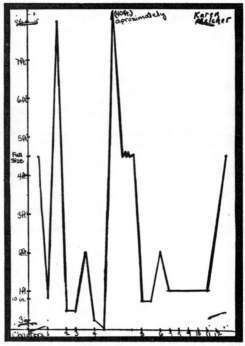

A Graph on Alice's Shrinking and Growing

SAFE Demonstration Lesson Plan 10.6: Pigmania
Grade Levels: 7–10

OBJECTIVES

Students will

1. plan a party based on a theme.
2. design invitations, decorations, refreshments, and entertainment.
3. have a Pigmania party for other students in the school.

BRIEF DESCRIPTION

After *The Pigman* has been read and enjoyed, it is time to celebrate the joy of discovering such a wonderful modern classic. Mr. Pignati's pig collection is the inspiration for pig-shaped invitations, place mats, a pig piñata, and many other ideas of which students will think. Even the refreshments served at the party can be reminiscent of food in the book. Each student is allowed to invite one friend from another class. But don't forget the entertainment. Scenes from the story can be reenacted for the guests.

PROCEDURES

Stimulus

The class reads Paul Zindel's *The Pigman*.[5] If it is a high school group or independent readers, they can simply be assigned a date by which to have the book completed. In an average class or with a group of poorer readers, it is best to have the class "track" while you read one chapter each day.

Activity

Challenge the class to plan a party to celebrate *The Pigman*. Once the challenge is accepted, brainstorm all the necessary components of a party (invitations, decorations, refreshments, favors, entertainment, and so forth.) Keep the theme of pigs in the designing and creating of all party components. Have the class decide on refreshments suitable for the party. (Chocolate-covered raisins are an agreeable substitute for the chocolate-covered ants of the story.)

Have the class select key scenes from the novel and write scripts. Have tryouts for the parts and start rehearsals. Decide who will be invited to the party (one friend each or perhaps a whole class). Finally, "mail" the invitations.

Follow-Up

Hold the party during a regular class period. Be sure to get permission from the administration for this unusual activity and inform other teachers, whose students might be invited, ahead of time.

Evaluation

Evaluate how closely the party theme matches the book. Note feedback from invited students and from other teachers who also catch the excitement of the book *The Pigman*. Gauge the excitement that reading this book produces in students.

BEGIN WITH A TOPIC: SAFE DEMONSTRATION LESSON PLANS

Other journeys across the curriculum might begin with topics presented in the textbook. The mention of a fascinating person might intrigue students enough to want to investigate the person's life further—for example, Christopher Columbus, Franklin D. Roosevelt, Mother Teresa, Raoul Wallenberg, or Andrei Sakharov. Lesson Plan 10.7 focuses on King Tut. The historical find by a famous archaeologist and his ensuing telegram to his sponsor furnish a dramatic starting point for an item-by-item analysis of many of the artifacts in the great collection of King Tut's tomb.

Great events may trigger an interest in students who want to pursue their own family history. Students in an American history class at any grade level can be led to appreciate their own heritage in Lesson Plan 10.8. Other units might focus on the Revolutionary War, the Westward Movement, the Gold Rush, the Civil War, or the Great Depression.

In an elementary self-contained classroom or in a junior high school core class, students welcome the chance to do something that has to do with advertising and, even more important, eating. Lesson Plan 10.9 is an idea that can be used in part as a single lesson or as a full-blown unit to review any geographic part of the world studied by a class.

SAFE Demonstration Lesson Plan 10.7: Re-creating the King Tut Exhibit Grade Levels: 5–7

OBJECTIVES

Students will

1. imagine the excitement of archaeology.
2. research the media and designs used to create ancient artifacts.
3. invent facsimiles of ancient Egyptian artifacts.

BRIEF DESCRIPTION

When elementary or junior high students are asked to replicate the objects from the King Tut exhibit, they become concerned about the media used in ancient Egypt, the design elements of the objects, and the uses and significance of each item. In this lesson that takes several days or even weeks to accomplish depending on the amount of time allowed daily, students are given the task of re-creating the King Tut exhibit, in part. Of the fifty-five objects, which toured the United States and are beautifully depicted on slides and in catalogues, students are given a choice of objects to re-create in small groups of four.

PROCEDURES

Stimulus

If available, show slides of the King Tut exhibit. Then duplicate the telegram sent by Howard Carter to his sponsor Lord Carnarvon when Carter first discovered the tomb. Before passing out the actual telegram to the class, have the students write their own version of what it probably said.

> AT LAST HAVE MADE WONDERFUL DISCOVERY IN VALLEY: A MAGNIFICENT TOMB WITH SEALS INTACT: RE-COVERED SAME FOR YOUR ARRIVAL: CONGRATULATIONS.

STATUE OF THE KING UPON A LEOPARD

By: Vivian Fu
Dino Dedes
Nathan Hagan
Jesus Villanueun

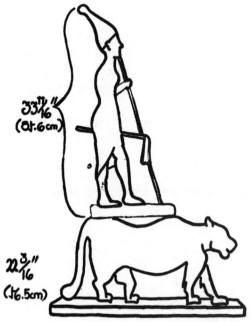

33 11/16"
(0t. 6cm)

22 3/16"
(56.5cm)

King Tut Exhibit

~ How to make ~
the statue

~ Materials ~
1. A doll
2. A panther
3. A 20 cm long stick
4. One 3" x 6" box
5. One 5" x 10" box
6. A toothpick
7. Clay
8. paper
9. Gold paint
10. Black paint

~ Equipment ~
1. scissor
2. Paint brush
3. tape
4. newspaper
5. A sharp pencil

If available, show the class *Treasures of Tutankhamun*,[6] a catalogue of the King Tut exhibit. Reproduce the list and descriptions of the fifty-five objects.

Activity

Divide the class into groups of four, taking care to balance each group with students of different abilities. Have each group select a first-, sec-ond-, and third-choice object from the list and descriptions to duplicate. (Do not allow duplicates within the class.) Inform each group of its object and begin planning sessions.

Before any actual craft work begins, insist that all proper research be accomplished by each group. Have groups work on their projects with the knowledge that they will be judged on the basis of aesthetics, authentic-ity, scale, and original use of materials (which depict the original objects the best).

Follow-Up

Each object must be displayed properly with a background or base. Each object must be accompanied by a complete description of the original item and by an explanation of the media used to replicate it by the students. (See "King Tut Exhibit.") Each object must be numbered and labeled when it is displayed with the other objects of the exhibit.

Evaluation

Judges such as school board members, principals from other schools, the art teacher, and other staff members may be asked to judge the exhibit and select winners in the following categories: Most Authentic, Most Aesthetic, Most Original, Best Displayed, and, of course, the Sweepstakes Winner over all the rest.

After so much effort, students also deserve evaluation by the teacher for their objects.

SAFE Demonstration Lesson Plan 10.8: Searching for Your Ancestors
Grade Levels: 8–11

OBJECTIVES

Students will

1. identify their heritage.
2. examine historical information in the community.
3. research an American art or craft.
4. synthesize family history with researched history.
5. apply knowledge gained about a craft through a project.

BRIEF DESCRIPTION

After investigating actual family history, students will be shown how to narrow down their search to a particular aspect of American history such as the Gold Rush. Using their imaginations and collected data, they write a colorful report about an actual or imagined ancestor. Finally, students choose a particular American craft such as quilt making or furniture building and relate the art or skill to their ancestor in the form of a project.

PROCEDURES

Stimulus

Using an American history textbook, select periods that might fit the ancestry of the class. For example, these might include the Gold Rush, the early California Mission period, the Civil War, Indian life, pioneer life at various stages, or the Westward Movement.

Tell the class about your own ancestry. Finally, show the class several films, filmstrips, or illustrations of actual American arts and crafts such as spinning, weaving, quilt making, silver smithing, glass blowing, or furniture building.

Activity

Start the class on an ancestry investigation of their own. Use the following directions: "Search, question, investigate, pry from your parents, grandparents, or other elderly relatives information about your ancestry. With permission, check old trunks, boxes, foot lockers, drawers, nooks, crannies in the basement, attic, or garage. Try to locate old musty, dusty stuff including photos, souvenirs, invitations, pictures, and letters that belonged to your great grandparents, or others in your family."

Follow-Up

Instruct students to narrow down their investigation to one ancestor such as their great grandfather or great grandmother. Have students establish the dates of his or her life (if possible), where he or she was from, whether it was another state or another country. Finally, have the student try to connect the ancestor to a particular event of the second half of the nineteenth century (see the previous suggested list).

Have students write an interesting, colorful report about their ancestor, being sure to include all the information they were able to locate. Inform students that they will be sharing their reports with the rest of the class.

Have students investigate a possible craft or skill that their ancestor may have performed. American arts such as spinning, weaving, quilt making, silver smithing, glass blowing, and furniture building are good candidates. Students should be assigned to write a brief description of how the craft was done. Some students may be able to furnish examples of handmade things. Quilt patterns offer a fascinating source for discovery. Students may want to draw patterns to scale to share as part of their projects. The découpage technique for preserving old letters, photos, or keepsakes might become a continuation of this project.

Evaluation

Monitor and evaluate students as they make their investigations. Estimate the validity of the students' correlations with real historical events. Measure the depth of student interest by the correlations made to actual American arts and crafts.

SAFE Demonstration Lesson Plan 10.9: International Bazaar and Travelog Grade Levels: 4–8

OBJECTIVES

Students will

1. locate resources and gather data about a specific country.
2. examine international cookbooks and select one recipe to test at home.
3. invent a restaurant for a city of a particular country.
4. plan an itinerary for a one-week visit to a particular country.
5. design and draw a travel poster.

BRIEF DESCRIPTION

This unit can be used as a contract during which time the class is divided into three major groups who take turns at three stations or separate areas of the classroom. The three areas would be a filmstrip-viewing area where three or four individual filmstrip projectors and strips representing all the countries studied in the unit are available, a cookbook "corner" where a large collection of international cookbooks (from the library) is located, and a travel agency where art supplies for making posters are available.

PROCEDURES

Stimulus

One-third of the class (in pairs) selects and views one filmstrip from a collection (from the school library) and answers questions about their country pertaining to basic geographic features and culture.

One-third of the class (in pairs) studies several tables of contents from a large number of international cookbooks (from the school library) and reads recipes in order to choose one that they will share with the class.

One-third of the class (in pairs) reads several travel brochures in order to grasp the style of typical travel-brochure language.

Activity

Students who are viewing filmstrips answer the following questions:

1. The population of _____ is _____. The density is _____.

2. The capital of _____ is _____. Its population is _____.

3. The chief exports of _____ are _____, _____, _____, _____.

4. The chief language spoken in _____ is _____.

5. The climate of _____ is _____.

6. The natural regions of _____ are _____, _____, _____, and _____.

(Some of these questions may have to be answered with the textbook.)

Students who are examining cookbooks select foods appropriate to their country and begin planning a restaurant and menu. *Directions:* Invent a restaurant that will be visited by tourists on a guided tour of your country. Design and make a menu that presents some of the most typical foods. Give your restaurant a name and print it on your menu (tagboard material provided in class). Completed menus will be displayed in class and later bound into a class book.

Students who have been examining travel brochures are ready to begin writing their tour itinerary. *Directions:* From information gathered in your text (and later, from your filmstrip), plan an itinerary (schedule of stops) for a one-week visit to _____ (your country). Each stop should focus on a major sight. The plan should explain in detail what the visitors will be doing (see the following examples).

Saturday: Jaipur/New Delhi. By elephant, ride up to the Amber Fort. You will be accompanied by musicians playing the traditional "Sarangi" music. Also visit the City Palace, Museum, and open-air observatories. Then fly to New Delhi, India's bustling capital.

Second Day, Sunday: Ireland. In Shannon, Ireland, we are met at the airport and escorted to our hotel. The afternoon is free, and tonight we are invited to a merry medieval welcome dinner at Dunratty Castle. Colleens serve us victuals of yesteryear to the mellow sound of harp music.

Eighth Day: Mombasa. Morning sightseeing shows us the old Arab section and Fort Jesus, built by the Portuguese in 1593. We also visit an African handicrafts locale, where wooden animals are made and sold. Afternoon at leisure for beaches, swimming, a dugout-canoe trip, perhaps—just as we please.

Follow-Up

Once all students have been exposed to all three stations, they are ready to begin work on the final drafts of their projects (that is, restaurant menu, travel itinerary). Have each pair of students pick one or more major sights of their country and design a travel poster that includes drawings or pictures of it or them. They should make up a catchy phrase for their poster, which will interest tourists in a trip to their country. (Have actual travel posters available as examples; travel agencies will often donate old ones to teachers.)

Evaluation

All of the above activities should lead to a culminating sharing time. At an "International Bazaar and Travelog," evaluate the overall success of the project and the individual effort put forth by each partnership. Provide an audience for this project by inviting parents or another class.

BEGIN WITH ART: SAFE DEMONSTRATION LESSON PLANS

Art is atypical as a beginning point, yet the rewards for following the directions it leads are limitless and lasting. Becoming aware for the first time of a great cathedral or discovering a work of art as a life-long pleasure profoundly affects students' thinking.

The cultural epoch or style-period approach so typical of college humanities courses works well in high school although it need not be confined to the upper grades. Medieval cathedrals can be the starting point for high school, elementary, or junior high school students who are taken on a "pilgrimage" with cathedral music in the background and slides of Chartres (Lesson Plan 10.10).

Sometimes the approach in interdisciplinary studies can begin with an element of art such as design (Lesson Plan 10.11). Teaching the distinction between curvilinear design of ancient Crete juxtaposed with geometric designs of the later Greek period can form a basis for understanding the epithets and many of the other traditional aspects of *The Odyssey*. And so art leads to literature.

Timing is essential in a good interdisciplinary course where opportunities must be taken whenever they occur. When the curiosity is there, the teacher must take advantage by interrupting the current lesson and capitalizing on the interest of the students. The opportunity to tie Impressionism to the art of writing a good essay occurred in a seventh-grade language arts class. One day, the class came upon one of van Gogh's "Sunflowers" reproduced on a page of its language arts text. "Oh, I could do that" or "What's so great about this painting?" piqued the teacher enough to cause her to bring in her special collection of slides purchased years before at a famous museum in Amsterdam. Lesson Plan 10.12 demonstrates how to look at a painting.

Fine art is probably the most neglected aspect of the humanities in schools today. Art classes usually devote most of their time to crafts, leaving an appreciation of the great works of artists to die on the vine. But Lesson Plan 10.13 presents a way to make it a vital concern of students in any class where journals are kept.

SAFE Demonstration Lesson Plan 10.10: A Pilgrimage to Chartres
Grade Levels: 4–12

OBJECTIVES

Students will

1. experience a sixteenth-century pilgrimage.
2. describe a medieval cathedral.
3. select a subtopic to study concerning medieval cathedrals.
4. compose an essay, story, or poem.

BRIEF DESCRIPTION

Using a slide collection of Chartres or of any medieval cathedral, the class is taken on a "pilgrimage." Using whatever background music is available (this example uses sixteenth-century music), the class is treated to a slide show complete with commentary to help them experience the grandeur of these masterpieces of the Middle Ages. Students of all ages will want to embark in various directions to study Gothic architecture, stained-glass windows, illuminated manuscripts, the medieval village, and much more.

PROCEDURES

Stimulus

Play a record ("Echoes from a 16th Century Cathedral," Roger Wagner Chorale) and show a series of slides of Chartres that begins with a view of Chartres in the distance and progressively brings us closer and closer and eventually inside.

As the slides and music are presented, read the following commentary aloud: It is the sixteenth century and you are on a pilgrimage to the cathedral of Notre Dame de Chartres. You have been traveling for several days when suddenly, at the crest of a distant hill, you at last see your destination. As you continue your approach, a host of feelings begins to arise in you. The strains of the distant choir begin to be heard, becoming louder and louder as you continue toward the spires of the medieval church. You realize that you are no longer tired. You become totally unaware of the distinctiveness of this great edifice, unaware of the texture of the music you hear—but simply overcome by the emotions you feel as you get closer and closer and finally enter Chartres Cathedral. (Once inside the cathedral, the commentary can stop so that students can simply experience the stained-glass windows with the light shining through as well as the exquisite statuary.)

Activity

During the above presentation, the students may take notes that reflect their feelings, including sensory descriptions.

Follow-Up

Tie the study of medieval cathedrals into the course of study by giving a brief background on Gothic architecture to students. Next subdivide the broad subject into parts of the whole and organize the class into small groups to study the following: stained-glass windows, Gothic architecture, illuminated manuscripts, Gothic sculpture, the medieval village, and any other areas that students have an interest in. Then launch the class into a study of several particular cathedrals other than Chartres such as Amiens, Reims, Notre Dame de Paris, Leon, Beauvais. Finally, have students use original notes from the "Activity" along with information gathered in their special study as a basis for an essay, story, or poem.

Evaluation

Judge the success of the project by the interest of the students. Note the degree of synthesis students are able to achieve in their completed essays, stories, or poems.

SAFE Demonstration Lesson Plan 10.11: From Pottery to Poetry
Grade Levels: 8–12

OBJECTIVES

Students will

1. recognize basic principles and elements of design.
2. observe basic techniques involved in pottery making.
3. compare and contrast design of ancient Greece.
4. distinguish between characteristic designs of pottery in two periods.
5. interpret the style of Homer's description of "things" in *The Odyssey*.
6. Interpret the epithets in *The Odyssey*.
7. cite the balance of harmony in the relationship between gods and goddesses and humans.
8. value rhythmic repetition.

BRIEF DESCRIPTION

This is an unusual way to approach a study of *The Odyssey*.[7] Because the Homeric poems are rooted in the Bronze Age of the myths, the age of Neptune, we can help students grasp an understanding of the fundamentals of this epic form through a comparison of vase designs from that time. *The Odyssey* is a Bronze Age poem dealing with Bronze Age legends and a Bronze Age hero and heroine all shaped into a special epic form or tradition. This lesson (which requires several days) could serve as an introduction to the great classic.

PROCEDURES

Stimulus

Acquaint students with the basic elements of art including design, line, pattern, shape and composition using a book such as Marion Downer's *Discovering Design*[8] or a magazine such as *Artist Junior, the Art Magazine for the Classroom*.[9]

Introduce the technique of pottery making to students through a filmstrip ("Ceramics," Charles A. Bennett Co., Inc.). Finally, show students pictures of both Bronze Age vases and geometric period vases using Reynold Higgins' *Minoan and Mycenean Art*[10] and Homann Wedeking's *The Art of Archaic Greece*.[11]

Activity

Elicit from students the contrasting characteristics of the two styles of vase painting (*Minoan* and *Mycenean:* feminine, organic, disorganized, impressionistic, curvilinear, decorative, natural subjects, informal, growth, vitality; *Geometric:* masculine, inorganic, organized, symbolic, rectilinear, abstract, formal, powerful, patterns inspired by weaving).

Call attention in Book I, pp. 28–29 (E. V. Rieu translation) of *The Odyssey* to the description of things: "great pillars," "wooden rack," "carved chair," "inlaid easychair," "handsome golden jug," "silver basin," "polished table," and "gold cups." Have students continue this list. Test whether students can grasp the blend of styles represented by these descriptions as being preserved sentiments of an ideal world.

Do the same thing also in Book I with epithets such as "that powerful goddess, the Nymph Calypso," "the heroic Odysseus," "Hermes, the keen-eyed Giant-slayer," "the goddess of the flashing eyes, Athene," "the wise Odysseus," and begin a class list of these stock phrases so that students can see how such character descriptions operate as both controlling factors of form as well as the life blood of the story.

Follow-Up

Working in small groups of four, five, or six, have students prepare oral readings of various books of *The Odyssey*. Suggest that they devise a way to suggest the repetitive stylistic form of the epithets and descriptions of objects as a part of their presentations. (Face masks could be constructed using paper plates, and cardboard objects representing the special "things" could be constructed.)

Divide the class into specialized groups to take a close look at the following aspects of *The Odyssey:* the religious significance of gods and goddesses who continually transform and man's relationship to them, the social order as represented in the poem, and the relationship between male and female. If the same topic is given to at least two different groups, a panel discussion might be staged or even a debate if opposing opinions emerge.

Evaluation

Note the ability of students to apply the underlying principle of this lesson in "Follow-Up" extensions. Note also the degree of synthesis students are able to make between the two vase painting styles as the basic epic form in *The Odyssey*.

SAFE Demonstration Lesson Plan 10.12: Looking at a Painting
Grade Levels: 3–9

OBJECTIVES

Students will

1. analyze the ideas held by the artist of a painting.
2. assess a painting objectively.
3. compose topic sentences for a paragraph on a painting.

BRIEF DESCRIPTION

Students analyze famous paintings to determine the most important elements. They create topic sentences to describe these ideas.

PROCEDURES

Stimulus

Show several slides of famous paintings to the class. (It is best to keep them all within the same art period or style.) Choose one slide and have the class name everything they see in the picture as the list is recorded on the board. Have the class decide the order of importance of each named thing. With the class, cross out the least important items. Have the class compose topic sentences that include the most important features on the list. Have the class vote on the best topic sentence.

Activity

Show another painting and have each student do the same exercise independently. Have volunteers share their topic sentences. Divide the class by rows and have them gather around one reproduction each of a painting (from art books in the school library) and perform the same exercise as a group. Each row or group must reach agreement on one topic sentence for its painting. Share each painting and topic sentence with the entire class.

Follow-Up

Write each topic sentence on the board near its painting. Then have each student choose one of the topic sentences and its painting and write a complete paragraph about the painting. Next have the students pair up to read their completed paragraphs to each other. Finally, call for a volunteer to read a paragraph about each painting.

Evaluation

Evaluate the topic sentences and give a "row" or group grade. Collect and evaluate each paragraph for its objectivity.

SAFE Demonstration Lesson Plan 10.13: Art Treasure Hunt
Grade Levels: 7–12

OBJECTIVES

Students will

1. locate ten works of art that represent personal values.
2. examine and classify art by medium.
3. characterize art by style period.
4. document the content of ten works of art.
5. conclude the meanings of ten works of art.

BRIEF DESCRIPTION

This lesson, which can be ongoing for several weeks, allows students to choose works of art to study, which represent their own preferences. Each student is instructed to hunt for ten works each representing a specific ideal or favorite aspect such as "my ideal mate" or "my favorite colors" in an abstract work of art. A journal entry for each choice is carefully made and includes not only a sketch of each work but also a written explanation of the medium used. In other words, the student addresses three questions about each work selected: How? What? Why?

PROCEDURES

Stimulus

Check out a cart of art books from the school library. Share with the class some of your favorite works from the following categories:

- Your ideal mate in art
- Your ideal child in art
- Your ideal hero or heroine in art (young or old)
- Your ideal place to spend your leisure hours
- Your ideal place to live
- Your ideal place to work
- Your favorite thing(s)
- Your favorite animal in art
- An abstract work with your favorite colors
- An abstract work in a design that you really like

Share also the particular medium of each choice (for example, watercolor, oil, ink drawing, collage, statue, and so forth.) Tell students the name of the style period each work represents (for example, Renaissance, Gothic, Romanticism, and so forth.)

Activity

Assign students the task of hunting for and finding ten treasures of their own. Each student must find one work for each of the above categories. (You may want to spread this over an entire quarter and assign one category a week.)

Illustrate how each "find" is to be entered into a journal. There should be two pages for each entry (a left and a right together). The student should attempt to draw a small pencil sketch of each choice on the first page (no one's lack of art ability will be counted against him or her). This sketch is for identifying the work and helping the student to remember it. The right-hand page is to be divided into thirds and labeled with the following subtitles: "Technique" (How), "Subject Matter" (What), and "Content" or "Meaning" (Why).

Follow-Up

Plan periodic sharing periods during which volunteers will share the choices they have made as well as the journal entries. Use these sharing sessions to discuss problems and to make decisions on appropriate supplementary lessons to give the class. There are many films and filmstrips available on art techniques that would fit perfectly into the curriculum at this point. Let the interest and enthusiasm of the class be your guide.

Evaluation

Evaluate these lessons on the basis of students' enthusiasm. If students begin to check out biographies of famous artists and books on various aspects of art from the library, assume that the project has been a success.

SUMMARY

The most effective way to engage students in thinking is to introduce a broad theme or issue in which all can become involved. Each student can operate at his or her individual level of ability as part of the group process. Students have an opportunity to apply varied levels of thinking as they gather data, then analyze, compare, and evaluate. Automatically, they will discover the need to return to the data-collection stage. Throughout this integrative learning experience, students share information orally and in writing, and they can be encouraged to use innovative ways of publishing their final report to the class or to a larger audience. Such integrative studies cross levels and the usual discipline divisions. Student involvement in planning and conducting these studies engages student interest so that thinking really does take place. Thus, the classroom becomes a learning laboratory in which students enjoy working with a teacher who is a guide, facilitator, and resource. The classroom becomes a center of inquiry.

CHALLENGE

Develop a lesson that is based on a work of literature, an aspect of a social studies text, or that is grounded in architecture, painting, sculpture, or some other art medium. Plan the lesson so that students will move to a different discipline from which they began.

Following the models in this chapter, develop a lesson that begins in your discipline but crosses to some aspect of music, art, literature, history, or philosophy.

Obtain a slide set of a major architectural edifice (for example, a medieval cathedral, an ancient Greek or Roman ruin, an Egyptian monument), select background music, and write a guided fantasy to accompany both. Use these to introduce the study of a period in history or art.

Select a classic work of literature that can represent, due to its universality, a unit in social studies. Prepare lessons that integrate a variety of other disciplines.

NOTES

1. James Moffett, *Teaching the Universe of Discourse* (Boston: Houghton Mifflin, 1983), Chapter 7, Conclusion.
2. J. R. R. Tolkien, *The Hobbit* (New York: Ballantine Books, 1965).
3. Kenneth Grahame, *The Wind in the Willows* (New York: Grossett & Dunlap, 1966).
4. Lewis Carroll, *Alice in Wonderland* (New York: Macmillan, 1963).
5. Paul Zindel, *The Pigman* (New York: Dell, 1968).
6. Katherine Stoddert Gilbert, Joan K. Holt, and Sara Hudson, eds., *Treasures of Tutankhamun* (New York: The Metropolitan Museum of Art, 1976).
7. E. V. Rieu, trans., *Homer* (Baltimore: Penguin Books, 1955).
8. Marion Downer, *Discovering Design* (New York: Lothrop, Lee and Shepard Co., 1947).
9. *Artist Junior, The Art Magazine for the Classroom;* "Design" 3, no. 5; "Magic of Line" 4, no. 5; "Pattern" 6, no. 4 (Feb. 1965); "Shape" 7, no. 3 (Jan. 1966); "Composition" 5, no. 2 (Nov. 1963).
10. Reynold Higgins, *Minoan and Mycenean Art* (New York–Washington: Praeger, 1967).
11. Homann Wedeking, *The Art of Archaic Greece.*

EXPLORING FURTHER

Eisner, E., ed. *Learning and Teaching the Ways of Knowing. 84th Yearbook of the National Society for the Study of Education, Part II.* Chicago: University of Chicago Press, 1985.

Perkins, David, and Barbara Leondar, eds. *The Arts and Cognition.* Baltimore: Johns Hopkins University Press, 1977.

Phillips, R. C. *Teaching for Thinking in High School Social Studies.* Reading, Mass.: Addison-Wesley, 1974.

Sinatra, R. *Visual Connections to Thinking, Reading, Writing.* Springfield, Ill.: Thomas, 1986.

Thaiss, Christopher, and Charles Suhor, eds. *Speaking and Writing, K–12: Classroom Strategies and the New Research.* Urbana, Ill.: National Council of Teachers of English, 1984.

It's good to make plans, to dream of a distant goal, but only if the dreaming is accomplished by realistic effort on our part.

Margaret Mead

The principal goal of education is to create men who are capable of doing new things, not simply of repeating what other generations have done — men who are creative, inventive, and discoverers. The second goal of education is to form minds which can be critical, can verify, and not accept everything they are offered.

Jean Piaget

The mere formulation of a problem is often far more essential than its solution, which may be merely a matter of mathematical or experimental skill. To raise new questions, new possibilities, to regard old problems from a new angle requires creative imagination and marks real advances in science.

Albert Einstein

I found that I could say things with color and shapes that I couldn't say in any other way — things that I had no words for.

Georgia O'Keeffe

CHAPTER 11

Reflection: Infusing Thinking into All Instruction

We wrote this book because we wanted to have an impact on teaching, to improve what we offer students in K–12 classrooms across the country. In this book, we have given you an overview of the many types of thinking that make up the learning process. We have made a sincere effort, furthermore, to provide you with practical lesson plans that carry out the theory and research available to us, lessons that you can implement in your own classroom. Within this book are ideas sufficient to enhance the curriculum of every elementary school, every middle school, every high school in the nation.

Yet, our efforts will have little significance unless what we have presented here is translated into practice by thousands of you who teach in classrooms with children and young adults in public and private schools. Now, we face the reality to which Margaret Mead refers on the opposite page. In this chapter, we want to talk with you, therefore, about applying what we have introduced in your daily instructional activities.

We would like to reflect on thinking instruction together, restating what we believe about teaching thinking. We need to face the obstacles that impede the teaching of thinking as well as to consider possible ways we think it could realistically happen. We would like to publicize exemplary practices with the hope that other teachers, schools, and school districts will move in similar directions. In this concluding chapter, we will address the following:

A Review of Our Beliefs
    The Underlying Assumptions
    Desired Outcomes for Every Student
Obstacles That Prevent Success
    Limited Definitions of "Thinking"

A Review of Our Beliefs

We began in Chapter 1 with an explanation of what we hoped to present in this book. Chapter by chapter we discussed different perspectives of the thinking process and related ideas. Many writers are entering the field who represent varied points of view and degrees of knowledge. We know that our ideas differ from others who are speaking out.

Informed by practice and in-depth knowledge of language and literacy development, we present thinking as a spiraling process that cannot be fractionated into discrete skills that students apply in linear fashion. We would like to summarize our beliefs for you and for ourselves because we feel that they should be made very clear if we are to carry them out.

THE UNDERLYING ASSUMPTIONS

To avoid having these beliefs remain as "underlying assumptions," we want to make a succinct statement of these understandings. We take this opportunity, therefore, to make explicit what we believe about teaching students to think, which becomes for us, teaching *for* thinking.

1. All children are eager and able learners. Any child who learns to speak has demonstrated the ability to think at the most advanced levels without instruction.

2. Thinking requires a broad definition that includes creativity, criticism, intuition, reflection. It is both affective and cognitive. Thinking skills are not clearly linear or sequential nor are they hierarchical in the sense that some thinking is better than others. From data collection to evaluation, skills are used recursively as needed during learning experi-

ences from preschool years through adulthood; all skills are necessary and they operate interdependently.

3. The unique aspect of thinking that teachers can introduce to students is metacognition as learners of all ages become aware of the thinking processes in which they do engage. As students consciously monitor their thinking processes, they will become more reflective thinkers, and real learning (change) will occur.

4. Teachers must also work consciously with metacognitive processes to become reflective practitioners who are aware of what they are thinking, what is happening in the classroom, and why they choose specific strategies. Only through such awareness will traditional instructional practices be improved.

5. Thinking is more than a set of discrete skills that students must be taught, and thinking instruction must be more than a package of prepared lessons to insert into the curriculum. Thinking begins naturally with language learning in a holistic unstructured context. Instruction plans should include opportunities for thinking to continue to grow as students grapple with ideas and issues according to their mental ability and maturity. Direct instruction can provide a context and scaffolding for growth as students encounter the literature and content of varied fields. Students will be motivated to inquire into studies that they help to select, plan, and evaluate. Focus in the classroom should be chiefly on teaching *for* thinking.

6. Thinking processes are an integral part of every subject studied and of every instructional activity. We need to recognize that thinking is infused throughout the total curriculum and be aware of the thinking processes that we are trying to stimulate through instruction. We cannot prevent students from thinking, but we do influence how and what they share with us.

7. The teaching of thinking should not be a class set apart from all other learning. As thinking is infused, so thinking instruction should be infused throughout the total curriculum at all levels. Instruction must always begin with recognition of students' prior knowledge and experience.

8. Many strategies used today by the skillful teacher engage students in thinking. We need to help teachers recognize when they are already teaching for thinking and then help them to increase the opportunities for thinking to occur in their classrooms. To be successful, thinking instruction must evolve from within rather than be imposed from outside.

9. The best way to teach for thinking is through integrated studies that engage students in making choices, decisions, and generalizations in real life contexts working with varied content. Writing *for* teachers or working *for* grades in school is not a real-life situation.

10. Thinking in classrooms must involve students in data collection, data processing, and data publication (orally, in writing, or through other media). Students at all levels must have opportunities to think intuitively, creatively, critically, and reflectively.

Thinking and language learning occur together beginning at birth in a very natural, unstructured way. Our fear is that well-meaning educators could endanger the students' learning to think by forcing students to drill on fragmented thinking exercises that stifle creativity and reflection. It has been said that if schools taught children how to speak, they would never learn. We made this mistake with reading instruction, making the task as difficult as we could, and we are only now beginning to recognize emergent literacy as the natural, and most effective, way for children to learn to read. We should be smart enough not to make the same mistake twice so soon again. Those who are engaging in thinking instruction should study carefully current development in literacy instruction, for it has much to say to us who would encourage student thinking.

We have drawn from many sources in refining our ideas about thinking instruction. Selected sources are listed at the end of this chapter. We would caution you, however, to trust your own judgment and above all, to observe how students do engage in thinking right before your eyes. Then apply all that you know about effective teaching; step down from the podium and join with students in what they are trying to do.

DESIRED OUTCOMES FOR EVERY STUDENT

What are the objectives for a thinking instruction program? What are we trying to achieve? Based on the preceding statement, we see goals and objectives in terms of student outcomes as we work with a student-driven, rather than a teacher-dominated curriculum. During any period of instruction, we would want students to

1. be aware that they do think all the time.
2. see their own thinking as having value and demonstrate a growing sense of self-esteem.
3. take time to think, to reflect on what they are doing and recognize that emotions affect thinking.
4. take pleasure in original, creative thinking, including humor, their own and that of others.
5. recognize the importance of collecting data to substantiate decision making and to reflect on the process. Demonstrate willingness to change a decision based on new evidence.
6. express their opinions in speaking and writing providing evidence to substantiate their opinions; present an argument; recognize different perspectives from which we can view issues.

7. engage in individual and group problem solving; respect ideas contributed by others, different points of view.

8. engage actively in constructing meaning as they interact with others, including the authors of literature that they read.

9. question the thinking of others—underlying assumptions, knowledge, expertise—but also recognize the existence of different perspectives; willingness to try on different points of view.

10. act as informed young citizens who know and care about what is happening in the world around them.

This summary may sound ideal, but it should and could be occurring in classrooms at all levels. It is the kind of thinking that undergirds multicultural education. It is the kind of thinking that can happen only in student-centered classrooms in which the teacher strives to support rather than dominate student learning.

Obstacles That Prevent Success

We can identify elements of teaching, curriculum, and the school that make quality thinking instruction difficult or impossible to achieve. Once we identify these elements, it is hoped that we can alleviate or eliminate them.

LIMITED DEFINITIONS OF "THINKING"

For many teachers and administrators, thinking is equated with "critical or higher-order thinking skills." This definition presupposes a required sequence of skills that build on one another, mounting in linear fashion to the highest or best skills. Teachers operating with this definition search out a set of published materials through which students must work to acquire these thinking skills in order of difficulty. This definition tends to omit intuitive, creative, and reflective thinking.

Teachers who are broadly aware of constructs proposed through the years by Freud, Skinner, and Piaget, to mention only a few theoreticians, are critical of definitions derived from only one perspective, recognizing how knowledge evolves. Aware of developments in the study of language and literacy acquisition, for example, they see the connections between such learning and our knowledge about thinking ability. They operate with a broader, less confining definition of thinking that includes creative, critical, and reflective thinking. They recognize, too, the importance of intuitive thinking and the influence of emotion on thinking, and they are aware of knowing as being both affective and cognitive. The informed teacher will step down from the lecturer's podium to work as a learner with students as they undertake an exciting voyage of discovery together.

THE TEACHER-DOMINATED CLASSROOM

Traditionally, the classroom has been teacher-dominated. The teacher plans instruction, including content, delivery, and evaluation. Students do what the teacher assigns, writing to please the teacher, striving to get a top grade from the teacher. The dominant teacher *tells* students, trying to give them all that he or she has learned. The teacher uses a published textbook to assist in delivering instruction with a typical assignment being to read a chapter and to answer the questions printed at the end. This teacher knows the right answers and, even though kindly, teaches chiefly for error avoidance, teaching students thus to fear making a mistake. Most parents would respect and support this kind of teaching.

As we learn more about thinking, however, we realize that a teacher who has greater ego strength is not afraid to relinquish the authority role or to say, "I don't know." This teacher observes how students learn, what motivates student learning, and respects student thinking. Thus, the classroom becomes student-centered with the teacher's role being to help students do what they are trying to do. At times students may assume a teaching role and the teacher will be a learner with the rest of the class. The secure teacher will schedule time for students to discover information, to experience problem-solving processes, to share the wonder of knowing. And, evaluation will reflect expectations congruent with the objectives implicit in the student-centered classroom.

Teacher-training institutions must rethink their programs so that teachers at all levels learn how to work more flexibly with students. Teacher education must provide information about the thinking processes and the best methods of promoting thinking in the classroom. New teachers entering the field with such training can serve as models for teachers who were trained in earlier years.

THE PRESCRIBED CURRICULUM

Seldom do teachers and students have great flexibility in deciding what happens in a classroom, for classroom instruction is regulated in many ways. Curriculum content is usually spelled out in a state course of study, and the state-level regulations are reflected in a districtwide course of study that is distributed to each teacher. Textbooks, sometimes selected at the state level, are often permitted to dictate the content and the method of delivering the curriculum for each grade or subject. Finally, testing also dictates curriculum content as parents and schoolboards evaluate teacher success based on student scores.

Determining curriculum is an area in which teachers are justified in exerting their professional expertise. Unless teachers have flexibility in selecting content and the method of delivery, it is unlikely that teaching an integrated program that maximizes the connections among skills and content areas will be possible.

THE STRUCTURE OF THE SCHOOL

Most secondary schools are structured for teaching in isolated classrooms focusing on one subject at a time. Instruction is divided, furthermore, into rigid segments of time, a particular disadvantage in middle school and high school instruction. Each day students must deal with a number of discrete subjects, preparing to please a number of different instructors. The self-contained elementary classroom is a pleasant exception to this segmentation.

Another aspect of the school structure that proves problematic is governance that remains "top-down." The principal communicates decisions made by the board and superintendent, and teachers carry them out. There exists, too, an unnatural distancing between school administrators and the teaching staff, an unhealthy distrust. Seldom is shared decision making an actuality. We need to recognize that all of us are working toward a common goal from preschool through higher education. We need to work together to achieve a method of providing education for young people that constantly considers the good of the learner above all else.

TESTING AND EVALUATION METHODS

Testing—assessment, measurement, evaluation—has been overdone in our school system as a whole. Students spend much of instructional time taking tests. Published test scores in local newspapers compare one school to another with no consideration of the factors that may be involved. Teacher evaluation based on student performance on test scores pushes teachers to teach for the test so that tests determine the curriculum to a large extent. Tests are usually objective and not always well-constructed. Published by outside experts, they seldom reflect what a teacher, school, or district is trying to do.

We need new methods of evaluating student performance. If instruction is to be individualized, if it is to be integrated so as to aid students in recognizing important relationships, evaluation must also be designed for the specific task and the individual students involved. Furthermore, evaluation should not always be determined by outsiders. Students and teachers can work together to identify the criteria by which a task or performance is to be evaluated, and then the students can help to apply the criteria as they learn to think and to evaluate their work and that of their peers.

SUMMARY

Obstacles do exist, but they are not insurmountable. The problems we have identified in this section can be overcome by teachers and administrators working in schools together, and it is beginning to happen.

Promising Practices and Ideas in Teaching Thinking

Exemplary practices do exist. We can point out ideas and projects that do promote the growth of thinking abilities much as we would hope. These practices must receive publicity so that others will recognize their worth and strive to emulate them. Other ideas recommended here are just beginning to evolve.

TEACHERS AS RESEARCHERS

An exciting movement that is springing up across the country is research conducted by classroom teachers. Sometimes organized into course structures, or more often informally as groups that meet to share what they are doing, teacher–researchers are discovering the excitement and importance of monitoring their own instruction.

Observing with a clinical eye, teachers may focus on motivation, self-esteem, thinking, or another interest or concern of their choice. How are the students performing, and what are they as teachers doing in response? As they observe, they shape their methods. They may involve students directly in the study: Let's decide what will motivate you to learn and see if it works. The focus for this classroom research is selected by the individual teacher, an informed insider.

Through such self-motivated reflection on teaching, change does happen. Listed here are books that may suggest possibilities to you:

Dixie Goswami and Peter Stillman, eds. *Reclaiming the Classroom: Teacher Research as an Agency for Change.* Upper Montclair, N.J.: Boynton/Cook, 1987.

Marian Mohr and Marion Maclean. *Working Together: A Guide for Teacher-Researchers.* Urbana, Ill.: National Council of Teachers of English, 1987.

A. Wotring and R. Tierney. *Two Studies of Writing in High School Science.* San Jose, Calif.: Bay Area Writing Project, 1982.

SELF-ESTEEM, THE BOTTOM LINE

We have rediscovered the importance of self-actualization and developing an "I can" attitude in each student. We realize that students with a strong sense of self-esteem are better prepared to get along with other persons who may come from different ethnic groups; thus, the groundwork is laid for true multicultural education. Self-esteem may also prove to be a key factor in persuading "at risk" students to remain in school rather than dropping out at the first opportunity. The growth of self-esteem begins at birth, so the preschool years are crucial. Self-esteem is, indeed, the bottom line.

We are learning, too, that self-esteem is also essential for the teacher. Only the psychologically secure teacher can step back to permit young learners to discover; this teacher has no need to represent the authority, the source of all knowledge. The strong teacher is not afraid to say, "I don't know. Let's find out together." The following books suggest ideas you may find helpful:

Matthew McKay and Patrick Fanning. *Self-Esteem*. New York: St. Martin's, 1987.

Pamela Tiedt and Iris Tiedt. *Multicultural Teaching*. Needham Heights, Mass.: Allyn and Bacon, 1986.

WRITING AS THINKING

The National Writing Project initiated ongoing staff development on the teaching of writing in K–14 classrooms across the country. Out of this effort evolved understandings and methods that support student thinking—for example, teaching students to work in small groups to edit each other's writing. Soon, teachers recognized that thinking precedes writing, that writing expresses thinking, and that writing also serves to extend thinking. Students learned, too, to write for audiences other than the teacher and to work for greater rewards than the grade given by the teacher. Our book was written by teachers who worked with one site of the National Writing Project. Other books you may find helpful include the following:

Julie Jensen, ed. *Composing and Comprehending*. Reston, Va.: ERIC Clearinghouse on Reading and Communications Skills, 1984.

Judith Langer and Arthur Applebee. *How Writing Shapes Thinking: A Study of Teaching and Learning*. Urbana, Ill.: National Council of Teachers of English, Research Report No. 22, 1987.

James Squire, ed. *The Dynamics of Language Learning*. Urbana, Ill.: National Conference on Research in English, 1987.

Iris Tiedt. *Writing: From Topic to Evaluation*. Needham Heights, Mass.: Allyn and Bacon, 1989.

TEACHER EDUCATION FOR EMPOWERMENT

The reform-in-education movement continues to cry for improved training for teachers. Chiefly, this effort focuses on ensuring that all teachers first have a strong major content field with no competition from pedagogy during the first four years of university study. Certification for teaching is then deferred until a fifth year of education. Programs that offer teacher training within the undergraduate four years are suspect and are expected to be phased out.

Those who advocate reform are missing the opportunity to press for teacher education that truly empowers the teacher to think and to stimulate the thinking of his or her students. More content courses will be beneficial as a foundation for teacher education only if they model the thinking processes we have described thus far. Students who experience a model designed for empowerment will expect to work in similar ways with the students they teach. Thus, the cycle will continue. The literature is yet to be written explicating teacher education for empowerment, but some authors have presented a case for integrated, student-centered instruction, as in the following books:

James Moffett, and Betty Jane Wagner. *A Student-Centered K–13 Language Arts and Reading Curriculum.* Boston: Houghton Mifflin, 1983.

Olson, Carol. *Thinking/Writing: Fostering Critical Thinking Skills Through Writing.* Irvine: University of California at Irvine Writing Project, 1984.

THE SCHOOL AS A CENTER OF INQUIRY

Appearing in education journals today is a call for total restructuring of the school. We need a new metaphor for the school, not a jail, a fountain of wisdom, a library. The idea of the school as an inquiring mind is a possibility that has merit. We can visualize this center of inquiry with researchers moving into and out of its walls working in the community as well as inside the school in laboratories, study carrels, and seminar rooms. Daring designers must work with enlightened educators to create housing that encourages data collection, data processing, and data publication initiated and carried out by young researchers working with teacher–researchers. Here is an exciting idea whose time may have come. You might explore the writing of Lauren Resnick:

Lauren Resnick. *Education and Learning to Think.* National Academy Press, 1987.

———. "Learning in School and Out." *Educational Researcher* 16, no. 9 (Dec. 1987): 13–20.

QUESTIONING AS A WAY OF LEARNING

We are recognizing the significance of the questions we formulate as an essential aspect of teaching and learning. Teachers are learning to ask questions that challenge students to think beyond the factual level, questions that require creative, reflective responses. Such questions often lead to metacognition as students are guided to analyze their own thinking processes. Teachers are learning also to encourage students to initiate the questions in the classroom, helping students to recognize the questions that are easy to answer and those that demand further processing. Students are involved in designing test questions, methods of evaluating their own progress, and identifying problems. Such approaches fit with the perception of the school as a center of inquiry.

Investigate ideas presented in these writings:

John Barell et al. "Fostering Thoughtful Self-Direction in Students." *Educational Leadership* 45, no. 7 (April 1988): 14–17.

Francis Hunkins. *Questioning Strategies and Techniques.* Needham Heights, Mass.: Allyn and Bacon, 1972.

Iris Tiedt. "Thinking as a Language Skill." In *The Language Arts Handbook.* Englewood Cliffs, N.J.: Prentice-Hall, 1983, 63–87.

LITERATURE-BASED INSTRUCTION

Opening the door to literature, particularly in elementary school literacy programs, represents informed practice that permits students to learn to read by reading whole language. Students are highly motivated to learn by reading well-written fiction. As they enter into transactions with authors, making meaning together, they engage in thinking in the most natural way possible. Once engaged with literature, they will continue to enjoy both fiction and nonfiction, prose and poetry, discovering a world of thinking. Literature is also being discovered as an essential part of learning across the curriculum as students read essays by Lewis Thomas, drama by Federico García, accounts by James Herriot, poetry and prose by Alice Walker, and on and on. Literature presents ways of thinking that may not be easily categorized to be presented in a scope and sequence of thinking skills. Consider, for example, the thinking of Shakespeare! Explore the sources listed here:

Bill Corcoran, and Emrys Evans, eds. *Readers, Texts, Teachers.* Upper Montclair, N.J.: Boynton/Cook, 1987.

Ben Nelms, ed. *Literature in the Classroom: Readers, Texts, and Contexts.* Urbana, Ill.: National Council of Teachers of English, 1988.

ECONOMIC CONCERN FOR EDUCATION

Perhaps the greatest hope for support for the kind of education we are envisioning lies in national recognition that improving education is essential for the economic welfare of the country. Everyone working in the field of education should know such reports as:

Becoming a Nation of Readers. Commission on Reading, National Academy of Education, 1985.

E. D. Hirsch, Jr. *Cultural Literacy.* Boston: Houghton Mifflin, 1987.

A Nation Prepared: Forum on Education and the Economy.

A Nation at Risk. The National Commission on Excellence in Education, 1983.

Teachers for the 21st Century. Carnegie, 1986.

Tomorrow's Teachers: The Holmes Report. Carnegie, 1986.

We should know such works so that we can critique what these groups have to say and then guide such efforts toward teaching for thinking, the kind of teaching and learning that we advocate.

INTERVENTION AT PRESCHOOL LEVELS

Part of the expressed fear for the loss of potential workers and the need for an educated workforce is the focus on learning at the preschool level. Economists and educational leaders recognize that many children come to school disadvantaged because their early years have not included rich learning experiences. Such children often become drop-outs in junior and senior high school. Here again, we need to be informed and ready to assume leadership in seeing that early childhood programs exist and that they reflect teaching for thinking and all that it entails.

A Final Word

Teaching for thinking is in the developmental stages. Considered by some to be a current fad in education, it is drawing input from many directions. We all need to continue to read, to listen, and to reflect on what we are hearing, recognizing the perspective from which each speaker or writer views the world.

Gradually then, we need to form our own position about thinking instruction. There is no one right answer, and no one person has all the answers. We need, therefore, to continue puzzling over the questions that arise.

1. Is the best thinking always rational and logical? What about Shakespeare, Churchill, Mozart, Magellan, van Gogh?
2. Is thinking separate from learning? Are we trying to establish a false dichotomy?
3. How do language and thinking develop together? What does language reveal about a student's thinking?
4. How can we reconcile skills with innate talents? What else is involved in thinking besides skill and knowledge?

5. What is the best context in which students can learn? What are the conditions that promote thinking?

Out of this reflection will come your personal perspective, your personal philosophy for teaching thinking.

CHALLENGE

Now is the time for you to begin reflecting on what you believe about teaching thinking.

1. Select an aspect of thinking that you might investigate in your classroom(s). You might consider, for example:
   • Questions asked by students—quantity and quality
   • Student awareness of thinking processes as revealed by writing in thinking logs
   • The development of self-esteem in one or two students
   Begin monitoring whatever you select. Note your findings in a three-ringed notebook.
2. Keep a dialectical journal as you read a literature selection that you plan to teach. Divide each page in half vertically. In the left-hand column, note ideas, values, assumptions presented by the author. Then in the right-hand column, record your personal questions, comments, and teaching notes. Use this journal in planning learning activities for students.
3. Began writing a position paper explicating your ideas about teaching thinking at whatever level you teach. Store the paper in your thinking file. Bring it out periodically to review, making changes that seem appropriate. Reflect on the learning process that is occurring for you.

EXPLORING FURTHER

This list differs from the references that appear at the end of other chapters. The resources listed here are ones that we recommend your buying for your own resource library. Therefore, we include addresses to facilitate your obtaining copies.

Arthur Costa. *Developing Minds: A Resource Book for Teaching Thinking.* Association for Supervision and Curriculum Development (125 N. West St., Alexandria VA 22314), 1985.
   A good overview of strategies and ideas to challenge your thinking.

Jeff Golub, ed. *Activities to Promote Critical Thinking.* National Council of Teachers of English (1111 Kenyon Rd., Urbana IL 61801), 1986.
   Articles written by teachers at different levels describing classroom practices.

Robert Marzano et al. *Dimensions of Thinking: A Framework for Curriculum and Instruction.* Association for Supervision and Curriculum Development (125 N. West St., Alexandria VA 22314), 1988.

> Co-authored by a group of seven persons and sponsored by a collaboration of many educational organizations, this framework based on cognitive psychology attempts to identify skills and processes of thinking.

Barbara Presseisen. *Thinking Skills: Research and Practice.* National Education Association (1201 Sixteenth St., N.W., Washington, DC 20036), 1986.

> A thirty-two-page summary of current research about thinking designed to "open teachers' minds to new ideas."

Peter Smagorinsky et al. *Explorations: Introductory Activities for Literature and Composition, 7–12.* National Council of Teachers of English (1111 Kenyon Rd., Urbana IL 61801), 1987.

> A small book of good ideas for connecting reading comprehension and writing instruction.

James Squire, ed. *The Dynamics of Language Learning: Research in Reading and English.* National Conference on Research in English (1111 Kenyon Rd., Urbana IL 61801), 1987.

Pamela Tiedt and Iris Tiedt. *Multicultural Teaching.* Allyn and Bacon (160 Gould St., Needham Heights MA 02194), 1979, 1986, 1989.

> The third edition presents a new perspective of multicultural education for all students beginning with their self-culture and self-esteem; contains strong thinking, language, and literature bases.

United States Department of Education. *What Works: Research about Teaching and Learning.* Volumes I and II. Government Printing Office (Washington DC 20402), 1986, 1987.

> Two succinct presentations of research that should make a difference in teaching.

Appendix

Additional Resources for the Teacher

In this appendix, we have listed additional sources of information about thinking. Refer also to the lists at the end of each chapter for references related to specific topics within the broad focus on thinking instruction. These resources will be especially helpful for staff development efforts as whole districts focus on improving the teaching of thinking. The list is divided into the following sections:

- Books and Materials for the Teacher
- Books and Materials for the Student
- Directory of Publishers

BOOKS AND MATERIALS FOR TEACHERS

Here are general books that provide information about thinking and metacognition.

Background Information

Almy, Millie et al. *Young Children's Thinking: Studies of Aspects of Piaget's Theory.* New York: Teachers' College Press, 1966.

Anderson, John. *Cognitive Skills and Their Acquisition.* Hillsdale, N.J.: Erlbaum, 1981.

Bossone, Richard. *The Fourth R: Reasoning.* New York: City University of New York, 1983.

Bruner, Jerome. *The Process of Education.* New York: Vintage, 1960.

Chall, Jeanne, and Allan Mirsky, eds. *Education and the Brain.* Seventy-seventh Yearbook of the National Society for the Study of Education. Chicago: University of Chicago Press, 1978.

Cohen, Josef. *Thinking.* Skokie, Ill.: Rand McNally, 1971.

Chipman, S.; J. Siegel; and R. Glaser, eds. *Thinking and Learning Skills: Current Research and Open Questions* (2 vols). Hillsdale, N.J.: Erlbaum, 1984.

De Bono, Edward. *New Think.* New York: Basic Books, 1967.

Dewey, John. *How We Think.* Boston: D. C. Heath, 1933.

Halpern, Diane. *Thought and Knowledge: An Introduction to Critical Reasoning.* Hillsdale, N.J.: Erlbaum, 1984.

Kneller, George. *The Art and Science of Creativity*. New York: Holt, 1965.

Machado, Luis. *The Right to Be Intelligent*. Elmsford, N.Y.: Pergamon Press, 1980.

Popp, Leonard et al. *The Basic Thinking Skills*. Ontario, Canada: Ontario Institute for the Study of Education, July, 1974.

Instructional Strategies

Adams, M. J. et al. *Teachers Manual. Prepared for Project Intelligence: The Development of Procedures to Enhance Thinking Skills*. Cambridge, Mass.: Harvard University Press, 1982.

Anderson, Philip, ed. *Integrating Reading, Writing, and Thinking*. Urbana, Ill.: National Council of Teachers of English, 1983.

Aylesworth, Thomas and Gerald Reagan. *Teaching for Thinking*. New York: Doubleday, 1965.

Bloom, Benjamin. *All Our Children Learning*. New York: McGraw-Hill, 1981.

Copple, C.; I. Siegel; and R. Saunders. *Educating the Young Thinker: Classroom Strategies for Cognitive Growth*. Hillsdale, N.J.: Erlbaum, 1984.

Covington, Martin; R. Crutchfield; L. Davies; and R. M. Olton. *The Productive Thinking Program: A Course in Learning to Think*. Columbus, Ohio: Merrill, 1974.

Cronbach, L. J., and R. E. Snow. *Aptitudes and Instructional Methods*. New York: Irvington, 1977.

De Bono, Edward. *Teaching Thinking*. New York: Penguin Books, 1980.

Hart, Leslie. *Human Brain and Human Learning*. New York: Longman, 1983.

Lipman, M.; A. Sharp; and F. Oscanyan. *Philosophy in the Classroom*, 2d ed. Philadelphia: Temple University Press, 1980.

Lochhead, Jack, and A. Whimbey. *Instructor's Guide for Problem-Solving and Comprehension: A Short Course in Analytical Reasoning*. Philadelphia: Franklin Institute Press, 1982.

Mearns, Hughes. *Creative Power: The Education of Youth in the Creative Arts*, rev. ed. New York: Dover, 1958.

McPeck, John. *Critical Thinking and Education*. New York: St. Martin's Press, 1981.

Nickerson, Raymond; David Perkins; and Edward Smith. *Teaching Thinking*. Orlando, Fla.: Academic Press, 1985.

Osborn, Alex. *Applied Imagination*. New York: Scribner, 1957.

PAR Thinking Skills Resource Panel. "Thinking about the Teaching of Thinking." In *Practical Applications of Research: Newsletter of Phi Delta Kappa's Center on Evaluation, Development, and Research* 3, no. 1 (Sept. 1980).

Segal, J.; S. Chipman; and R. Glaser. *Relating Instruction to Basic Research*. Hillsdale, N.J.: Erlbaum, 1983.

Zepezauer, Frank. "Consciousness Shifting: Intellectual Training in the Schools." *California English* (March–April 1981).

Problem Solving

Jacobs, Paul, and M. Meirovitz. *Brain Muscle Builders: Games to Increase Your Natural Intelligence*. Englewood Cliffs, N.J.: Prentice-Hall, 1983.

Polya, Gyorgy. *How to Solve It*. New York: Doubleday, 1957.

Snow, R.; P. Federico; and W. Montague, eds. *Aptitudes, Learning, and Instruction*, vol. 1. Hillsdale, N.J.: Erlbaum, 1980.

Whimbey, Arthur, and Jack Lochhead. *Problem Solving and Comprehension: A Short Course in Analytical Reasoning*, 3d ed. Philadelphia: Franklin Institute Press, 1982.

Whimbey, Arthur, and Jack Lochhead. *Beyond Problem Solving and Comprehension*. Philadelphia: Franklin Institute Press, 1984.

Creativity

Adams, James. *Conceptual Blockbusting: A Guide to Better Ideas*. 2d ed. New York: Norton, 1980.

Barron, Frank. *Creative Person and Creative Process*. New York: Holt, 1969.

Bartel, Roland. *Metaphors and Symbols: Forays into Language*. Urbana, Ill.: NCTE, 1983.

De Bono, Edward. *Lateral Thinking: Creativity Step by Step*. New York: Harper, 1970.

Getzels, Jacob, and Philip Jackson. *Creativity and Intelligence*. New York: Wiley, 1962.

Goertzel, Victor, and Mildred Goertzel. *Cradles of Eminence*. Boston: Little, Brown, 1962.

Guilford, Joy. *Personality*. New York: McGraw-Hill, 1959.

Koestler, Arthur. *The Act of Creation*. New York: Macmillan, 1964.

LeBoeuf, Michael. *Imagineering: How to Profit from Your Creative Powers*. New York: McGraw-Hill, 1982.

MacKinnon, Donald W., ed. *The Creative Person*. University of California, 1962.

Parnes, Sidney J., and Harold H. Harding, eds. *A Source Book for Creative Thinking*. New York: Scribner, 1962.

Parnes, Sidney J. et al. *Guide to Creative Action*. New York: Scribner, 1977.

Perkins, David. *The Mind's Best Work: A New Psychology of Creative Thinking*. Cambridge, Mass.: Harvard University Press, 1983.

Rothenberg, A. *The Emerging Goddess: The Creative Process in Art, Science, and Other Fields*. Chicago: University of Chicago Press, 1982.

Simonton, Dean K. *Genius, Creativity and Leadership: Historiometric Inquiries*. Cambridge, Mass.: Harvard University Press, 1984.

Torrance, E. Paul. *Guiding Creative Talent*. Englewood Cliffs, N.J.: Prentice-Hall, 1962.

Torrance, E. Paul. *Education and the Creative Potential*. Minneapolis: University of Minnesota Press, 1963.

Torrance, E. Paul. *What Research Says to the Teacher: Creativity*. Washington, D.C.: National Education Association, 1963.

Von Oech, Roger. *A Wack on the Side of the Head: How to Unlock Your Mind for Innovation*. Warner Books, 1983.

Philosophy of Mind and Thinking

Berthoff, Ann E. *The Making of Meaning*. Upper Montclair, N.J.: Boynton/Cook, 1981.

Kahane, Howard. *Logic and Contemporary Rhetoric*. Belmont, Calif.: Wadsworth, 1980.

Matthews, Gareth. *Philosophy and the Young Child*. Cambridge, Mass.: Harvard University Press, 1980.

Radner, Daisie and Michael Radner. *Science and Unreason*. Belmont, Calif.: Wadsworth, 1982.

Rico, Gabriele. *Metaphor and Knowing: Analysis, Synthesis, Rationale.* PhD dissertation, Stanford University, 1976.

Rico, Gabriele et al. *A Metaphor Curriculum in Art.* Los Altos High School District, Los Altos, Calif., 1976.

Ruggerio, Vincent. *The Art of Thinking.* New York: Harper, 1984.

Learning to Learn

Baddely, A. *Your Memory: A User's Guide.* New York: Macmillan, 1982.

Brown, S., and M. Walter. *The Art of Problem Posing.* Philadelphia: Franklin Institute Press, 1983.

Novak, J. D., and R. D. Gowin. *Learning How to Learn.* Cambridge University Press, 1984.

O'Neil, H. F., and C. D. Splielberger, eds. *Cognitive and Affective Learning Strategies.* New York: Academic Press, 1979.

Visual, Oral, and Symbolic Communication

Arnheim, Rudolph. *Visual Thinking.* University of California Press, 1976.

Gardner, Howard, and Hope Kelly, eds. *Viewing Children Through Television.* San Francisco: Jossey-Bass, 1981.

Greenfield, Patricia. *Mind and Media: The Effects of Television, Video Games, and Computers.* Cambridge, Mass.: Harvard University Press, 1984.

Johnson-Laird, P. N. *Mental Models: Toward a Cognitive Science of Language, Inference, and Consciousness.* Cambridge, Mass.: Harvard University Press, 1983.

Luria, A. R. *Cognitive Development: Its Cultural and Social Foundations.* Cambridge, Mass.: Harvard University Press, 1976.

Moffett, James. *Teaching the Universe of Discourse.* Boston: Houghton Mifflin, 1983.

Moffett, James, and Betty Jean Van Wagner. *The Student-Centered Language Art and Reading Curriculum: A Teacher's Handbook.* Boston: Houghton Mifflin, 1983.

Morris, P., and P. Hampson. *Imagery and Consciousness.* Orlando, Fla.: Academic Press, 1983.

Paley, Vivian. *Wally's Stories.* Cambridge, Mass.: Harvard University Press, 1981.

Vygotsky, L. S. *Thought and Language.* Cambridge, Mass.: MIT Press, 1962.

Artificial Intelligence and Computers

Papert, Seymour. *Mindstorms: Children, Computers, and Powerful Ideas.* New York: Basic Books, 1982.

Turkle, S. *The Second Self: Computers and the Human Spirit.* New York: Simon & Schuster, 1984.

Brain Functioning and Neurobiology

Annett, Marian. *Left, Right, Hand and Brain: The Right Shift Theory.* Hillsdale, N.J.: Erlbaum, 1985.

Bloom, F. E.; L. Hofstadter; and L. Arlyne. *Brain, Mind, and Behavior.* San Francisco: Freeman, 1984.

Bogen, Joseph. "The Other Side of the Brain VII: Some Educational Aspects of Hemispheric Specialization." *UCLA Educator* 17 (1975): 24–32.

Martin, Kathi. "Righting the Left-Sided Tilt." *New Realities* (April 1979).

Restak, Richard. *The Brain.* New York: Bantam Books, 1984.

Rico, Gabriele. "Metaphor, Cognition, and Clustering." In *Creative Thinking,* edited by Stephen Carmean and Burton Grover. The Eighth Western Symposium on Learning, 1977.

Samples, Bob. "Holonomic Knowing: A Challenge for Education in the 80's." In *Education in the Eighties: English,* edited by R. Baird Shuman. Washington, D.C.: National Education Association, 1981.

Tarnapol, Lester, and Muriel Tarnopol, eds. *Brain Function and Reading Disabilities.* University Park, Md.: University of Maryland Press, 1976.

Wittrock, M. C., ed. *The Brain and Psychology.* New York: Academic Press, 1980.

Reasoning and Critical Thinking

Kahneman, D.; P. Slovic; A. Tversky, eds. *Judgment Under Uncertainty: Heuristics and Biases.* Cambridge University Press, 1982.

Nisbett, R., and L. Ross. *Human Inferences: Strategies and Shortcomings of Social Judgment.* Englewood Cliffs, N.J.: Prentice-Hall, 1980.

Smith, Frank. *Comprehension and Learning.* New York: Holt, 1975.

Cognitive Development

Almy, Millie et al. *Young Children's Thinking: Studies of Some Aspects of Piaget's Theory.* New York: Teachers College Press, 1966.

Boden, Margaret. *Jean Piaget.* New York: Viking Press, 1980.

Flavell, J. *Cognitive Development.* Englewood Cliffs, N.J.: Prentice-Hall, 1977.

Flavell, J. *The Developmental Psychology of Jean Piaget.* New York: Van Nostrand, n.d.

Gardner, Howard. *Developmental Psychology: An Introduction.* Boston: Little, Brown, 1982.

Hayakawa, S. I. *Language in Thought and Action.* New York: Harcourt, 1972.

Kohlberg, Lawrence et al. *Moral Stages: A Current Formulation and a Response to Critics.* Karger, 1983.

Meadows, S., ed. *Developing Thinking: Approaches to Children's Cognitive Development.* New York: Methuen, 1983.

Sugarman, S. *Children's Early Thought: Developments in Classification.* Cambridge University Press, 1983.

Yussen, S. R., ed. *The Growth of Insight in Children.* Orlando, Fla.: Academic Press, 1985.

Intelligence

Baron, J. *Rationality and Intelligence.* Cambridge University Press, 1985.

Christenbury, Leila, and Patricia Kelly. *Questioning: A Path to Critical Thinking.* Urbana, Ill.: NCTE/ERIC Trip Booklet, 1983.

Gardner, Howard. *Frames of Mind: The Theory of Multiple Intelligences.* New York: Basic Books, 1983.

Hawkins, Thom. *Group Inquiry Techniques for Teaching Writing.* Urbana, Ill.: NCTE/ERIC Trip Booklet, 1976.

Moore, Linda P. *You're Smarter Than You Think: At Least 500 Fun Ways to Increase Your Intelligence.* New York: Holt, 1985.

National Council of Teachers of English. *Thinking Through Language,* Book 1 (Grades 7–8); Book 2 (Grades 9–12). Urbana, Ill.: NCTE, 1986.

Sternberg, R. J., ed. *Advances in the Psychology of Human Intelligence,* 2 vols. Hillsdale, N.J.: Erlbaum, 1984.

BOOKS AND MATERIALS FOR STUDENTS

Pattern Books That Guide Response

These books are great to share as a stimulus for thinking and for developing writing fluency at the beginning of the year for students of any age. They are particularly helpful in providing scaffolding for young writers and for older students who may need this help.

Allard, Harry. *I Will Not Go to the Market Today.* New York: Dial Press, 1979. Imaginative excuses.

Anglund, Joan. *A Friend Is Someone Who Likes You.* New York: Harcourt, 1958. Subject for class book; suggests pattern for other topics.

Bayer, Jane. *A, My Name Is Alice.* New York: Dutton, 1984. New twist to an old game.

Baylor, Byrd. *Everybody Needs a Rock.* New York: Scribner, 1974. Rules for choosing just the right rock.

Brown, Margaret. *The Important Book.* New York: Harper, 1968. Pleasant pattern based on familiar objects.

Charlip, Remy. *Fortunately.* New York: Parents, 1964. Contrasts good and bad luck.

Kalan, Robert. *Rain.* New York: Greenwillow, 1978. Explores a familiar topic.

Krauss, Ruth. *A Hole Is to Dig.* New York: Harper, 1952. Defines familiar objects suggesting an easy pattern.

Levine, Joan. *A Bedtime Story.* New York: Dutton, 1975. A funny role reversal of child and parents.

Martin, Bill. *Brown Bear, Brown Bear, What Do You See?* New York: Holt, 1963. Good pattern for making class book.

Mayer, Mercer. *What Do You Do with a Kangaroo?* New York: Four Winds, 1974. Stimulates imaginative solutions to a problem.

Mizumura, Kazue. *If I Were a Mother.* New York: Crowell, 1968. How would you behave if you were a mother? A father?

O'Neill, Mary. *Hailstones and Halibut Bones.* New York: Doubleday, 1961. Poetry pattern that children enjoy imitating.

Shaw, Charles. *It Looked like Spilt Milk.* New York: Harper, 1947. Tear white paper into shapes to write about.

Udry, Janice. *A Tree Is Nice.* New York: Harper, 1954. What trees are good for; same pattern for other things.

Viorst, Judith. *Alexander's Terrible, Horrible, No-Good, Very Bad Day.* New York: Atheneum, 1981. Students write about their horrible days or, for a change, a very good day.

Literature to Discuss and to Write About

Many of these titles could be read aloud to a class. Thinking and talking about the ideas presented then leads to writing.

Primary Grades

Allard, Harry. *It's So Nice to Have a Wolf Around the House.* New York: Doubleday, 1977. Breaks down stereotyped thinking about wolves.

Allard, Harry. *Bumps in the Night.* New York: Doubleday, 1979. Stimulates talk about a common fear.

Ets, Marie Hall. *Gilberto and the Wind.* New York: Viking, 1963. Good talk-about.

Hutchins, Pat. *Rosie's Walk.* New York: Macmillan, 1968. Requires close observation of illustrations.

Keats, Ezra Jack. *The Snowy Day.* New York: Viking, 1963. Realistic story about black child's adventures.

McDermott, Gerald. *Arrow to the Sun.* New York: Viking, 1975. Beautiful Indian folktale.

Parish, Peggy. *Amelia Bedelia.* New York: Harper, 1963. Humorous plays on words; see other titles.

Scott, Ann. *On Mother's Lap.* New York: McGraw, 1972. Beautiful Eskimo story about feelings of first-born child.

Sendak, Maurice. *Where the Wild Things Are.* New York: Harper, 1963. Fearful monsters, but Max returns safely.

Wood, Barbara. *The Napping House.* 1982. Cumulative tale that requires close observation of illustrations.

Yashima, Taro. *Crow Boy.* New York: Viking, 1967. Understanding one another's attributes.

Zemach, Harve. *The Judge.* New York: Farrar, 1969. Evaluation of decision.

Middle School

Allard, Harry. *Miss Nelson Is Missing.* Boston: Houghton, 1977. Funny spoof children enjoy; see also sequels.

Cameron, Polly. *I Can't, Said the Ant.* New York: Coward, McCann & Geoghegan, 1961. Wordplay in rhyme.

Digby, Desmond. *Waltzing Matilda.* Cleveland, Ohio: Collins, 1979. Lyrics to a familiar song.

Gwynne, Fred. *The King Who Rained.* New York: Windmill, 1970. Wordplay students enjoy.

Silverstein, Shel. *The Giving Tree.* New York: Harper, 1976. What kind of love is this?

Silverstein, Shel. *Where the Sidewalk Ends.* New York: Harper, 1978. Funny verses students enjoy chanting and using as models for writing.

Tresselt, Alvin. *The Dead Tree.* New York: Parents, 1972. The life cycle of a tree; poetic prose.

Middle School and High School

Carroll, Lewis. *Alice in Wonderland* and *Through the Looking Glass.* Various editions. A fantasy that stimulates thinking.

Packard, Vance. *The Hidden Persuaders*. New York: McKay, 1957. Provocative ideas to discuss.

Shannon, George. *Stories to Solve: Folktales from Around the World*. New York: Dutton, 1980. Folktales to use as part of a multicultural unit.

Viorst, Judith. *If I Were in Charge of the World and Other Worries*. New York: Atheneum, 1981. Humorous poems to share and talk about.

Directory of Publishers

Abelard, Schuman, Ltd. 666 Fifth Ave., New York, NY 10019

Abingdon Press. 201 Eighth Ave., South, Nashville, TN 37202

Abrams. 110 E. 59th St., New York, NY 10022

ACI Films. 35 West 45 Street, New York, NY 10036

Academic Press. 111 5th Ave., New York, NY 10003

Addison-Wesley Publishing Co. Reading, MA 01867

Aid/Rocap Textbook Program. c/o American Embassy, San Salvador, El Salvador

Aims. 20 East 30th Street, New York, NY 10016

Aims Instrumental Media Services. P.O. Box 1010, Hollywood, CA 90028

Aldine Publishing. 529 S. Wabash Ave., Chicago, IL 60605

Alemany Press. Box 5265, San Francisco, CA 94101

Aleut League. Star Route A, Box 289, Spenard, AK

Allyn and Bacon, Inc. 160 Gould St., Needham Heights, MA 02194

American Association for Jewish Education. 101 Fifth Ave., New York, NY 10003

American Council for Judaism. 309 Fifth Ave., New York, NY 10016

American Council for Nationalities Service. 20 W. 40th St., New York, NY

American Council on Education. 1785 Massachusetts Ave., NW., Washington, D.C. 20036

American Federation of Teachers. AFL-CIO, 1012–14th St., NW., Washington, D.C. 20025

American Folklore Society. Univ. of Texas Press, Box 7819, Austin, TX 78712

American Friends Service Committee, Children's Program, 160 N. 15th St., Philadelphia, PA 19102

American Heritage Press. 1221 Avenue of the Americas, New York, NY 10020

American Library Association. Publishing Services, 50 E. Huron St., Chicago, IL 60611

American Lithuanian Community. 6804 South Maplewood Ave., Chicago, IL 60629

American Personnel and Guidance Association. 1712 I St., NW., Washington, D.C., 20009

American Psychological Assn. 1200 17th St., N.W., Washington, D.C. 20036

American-Scandinavian Foundation. 126 East 73rd St., New York, NY 10021

American School Foundation. A.C., Calle Sur 136, No. 135, Mexico 18, D.F.

Anti-Defamation League of B'nai Brith. 315 Lexington Ave., New York, NY 10016

Applied Language Research Center. 1116 E. Yandell Dr., El Paso, TX 79902

Arco Pub. Co. 219 Park Ave. S., New York, NY 10003

Asia Society. 112 E. 64th St., New York, NY 10021

Aspira, Inc. 296 Fifth Ave., New York, NY 10001

Association for Childhood Education International. 3615 Washington Ave., NW., Washington, D.C. 20016

Association for the Study of Negro Life and History. 1538 9th St., NW., Washington, D.C. 20001

Association of Mexican-American Educators, Inc. (AMAE). California State College at San Bernardino, 5500 State College Pkwy., San Bernardino, CA 92407

Association on American Indian Affairs, Inc., 432 Park Ave. S., New York, NY 10016

Atheneum Publishers. 122 E. 42d St., New York, NY 10017

Augsburg Pub. House. 426 S. 5th St., Minneapolis, MN 55415

Avon Books, 959 Eighth Ave., New York, NY 10019

Babel Media Center. 1033 Heinz St., Berkeley, CA 94710

Ballantine Books. 201 E. 50th St., New York, NY 10022

Bantam Books. 666 Fifth Ave., New York, NY 10019

Barr Films. P.O. Box 7-C, Pasadena, CA 91104

Basque Studies Program. Univ. of Nevada, Reno, NV 89507

Beacon Press. 25 Beacon St., Boston, MA 02108

Behavioral Publication. 2852 Broadway, New York, NY 10025

Bell & Howell. 2201 West Howard, Evanston, IL 60202

Berkeley Pub. Corp. 200 Madison Ave., New York, NY 10016

Bilingual Demonstration and Dissemination Center. 2nd Floor—Navarro Elem. Sch., 623 South Pecos, San Antonio, TX 78207

Bilingual Educational Services. P.O. Box 669, 1603 Hope St., South Pasadena, CA 91030

Bilingual Publications Co. 1966 Broadway, New York, NY 10023

Bobbs-Merrill Co. 4300 W. 62d St., Indianapolis, IN 46268

Books for the People Fund, Inc. Pan American Union, Washington, D.C. 20006

Boston Music Co. 116 Boylston St., Boston, MA 02116

Boston Public Library. Copley Square, Boston, MA 02116

Stephen Bosustow Productions. 1649 11th St., Santa Monica, CA 90404

The R. R. Bowker Co. Xerox Education Group, 1180 Avenue of the Americas, New York, NY 10036

Bowmar Publishing Corp. 622 Rodier Dr., Glendale, CA 91201

Bradbury Press. 2 Overhill Rd., Scarsdale, NY 10583

Brigham Young University Center for International and Area Studies. Publications Services, Box 61, FOB, Provo, UT 84602

Brigham Young University Press. 204 University Press Bldg., Provo, UT 84602

British Council. English-Teaching Information Centre, State House, 63 High Holborn, London W.C. 1, England

Bro-Dart Foundation. 1609 Memorial Ave., Williamsport, PA 17101

Broadcasting Foundation of America. 52 Vanderbilt Ave., New York, NY

Wm. C. Brown Pub. 2460 Kerper Ave., Dubuque, IA 52001

Bureau of Jewish Education. 72 Franklin St., Boston, MA 02110

Burgess Pub. Co. 7108 Ohms Ln., Minneapolis, MN 55435

California Library Association. 1741 Solano Ave., Berkeley, CA 94707

California State Dept. of Ed. 721 Capitol Mall, Sacramento, CA 95814

California Test Bureau (Div. of McGraw-Hill). Del Monte Research Park, Monterey, CA 93940

Canada Council. Humanities and Social Sciences Div., 140 Wellington St., Ottawa, Ontario, Canada

Catholic Library Association. 461 W. Lancaster Ave., Haverford, PA 19041

Center for Applied Linguistics (ERIC Clearinghouse for Linguistics). 1717 Massachusetts Ave., NW., Washington, D.C. 20036

Center for Curriculum Development in Audio-Visual Language Teaching. The Irvin Building, Philadelphia, PA

Center for Inter-American Relations. 680 Park Ave., New York, NY 10021

Center for Teaching International Relations (CTIR). University of Denver, Denver, CO 80208

Center for Urban Education. 105 Madison Ave., New York, NY 10016

Central American Regional Textbook Prog. (Centro Regional de Libros de Textos). Departamento de Asuntos Culturales y Educativos, Organización de Estados Centro-americanos (ODECA), San Salvador, El Salvador

Centro Mexicano de Escritores. Apartado Postal 1298, Mexico D.F., Mexico

Centron Educational Films. 1621 W. Ninth, Lawrence, KS 66044

Changing Times Education Service. 1729 H Street, NW., Washington, D.C. 20006

Child Development Evaluation and Research Center. The Univ. of Texas at Austin, Austin, TX 78712

Child Study Assn. of America. Publications Dept., 9 E. 89th St., New York, NY 10028

Children's Book Council, Inc. 175 Fifth Ave., New York, NY 10010

Children's Music Center, Inc. 5373 West Pico Blvd., Los Angeles, CA 90019

Children's Press. 1224 W. Van Buren St., Chicago, IL 60607

Chilton Book Co. Radnor, PA 19089

Christopher News Notes. 12 E. 48th St., New York, NY 10017

Churchill Films. 662 N. Robertson Blvd., Los Angeles, CA 90069

Citation Press. 50 W. 44th St., New York, NY 10036

Clearvue. 6666 N. Oliphant Ave., Chicago, IL 60631

William Collins & World Publishing Co. 2080 W. 117th St., Cleveland, OH 44111

Columbia University Press. 562 W. 113th St., New York, NY 10025

The Combined Book Exhibit, Inc. Scarborough Park, Albany Post Rd., Briarcliff Manor, NY 10510

Commission on the Humanities in the Schools. P.O. Box 15212, Steiner St. Station, San Francisco, CA 94115

Committee for the Yiddish Schools. 426 West 58th St., New York, NY 10019

Computer Curr. Corp. Box 10080, Pittsburgh, PA 94303

Constitutional Rights Foundation. 1510 Cotner Ave., W. Los Angeles, CA 90025

Contemporary Press. Box 1524, San Jose, CA 95109

Continental Book Co. 11-03 46th Ave., Long Island City, NY 11101. Resources for Sp.-Eng. bilingual curriculum (Mexico and Puerto Rico).

Coronet Instructional Media. 65 E. South Water St., Chicago, IL 60601

Council on International Educational Exchange. 777 United Nations Plaza, New York, NY 10017

Council on Interracial Books for Children, Inc. 1841 Broadway, New York, NY 10023

Coward, McCann & Geoghegan. 200 Madison Ave., New York, NY 10016

George Cram. 301 S. LaSalle St., Indianapolis, IN 46206

Thomas Y. Crowell Co. 666 Fifth Ave., New York, NY 10019

Crown Publishers. 1 Park Ave., New York, NY 10016

Curriculum Inquiry Center. University of California, 405 Hilgard Ave., Los Angeles, CA 90024

The John Day Co. 666 Fifth Ave., New York, NY 10019

Dell/Delacorte Press. 1 Dag Hammarskjold Plaza, 245 E. 47th St., New York, NY 10017

Department of Foreign Languages. 1201 Sixteenth St., N.W., Washington, D.C. 20036

The Dial Press. 1 Dag Hammarskjold Plaza, 245 E. 47th St., New York, NY 10017

Dillon Press. 106 Washington Ave. N., Minneapolis, MN 55401

Disney, Walt, Educational Materials. 800 Sonora Ave., Glendale, CA 91201

Dodd, Mead & Co. 79 Madison Ave., New York, NY 10016

Doubleday & Co. 245 Park Ave., New York, NY 10017

Doubleday Multimedia. 1371 Reynolds Ave., Santa Ana, CA 92705

Dover Publications. 180 Varick St., New York, NY 10014

Dryden Press, 901 N. Elm, Hinsdale, IL 60521

E. P. Dutton & Co. 2 Park Ave., New York, NY 10016

Early Childhood Bilingual Education Project. Yeshiva U., 55 Fifth Ave., New York, NY 10003

East-West Center. Institute of Advanced Projects, Univ. of Hawaii, Honolulu, HI 96822

Editorial La Muralla, S.A. Carretas, 14, 5. 1–2, Madrid 12, Spain

Educational Development Corp. 202 Lake Miriam Dr., Lakeland, FL 33803

Educational Testing Service. Rosedale Rd., Princeton, NJ 08540

EMC Corp. 180 E. Sixth St., St. Paul, MN 55101

Encyclopaedia Britannica Educational Corp. 425 N. Michigan Ave., Chicago, IL 60611

English for Speakers of Other Languages Program (ESOL). Center for Applied Linguistics, 1717 Massachusetts Ave., N.W., Washington, D.C. 10036

Enoch Pratt Free Library. Baltimore, MD 21201

ERIC (Educational Resources Information Center). (Central ERIC Headquarters) U.S. Office of Education, Dept of Health, Ed., and Welfare, 400 Maryland Ave., S.W., Washington, D.C.

ERIC Clearinghouse on Adult Education. Syracuse Univ., Syracuse, NY 13210

ERIC Clearinghouse on Counseling and Personnel Services. Univ. of Michigan, Ann Arbor, MI 48104

ERIC Clearinghouse on the Disadvantaged. Teachers College, Columbia Univ., New York, NY 10027

ERIC Clearinghouse on Early Childhood Education. 805 W. Pennsylvania Ave., Urbana, IL 61801

ERIC Clearinghouse on Educational Administration. Univ. of Oregon, Eugene, OR 97403

ERIC Clearinghouse on Educational Facilities. Univ. of Wisconsin, Madison, WI 53703

ERIC Clearinghouse on Educational Media and Technology. Stanford Univ., Stanford, CA 94305

ERIC Clearinghouse on Exceptional Children. The Council for Exceptional Children, Washington, D.C. 20036

ERIC Clearinghouse on Higher Education. George Washington Univ., Washington, D.C. 20006

ERIC Clearinghouse on Junior Colleges. Univ. of Calif. at Los Angeles, Los Angeles, CA 90024

ERIC Clearinghouse on Library and Information Sciences. Univ. of Minnesota, Minneapolis, MN 55404

ERIC Clearinghouse on Linguistics. Center for Applied Linguistics, 1717 Massachusetts Ave., N.W., Washington, D.C. 10036

ERIC Clearinghouse on Reading, Indiana Univ., Bloomington, IN 47401

ERIC Clearinghouse on Rural Education and Small Schools. New Mexico State Univ., Box 3AP, Univ. Pk. Branch, Las Cruces, NM 88001

ERIC Clearinghouse on Science Education. Ohio State Univ., Columbus, OH 43221

ERIC Clearinghouse on Teacher Education. American Association of Colleges for Teacher Education, Washington, D.C. 10005

ERIC Clearinghouse on the Teaching of English. National Council of Teachers of English, Champaign, IL 61820

ERIC Clearinghouse on the Teaching of Foreign Languages. Modern Language Association of America, 62 Fifth Ave., New York, NY 10011

ERIC Clearinghouse on Vocational and Technical Education. Ohio State Univ., Columbus, OH 43210

ESL Demonstration Project Center. 2950 National Ave., San Diego, CA 92113

M. Evans & Co. 216 E. 49th St., New York, NY 10017

Farrar, Straus & Giroux. 19 Union Square West, New York, NY 10003

Fawcett Books, CBS. 600 Third Ave., New York, NY 10016

E. W. Faxon Co. 15 Southwest Park, Westwood, MA 02090

Fearon Teacher Aids. David Lake Publishers, 19 Davis Dr., Belmont, CA 94002

The Feminist Press. Box 334, Old Westbury, NY 11568

Follett Publishing Co. 1010 W. Washington Blvd., Chicago, IL 60607

Foreign Language Education Center. Sutton Hall 417, The Univ. of Texas at Austin, Austin, TX 78712

Foreign Language Innovative Curricula Study (FLICS). 550 City Center Building, 220 E. Huron, Ann Arbor, MI 48108

Foreign Policy Association. 205 Lexington Ave., New York, NY 10016

Four Winds Press. 50 W. 44th St., New York, NY 10036

Free Library of Philadelphia. 19th and Vine St., Philadelphia, PA 19103

Freedomway Associates, Inc. 799 Broadway, New York, NY 10003

Friendship Press. 475 Riverside Dr., New York, NY 10027

Garfield Elementary School. Del Rio ISD, Del Rio, TX

Garrard Publishing Co. 1607 N. Market St., Champaign, IL 61820

General Educational Media. 350 Northern Blvd., Great Neck, NY 10021

Gessler Publishing Co., Inc. 131 East 23rd St., New York, NY 10010

Glencoe Publishing. 15319 Chatsworth St., Mission Hills, CA 91345

Global Perspectives in Education. 218 E. 18th St., New York, NY 10003. West Coast Office: P.O. Box 9976, Mills College Station, Oakland, CA 94613

Golden Gate Junior Books. 1247½ N. Vista St., Hollywood, CA 90046

Golden Press (Western Publishing Co.). 850 Third Ave., New York, NY 10022

Goldsholl Associates. 420 Frontage Rd., Northfield, IL 60093

Grant, Allan, Productions. 808 Lockearn St., Los Angeles, CA 90049

Grosset & Dunlap. 51 Madison Ave., New York, NY 10010

Guidance Associates. 41 Washington Ave., Pleasantville, NY 10570

Hachette Teacher's Showroom and French Book Guild. 595 Madison Ave., New York, NY 10022

G. K. Hall & Co. 70 Lincoln St., Boston, MA 02111

Hammond, Dr. 211 S. Main, McAllen, TX 78501

Harcourt Brace Jovanovich. 1250 Sixth Ave., San Diego, CA 92101

Harper & Row, Publishers. 10 E. 53rd St., New York, NY 10022

Harvey House. 20 Waterside Plaza, New York, NY 10010

Haskell Institute. Lawrence, KS 66044

Hastings House Publishers. 10 E. 40th St., New York, NY 10016

Hawthorn Books. 260 Madison Ave., New York, NY 10016

Hayden. 50 Essex St., Rochelle Park, NJ 07622

D. C. Heath, 125 Spring St., Lexington, MA 02173

Heffernan Supply Co., Inc. 926 Fredericksburg Rd., Box 5309, San Antonio, TX 78201

Heinman. 1966 Broadway, New York, NY 10023

Hispanic-American Publications, Inc. 252 East 51st St., New York, NY 10022

Holiday House. 18 E. 56th St., New York, NY 10022

Holt, Rinehart & Winston. 383 Madison Ave., New York, NY 10017

Houghton Mifflin Co. 1 Beacon St., Boston, MA 02107

HRD/ROCAP. U.S. Embassy, Guatemala, Guatemala

Human Sciences Press. 72 Fifth Ave., New York, NY 10011

Indian Rights Association. 1505 Race St., Philadelphia, PA 19102

Indiana Univ. Press, 10th & Morton St., Bloomington, IN 47401

Information Center on Children's Cultures. U.S. Committee for UNICEF, 331 E. 38th St., New York, NY 10016

Institute for Personality and Ability Testing. 1602 Coronado Dr., Champaign, IL 61820

Institute for Research in Language Teaching. Central Corporus 108, 15 Agebacho, Shinjuku-ku, Tokyo, Japan

Institute for World Order. 777 United Nations Plaza, New York, NY 10017

Institute of Language Teaching. Waseda Univ., No. 647, 1-Chome, Totsuka-Machi, Shinjuku-ku, Tokyo, Japan

Instituto Lingüístico de Verano (Summer Inst. of Linguistics). Box 1960, Santa Ana, CA 92702

Instructor Publications. Dansville, NY 14437

Integrated Education Associates. 343 S. Dearborn St., Chicago, IL 60604

Inter-Agency Committee on Mexican American Affairs. 1800 G St., NW., Washington, D.C. 20506

Inter-American Ed. Center. Inter-American Institute, 2525 Tower Life Bldg., San Antonio, TX 78205

Inter-American Institute. The Univ. of Texas at El Paso, El Paso, TX 79999

Inter-American Prog. for Linguistics and Lang. Teaching/Programa Internacional de Lingüística y de Enseñanza de Idiomas (PILEI). El Colegio de Mexico, Guanajuato 125, México 7, D.F.

International Center for Research on Bilingualism. Cité Universitaire, 4530 Bibliothèque Générale, Ste-Foy 10, Québec, Canada

International Film Bureau Inc. 332 S. Michigan Ave., Chicago, IL 60604

International Reading Association. Box 695, Newark, DE 19711

Jewish Education Committee. 426 West 58th St., New York, NY 10019

Alfred A. Knopf. 201 E. 50th St., New York, NY 10022

Kosciuszko Foundation. 15 East 65th St., New York, NY 10021

Language Arts, Inc. 1205-C.W. 34th St., Austin, TX

Language Research Associates. 300 North State St., Chicago, IL 60610

Language Study Center. Philippine Normal College, Manila, Philippines

Learning Corp. of America. 711 Fifth Ave., New York, NY 10022

Learning Resources Co. P.O. Box 3709, 202 Lake Mirian Dr., Lakeland, FL 33803

Learning Tree Filmstrips. 934 Pearl St., P.O. Box 1590 Dept. 105, Boulder, CO 80302

Lerner Publications Co. 241 First Ave. N., Minneapolis, MN 55401

Libraries Unlimited. Box 263, Littleton, CO 80120

J. B. Lippincott Co. 521 Fifth Ave., New York, NY 10017

Little, Brown & Co. 34 Beacon St., Boston, MA 02106

Lorraine Music Co. P.O. Box 4131, Long Island City, NY 11104

Los Palomas De Taos, P.O. Box 3194, Taos, NM 87571

Lothrop, Lee & Shepard Co. 105 Madison Ave., New York, NY 10016

L'Union Saint-Jean Baptiste D'Amérique. 1 Social Street, Woonsocket, RI

Macrae Smith Co. Lewis Tower Bldg., 225 S. 15th St., Philadelphia, PA 19102

Macmillan Publishing Co. 866 Third Ave., New York, NY 10022

Maestros Para Mañana (Teachers for Tomorrow). 1705 Murchison Dr., Burlingame, CA 94010

McCormick-Mathers, Litton. 7625 Empire Dr., Florence, KY 41042

McGraw-Hill Book Co., 1221 Avenue of the Americas, New York, NY 10020

David McKay Co., Publishers. 750 3d Ave., New York, NY 10017

Media and Methods Institute. 134 N. 13th St., Philadelphia, PA 19107

Merrill, Charles E., Publishing Co. 1300 Alum Creek Dr., Columbus, OH 43216

Mershon Center, Ohio State University, 199 W. 10th Ave., Columbus, OH 43201

Julian Messner (A Division of Simon & Schuster). 1 W. 39th St., New York, NY 10018

Mexican-American Educators Coordinating Council. State Dept. of Ed., 721 Capitol Mall, Sacramento, CA 95814

Mid-America Program for Global Perspectives in Education. Indiana University, 513 North Park, Bloomington, IN 47405

Miller-Brody Productions. 711 Fifth Ave., New York, NY 10022

Modern Language Association. 62 Fifth Ave., New York, NY 10011

Modern Language Center. The Ontario Institute for Studies in Education, 102 Bloor St. West, Toronto 5, Ontario, Canada

William Morrow & Co. 105 Madison Ave., New York, NY 10016

Multicultural Resources. Box 2945, Stanford, CA 94305

Multi-Media Approach to Library Services for the Spanish Surnamed. Colorado State College, Greeley, CO

National Assn. for Bilingual Ed. 1201 16th St., NW., Washington, D.C. 20036

National Association for the Advancement of Colored People. 1790 Broadway, New York, NY 10019

National Assn. of Interdisciplinary Ethnic Studies. Iowa State U., Ames, IA 50011

National Association of Language Laboratory Directors. Brown Univ., Box E, Providence, RI 02912

National Carl Schurz Association (NCSA). 339 Walnut St., Philadelphia, PA

National Conference of Christians and Jews. 43 W. 57th St., New York, NY 10019

National Congress of American Indians. 1346 Connecticut Ave. N.W., Washington, D.C. 20036

National Council for the Social Studies. 1201 Sixteenth St. N.W., Washington, D.C. 20036

National Council of Teachers of English. 1111 Kenyon Rd., Urbana, IL 61801

National Council of Teachers of Mathematics. 1906 Assoc. Dr., Reston, VA 22091

National Education Association. 1201 Sixteenth St., N.W., Washington, D.C. 20036

National Geographic Society. Washington, D.C. 20036

National Instructional Television. Box A, Bloomington, IN 47401

Negro Bibliographic and Research Center, Inc. 117 R St., NE., Washington, D.C. 20002

Negro Book Club. 160 W. 85th St., New York, NY 10024

Thomas Nelson, 407 7th Ave., Nashville, TN 37202

Newbury House Publishers. 68 Middle Rd., Rowley, MA 01969

Newsweek, 444 Madison Ave., New York, NY 10022

New York Library Association. Children and Young Adult Services Section, 230 W. 41st St., Suite 1800, New York, NY 10036

New York Office of State History. State Education Dept., 99 Washington Ave., Albany, NY 12210

Nordmanns Förbundet. Minneapolis Chapter, 529 E. Minnehaha Parkway, Minneapolis, MN 55419

Northern Arizona Supplementary Education Center (NASEC). Northern Arizona Univ., Box 5618, Flagstaff, AZ 86001

W. W. Norton. 500 Fifth Ave., New York, NY 10036

Norwegian-American Historical Association, Northfield, MN

Nuffield Foundation. Nuffield Foreign Languages, Teaching Materials Project, 5 Lyddon Terrace, The University, Leeds 2, England

Oakland Public Library. 1457 Fruitvale Ave., Oakland, CA 94601

J. Philip O'Hara. 20 E. Huron St., Chicago, IL 60611

Oxford Films. 1136 North Las Palmas Ave., Los Angeles, CA 90036

Oxford University Press. 16-00 Politt Dr., Fair Lawn, NJ 07410

Pan American Union. 17th and Constitution Ave., NW., Washington, D.C. 20006

Pantheon Books, 201 E. 50th St., New York, NY 10022

Parents' Magazine Press. 52 Vanderbilt Ave., New York, NY 10017

Parnassus Press. 4080 Halleck St., Emeryville, CA 94608

Pathescope Educational Films. 71 Weyman Ave., New Rochelle, NY 10802

Peace Corps. 806 Connecticut Ave., N.W., Washington, D.C. 20515

F. E. Peacock Pub. 401 W. Irving Park Rd., Itasca, IL 60143

Penguin Books. 625 Madison Ave., New York, NY 10022

S. G. Phillips. 305 W. 86th St., New York, NY 10024

Pied Piper Productions. P.O. Box 320, Verdugo City, CA 91046

Plays. 8 Arlington St., Boston, MA 02116

Platt & Munk, Publishers. 1055 Bronx River Ave., Bronx, NY 10472

Pocket Books, 1230 Ave. of the Americas, New York, NY 10020

Polish-American Congress. 1520 West Division, Chicago, IL 60622

Polish-American Journal. 409–415 Cedar Ave., Scranton, PA 18505

Polish Institute of Arts and Sciences. 59 East 66th St., New York, NY 10021

Polish Teachers Assn. in America. 2653 W. Logan Blvd., Chicago, IL 60647

Portal Press, Inc., Publishers. 605 Third Ave., New York, NY 10016

Practical Drawing Co. 2205 Cockrell, Dallas, TX 75222

Praeger Publishers. 111 Fourth Ave., New York, NY 10003

Prentice-Hall. Englewood Cliffs, NJ 07632

Project Head Start. The Office of Economic Opportunity, 1111 18th St., NW., Washington, D.C. 10036

Project Libro. The Galton Institute, 319 S. Robertson Blvd., Beverly Hills, CA 90211

Proyecto Leer. La Casita, Pan American Union, Washington, D.C. 20006

Psychological Corporation. 304 E. 45th St., New York, NY 10017

Psychological Test Specialists. Box 1441, Missoula, MT

Puerto Rican Forum, Inc. 156 Fifth Ave., New York, NY 10010

G. P. Putnam. 200 Madison Ave., New York, NY 10016

Pyramid Films Corporation. P.O. Box 1048, Santa Monica, CA 90406

Q-ED Productions. P.O. Box 1608, Burbank, CA 91507

Rand McNally & Co. P.O. Box 7600, Chicago, IL 60680

Random House. 201 E. 50th St., New York, NY 10022

Random House Educational Media. Order Entry Department-Y, 400 Hahn Road, Westminster, MD 21157

Henry Regnery. 180 N. Michigan Ave., Chicago, IL 60601

The Reilly & Lee Co. 114 W. Illinois St., Chicago, IL 60610

Rosenzweig, Dr. Saul. 8029 Washington St., St. Louis, MO 63114

St. Martin's Press. 175 Fifth Ave., New York, NY 10010

Salinger Educational Media. 1635 12th St., Santa Monica, CA 90404

Santillana. S.A. de Ediciones, Elfo, 32, Madrid 17, Spain

Scarecrow Press. 52 Liberty St., Box 656, Metuchen, NJ 08840

Schloat Productions. 150 White Plains Rd., Tarrytown, NY 10591

Schmitt, Hall & McCreary Co. 110 N. Fifth St., Minneapolis, MN 55403

Scholastic Magazines. Audio Visual and Media Dept., 50 West 44th St., New York, NY 10036

Schools for the Future. P.O. Box 349, Cooper Station, New York, NY 10003

Science Research Associates, Inc. 259 East Erie St., Chicago, IL 60611

Scott, Foresman & Co. Educational Publishers, 1900 E. Lake Ave., Glenview, IL 60025

Screen Education Enterprises. 3220 16th Avenue West, Seattle, WA 98119

Charles Scribner's Sons. 597 Fifth Street, New York, NY 10017

Scroll Press, Publishers. 129 East 94th St., New York, NY 10028

The Seabury Press. 815 Second Ave., New York, NY 10017

See Hear Now! Ltd. 49 Wellington St., East, Toronto M5E 1C9 Canada

Simon & Schuster, Publishers. 630 5th Ave., New York, NY 10020

Society for French American Cultural Services & Educational Aids (FACSEA). 972 Fifth Ave., New York, NY

Society for the Advancement of Scandinavian Studies. Northeastern Univ., Evanston, IL

Sons of Norway Intl. Hdqtrs. 1455 West Lake St., Minneapolis, MN 55408

Southeastern Educational Corp. Box 10867, Airport Branch, Atlanta, GA 30304

Southern Regional Council, Inc. 5 Forsyth St., NW., Atlanta, GA 30303

Southwest Council for Biling. Ed. Box 497, The Univ. of Texas at El Paso, El Paso, TX 79999

Southwest Ed. Dev. Lab. Suite 550, Commodore Perry Hotel, Austin, TX 78701

Stanford Program on International and Cross-Cultural Education (SPICE). Lou Henry Hoover Bldg., Room 200, Stanford University, Stanford, CA 94305

Steck-Vaughn Co. Division of Intext Publishers Group, Box 2028, Austin, TX 78767

Studyscopes Productions. Box 25943, Los Angeles, CA 90025

Summer Institute of Linguistics. Wycliffe Bible Translators, Inc., Box 1960, Santa Ana, CA

Superintendent of Documents. U.S. Government Printing Office, Washington, D.C. 20402

Teachers College Press. 1234 Amsterdam Ave., New York, NY 10027

Teachers of English to Speakers of Other Languages (TESOL). School of Languages and Linguistics. Georgetown Univ., Washington, D.C. 20007

Teaching Research Division. Oregon State System of Higher Education, Monmouth, OR

Teaching Resources Films. Station Plaza, Bedford Hills, NY 10507

Technicolor, 299 Kalmus Dr., Costa Mesa, CA 92626

3M Company. Visual Products Division, Box 334, 3M Center, St. Paul, MN 55101

Trans-World Films, Inc. 332 South Michigan Ave., Chicago, IL 60604

Troll Associates. 320 Route 17, Mahwah, NJ 07430

Charles Tuttle. 28 S. Main St., Rutland, VT 05701

Union of Am. Hebrew Congregations. 838 Fifth Ave., New York, NY 10021

United Japanese Society of Hawaii. Honolulu, HI

United Nations. Rm. A-3315, New York, NY 10017

United States Aid Mission to Bolivia. Casilla 673, La Paz, Bolivia

U.S. Committee for UNICEF. P.O. Box 1618, Church St. Station, New York, NY

U.S. Dept. of Health, Education, and Welfare. U.S. Office of Education, 400 Maryland Ave., SW., Washington, D.C. 20202

U.S. Dept. of Interior. Bureau of Indian Affairs, 1951 Constitution Ave., NW., Washington, D.C. 20242

U.S. Dept. of State, U.S. Mexico Commission for Border Development and Friendship, 1800 G St., NW., Washington, D.C. 20525

U.S. Inter-Agency Committee on Mexican American Affairs. 1800 G St., NW., Washington, D.C. 20506

University of Chicago Press. 5801 Ellis Ave., Chicago, IL 60637

University of Pittsburgh Press. 127 N. Bellefield Ave., Pittsburgh, PA 15213

The Vanguard Press. 424 Madison Ave., New York, NY 10017

Van Nostrand-Reinhold Co. 450 W. 33d St., New York, NY 10001

The Viking Press. 625 Madison Ave., New York, NY 10022

Villa Jones. Centro Cultural Internacional, A.C., Chilpancingo 23, México 11, D.F.

Visual Instruction Bureau. Division of Extension, 18th and Sabine Sts., The Univ. of Texas at Austin, Austin, TX 78712

Henry Z. Walck, Publishers. 19 Union Square W., New York, NY 10003

Walker & Co. 720 5th Ave., New York, NY 10019

The Ward Ritchie Press (Anderson, Ritchie & Simon). 3044 Riverside Dr., Los Angeles, CA 90039

Frederick Warne & Co. 101 5th Ave., New York, NY 10003

Ives Washburn. 750 3d Ave., New York, NY 10017

Washington Square. See Pocket Books.

Franklin Watts. 730 5th Ave., New York, NY 10019

Western Psychological Services. 12031 Wilshire Blvd., Los Angeles, CA 90025

Westminster Press. Witherspoon Building, Philadelphia, PA 19107

Weston Woods, Weston, CT 06880

Albert Whitman & Co. 560 West Lake St., Chicago, IL 60606

The H. W. Wilson Co. 950 University Ave., New York, NY 10452

Windmill Books. 201 Park Avenue South, New York, NY 10003

Xerox Films. 245 Long Hill Road, Middletown, CT 06457

Young Scott Books. Reading, MA 01867

Index